Cultivating Connection

Cultivating Connection

A PRACTICAL GUIDE FOR PERSONAL AND RELATIONSHIP GROWTH IN ETHICAL NON-MONOGAMY

Sander T. Jones, LCSW, LISW-CP, CCH

Cast Net Books publishes its books in a variety of electronic and print formats. Some content that appears in print may not be available in electronic books, and vice versa.

Publisher: Cast Net Books
Title: Cultivating Connection: A practical guide for personal and relationship growth in ethical non-monogamy
Cover Layout: Pickawoowoo Publishing Group
Interior Layout: Pickawoowoo Publishing Group
Editor: Andrea Zanin
Interior Graphics: Hemlata Sarma

Printing & Distribution: Ingram (USA, UK, AUS, EUR)

ISBN: 979-8-9876647-0-4 (paperback)
ISBN: 979-8-9876647-1-1 (ebook)

First Printing, 2023

Table of Contents

Acknowledgements

This book, like all others, would not exist without the encouragement, support, and assistance of many wonderful people. I want to express my appreciation to all the people who have taught and trained me in my profession over the years, particularly the personal mentoring of Clerissa Cooper, LPC and Dr. Becky Beaton, and to all my clients, as I have learned from each and every one of you. I want to thank my own personal polycule for being such wonderful humans and for being willing to engage in communication work with open hearts and open minds, over and over again. I want to thank Dr. Eli Sheff for her coaching and encouragement when I was stuck, as well as Kitty Chambliss for her encouragement along the way. I want to thank Colleen McMahon for her early editing efforts and copy reading. And I want to thank John Adams for his early editing assistance, and multifaceted marketing skills—and also Desireé Stephens who helped with marketing guidance. I want to thank Andrea Zanin for her incredible professional editing skills, fabulous input, and caring encouragement. I want to extend my appreciation to the early readers—Rachael Zoreena, Dr. Rachel Kieran, Mikaela Corlette-Black, LPC, and Marla Stewart for their content input and title suggestions—and also Anna Baxter, LPC for help naming the book. And I want to thank all the people who helped me with exposure on their podcasts, blogs, groups, and channels.

Introduction

What's healthy in a relationship? How do we foster a strong, secure love with a partner or partners while also balancing that with our independence, particularly in ethical non-monogamy (ENM)? What are boundaries? How do we make them and how do we know when they are healthy and ethical? And how do we negotiate fairly and sensitively with partners with whom we may have varying degrees of commitment? When there's a conflict in our relationships, how do we defend our individual boundaries while still taking good care of our relationships and even strengthening the bond within them?

These are the questions I try to answer in this book.

After several years as a relationship therapist working with people in non-monogamous relationships, I noticed the greatest confusion for my clients seemed to be around personal boundaries, how to employ them, and how to balance individual needs with the needs of the relationship.

I saw people who gave away almost everything for their relationships and wondered why they still felt unloved and unappreciated. I saw people who felt so guilty asking for or requiring anything from their partners that they twisted themselves into pretzels to become a perfect match for someone who was not a good match for them.

I saw people make demands of their partners while throwing temper tantrums, making threats, and outright bullying them, and then wondering why their partners felt unsafe, were unwilling to speak their truth, felt increasingly resentful, and grew ever more distant from them.

I saw people struggle with their fear of abandonment, trauma triggers, and mental health disorder symptoms. I saw people desperately wanting understanding and compassion from their partners while asking for it in ways that would make most people feel defensive or would drive them away.

I wanted to help people understand the balance between taking good care of themselves and taking good care of their relationships. I believed that when the balance was right, and both (or all) people in the relationship were doing it, these processes—taking care of themselves and taking care of the relationship—would work together rather than in opposition.

I believed it was important to understand when a person was using personal boundaries appropriately and when they were employing them improperly. I began by thinking about what kinds of interactions foster growth, self-esteem, and self-compassion for us as individuals versus what kinds of interactions cause us harm and even trauma. I felt strongly that we have a fundamental human right to be treated in ways that are not inherently harmful.

I combined this with what I knew from relationship counseling litera-ture and training. What interactions lead to increased happiness and bond-ing in relationships, and what behaviors lead to harm and alienation? I also believe strongly that we are fundamentally very social beings and support-ive, encouraging, affectionate relationships are integral to our mental health and emotional happiness.

I came up with a list of rights that I believe a person has and must protect in order to remain a healthy individual. I also came up with a way of interact-ing and speaking that includes respecting each person's human rights, and also fosters bonding and connection in relationships. And finally, I came up with a system for determining what to do when one person's rights seem to impact or conflict with another person's rights.

As I sketched out what I believed relationship-related human rights should be, I knew that these rights needed to apply equally to every per-son involved in a relationship. However, this often led to situations where it appeared that one person's rights directly conflicted with someone else's rights.

There's an old saying, "Your right to swing your fist ends where my nose begins." Despite its violent imagery, what this adage means is that you have the right to control your body (your fist) but that right is limited by my right to control my body (my nose) and by the way the exercising of your right impacts me. I applied this principle to the rights that I was sketching out.

It began with a blog

In January 2018, I wrote and published my first blog post in an attempt to clarify what boundaries we have a right to make and when we cross the line out of rightful boundaries and into behavior that becomes controlling and unethical, and thus damaging to our relationships. Specifically, I wrote about how this might show up in non-monogamous relationships. That first blog post led to three more in which I clarified common obstacles to creating healthy boundaries and discussed how relationship agreements are key to resolving relationship conflicts.

As I continued working with clients, I referred them to my blog posts to help them understand what I was trying to teach them in relationship counseling. Over and over, clients responded positively and told me the blog posts were very helpful.

During this time, I was also doing presentations at local non-monogamy conventions (Atlanta Poly Weekend and Sex Down South) on relationship communication, attachment and bonding, and controlling and manipulative behavior. I received a lot of positive feedback from attendees and con organizers regarding these presentations and how useful they felt the information was in helping them reduce the pain in their relationship conflicts, better resolve those conflicts, and navigate their multiple, overlapping non-monogamous relationships more smoothly.

It was at this time that I began to consider writing a book. I knew I had a lot more to say about what was healthy for relationships and how to use these ideas about personal boundaries in a way that improved the bonding, trust, and intimacy in relationships. And I knew I wanted to share this information with many more people than I would ever reach in face-to-face settings.

How is this book different?

This book is my attempt at sharing a complete system for finding and creating that beautiful balance between fostering a healthy self and fostering healthy non-monogamous relationships.

This book is not a primer on polyamory. I will not focus on teaching what polyamory is, why you might want to try it, or how to get started. This book is specifically about teaching a system through which to examine and resolve the conflicts and disagreements that inevitably arise in any adult relationship, and it's written in a way that's friendly to polyamorous, LGBTQIA2+ (lesbian, gay, bisexual, transgender, queer, intersexed, asexual, Two-Spirit, and more) and kink/BDSM relationships.

What is my therapeutic approach?

I am a psychotherapist (Licensed Clinical Social Worker[1]) and I specialize in working with people in the polyamorous, kink, and BDSM communities, as well as the LGBTQAI2+ communities, and with sex workers. At present I am licensed in both Georgia and South Carolina, and I'm registered to do telemental health in Florida.

I've trained in a lot of modalities and I'm purposefully and decidedly eclectic in my approach to therapy. Clients come to therapy because they're in pain. My job is to help them reduce their pain, help them heal their mental and emotional injuries, teach them how to cope with symptoms they can't (or can't yet) eliminate, and create and sustain a happy, healthy life and relationships. I am interested in learning and using any modality that will help me to help them achieve these goals.

I believe there is a basic, fundamental human nature that scientists and clinicians are still working to understand. Brené Brown references it when she says, "You are neurobiologically hardwired to care what people think."[2] We care what people think, and thanks to mirror neurons, most of us can (imperfectly) read emotions on others' faces and use that as a clue to tell us what we believe others think of us.

Mirror neurons are specialized brain cells that allow us to watch someone else do a task and then mirror their behavior. This is also why we can imagine ourselves in the position of another person and imagine how they might feel. (If we then care about how they feel, that is empathy.) We also use this ability when we try to predict another person's intentions or state of mind based on their facial expressions, tone of voice, and behaviors.

---

1 Licensed Clinical Social Worker (LCSW) is the designation for my clinical license in Georgia. Licensed Independent Social Worker in Clinical Practice (LISW-CP) is the designation for my license in South Carolina. CCH stands for Certified Clinical Hypnotherapist, which means I've earned a certification in clinical hypnotherapy from the Anxiety and Stress Management Institute.

2 Sandra Respeto (director), 2019. *The Call to Courage*. Documentary, Netflix.

Human beings are neurobiologically hardwired as social creatures. In the formative times of our species, our individual survival depended on group cohesion, working together, and protecting one another. Deep emotional bonds, alliances, friendships, an awareness of power and influence, seeking acceptance, and avoiding rejection, humiliation, and shame are ways our individual emotions encourage behavior that benefits group cohesion and group survival and that secures our individual membership in the group.

We evolved hardwired with a strong desire to be valued, cared-for members of a group of other humans because that benefited our survival as individuals and the survival of our species as a whole in a world filled with predators and other perils. Human emotions are physical-mental states of being meant to motivate us toward certain behaviors. Any psychological or therapeutic intervention must work within the framework of our neurobiological human nature or it will fail to help and may also do harm.

Steven Porges' revolutionary work on polyvagal theory explains much more about human physiology of emotions than we ever understood before. Evolution is much like soil stratification: old systems remain, and new systems get layered on top of older systems. When interacting with our environment, we use our newest developed systems first. The ventral vagal system, or social engagement system, creates our "safe and social" mode. It's the newest layer, and is unique to mammals. Deb Dana, an international lecturer on polyvagal theory, explains:

> Connecting with others is a biological imperative. … We seek opportunities for co-regulation. The ability to soothe and be soothed, to talk, listen, to offer and receive, to fluidly move in and out of connection is centered in this newest part of the autonomic nervous system. Reciprocity, the mutual ebb and flow that defines nourishing relationships is a function of the ventral vagus. … In a ventral vagal state [the safe and social mode], we have access to a range of responses including calm, happy, meditative, engaged, attentive, active, interested, excited, passionate, alert, ready, relaxed, savoring, and joyful.[3]

_____

3 Deb Dana, 2018. *The Polyvagal Theory in Therapy: Engaging the Rhythm of Regulation.* W. W. Norton.

When we are in the safe and social mode, we try to stay in it. This is the mode where we are open and trusting. Porges' research shows that when we are in the safe and social mode, the activity in the vagal system is mostly between the face and heart. We are relaxed, open, and engaging with others.

If a threat arises, such as a person suddenly acting aggressively, we may find our first response is confusion and we may try to explain away the threat. We may offer up explanations for the behavior that allows everyone in the group to stay in safe and social mode. "I'm sure he didn't mean that. He's just overly tired."

However, once our amygdala (the threat detection center of the brain) registers danger, the activity in the vagal system drops into the trunk of the body and the limbs, adrenaline is pumped into the bloodstream and the arms and legs feel a surge of energy as the body is primed to fight or flee.

If the danger is such that we can't run, or the threat is too powerful to fight, the activity in the vagal system drops down further to the gut and we freeze or "play dead" in the hopes the threat goes away.

The fight, flight, or freeze response comes from two older evolutionary systems: the sympathetic branch of the autonomic nervous system and the dorsal vagal pathway of the parasympathetic branch. Once we have been activated down the polyvagal ladder into fight, flight, or freeze, we eventually seek safety and comfort in order to move back up the ladder and feel safe and social again. That safety can be created through self-comforting or through seeking comfort and co-regulation with others.

For relationships to be healthy and promote the mental and emotional health of those in the relationship, the people need to be attuned to one another. They need to feel safe enough to open up to each other and respond in ways that continue to create safety and security for each other. And when people become misaligned, they need a way to get back into alignment so they can return to providing that attunement, co-regulation, and reciprocity to one another. This is where happiness is found and created. And this is what I try to help my clients achieve.

Who am I?

At the time of this writing, I'm in my late fifties and I've been in a happy, healthy polyamorous relationship for 13 years. I've also happily cohabitated with my partner and metamour[4] (my partner's wife) for six years. I have a girlfriend who lives nearby with her wife. My partner and metamour have had many other relationships of varying degrees of commitment over the years.

Though I lived as and identified as a lesbian for most of my adult life, I now identify as nonbinary, genderqueer, and transmasculine, and have chosen to do some limited transitioning through surgery and hormones. I use either she or they pronouns, or no pronouns at all.

Acknowledging my bias

No writer can claim to be unbiased or objective. I believe one of the first steps in trying to make my written work more accessible and relatable is to acknowledge my bias as the writer.

A second step is to try to reference other perspectives and lived experiences that I, as a writer, have not lived.

A third step is to ask others with different life experiences to review the material before publication in an attempt to improve its inclusiveness.

Here are my biases: I was raised in the United States as a person recognized as Caucasian (a privileged position in a racist culture). "White" culture in the United States is unusually individualistic and my perspective on psychology and social psychology may be insensitive to the powerful group identities and responsibilities people of color can feel toward their family, extended family, tribe, race, or culture.

I was raised as a girl though I showed strong connection to a masculine identification at an early age. From my earliest memories, I strongly resisted and resented the double standards and unequal social expectations that were placed on people seen as girls and women (and thus placed on me). These gendered social rules and expectations restricted me from doing the things I found enjoyable, and they prescribed activities I found boring and tiresome. They also pressured me to be submissive or self-sacrificing when it didn't feel right or fair.

Even at four or five years old, I could see how gendered behaviors and traits were related to the social power and influence a person could effectively wield. And I was raised in an environment where interpersonal power

---

4 A metamour is your partner's other partner.

was often used to take advantage of others, manipulate or control others, and callously abuse and harm others. I saw and experienced the trauma, harm, and fragmented relationships first-hand and I became very interested in how power and influence are created, used, and abused, how abuses of power can be opposed or prevented, and how relationships in these circumstances can be repaired.

Additionally, my experience and knowledge in the kink and BDSM/ Leather communities informs my awareness of power dynamics in relationships, including both the potentially healing and potentially harmful uses of power. As such, my perspective is strongly egalitarian. I recognize that power is always present in relationships and that it's better for people to acknowledge it explicitly. I believe that if people desire a power dynamic, they should make this a conscious, consensual, and intentional choice.

I also feel strongly that if a person wishes to negotiate away some of their personal power, they should do so, at the beginning, as a person of equal power and respect. They should take the time they need to develop trust and safety with the person to whom they wish to give that power. And they should put mechanisms in place to express when something in the dynamic is hurting them, to request course correction, or to take back their power should they feel the need to do so.

This book is written primarily with a non-monogamous readership in mind. My perspective is that even in an extensive polycule (a group of people in interconnected romantic or sexual relationships), there is a relationship between each pair of people. Even in a triad, person 1 has a relationship with person 2, person 2 has a relationship with person 3, and person 3 has a relationship with person 1. And there is a relationship dynamic that includes all three people. The triad can be broken down into three couple relationships that each involve making space for the other two couple relationships. For this reason, I primarily refer to relationships as involving two people, though I also discuss group dynamics involving more than two people from time to time.

A note for monogamous people

Monogamous-minded people can benefit just as much from this book as non-monogamous ones. The system for communication and respecting individual rights is the same. All relationships can benefit from open, clear, compassionate communication about what expectations you both agree are fair. Monogamy is simply one of those expectations and agreements.

I feel this is one of the gifts that non-monogamous subcultures can offer to monogamous people. Because the expectation of monogamy is built into our culture, people typically engage in monogamous relationships without actually examining or discussing those expectations. They rarely actually sit down with each other and consciously agree or consent to those expectations.

For example, one person in a couple might believe that cheating only takes place if they actually have physical sex with another person. Their partner might believe that feeling romantic love for another person or sharing close, intimate feelings is "emotional cheating" and that it counts just as much as sexual cheating. If these two people haven't talked about what monogamy is to them and what constitutes cheating, they may be headed for a potential disaster somewhere down the road.

On the other hand, if they talk about it before it happens, they get a chance to spell out what counts as cheating to each of them, and to actively agree (or disagree and negotiate) the expectations and possible agreements they want to have that restrict their behavior.

About the system

This book provides a clear and easy-to-apply system for understanding what we have a right to expect from others, versus what we should present as a request. It discusses how to know when agreeing to a request is healthy or unhealthy and how to go about addressing these topics with our partner or partners, or even with other people in our lives such as friends, co-workers, or family members.

When (and how) to seek professional help

This book is not meant as a substitute for professional treatment or care. If you have mental health issues, especially if they threaten your safety or someone else's safety, please seek professional help. If your relationship does not improve with self-help resources (such as this book), please seek professional help.

If you are in an abusive relationship, please seek professional help and the support of organizations that can help protect you. When in an abusive relationship, standing up for yourself can increase the abuse directed at you, and leaving an abuser can increase the risk to your safety. There are organizations whose mission it is to keep people safe while helping them to exit an abusive relationship.

That said, I'm very aware that mental health help can be difficult and confusing to access, particularly in the United States. When I was 18 years old, I left the unfortunate circumstances I was raised in. I was on my own and also had very active symptoms of complex post-traumatic stress disorder, anxiety, depression, and substance abuse issues. I had not developed self-discipline or coping skills. I was unpredictable and undependable. In short, I was a mess.

I worked minimum-wage jobs, and barely avoided being fired. I was poor. And I had no health insurance. Had I known I needed mental health care, I wouldn't have known how to access it, or what it had to offer. Instead, I read self-help books and accessed self-help groups. Eventually I found a government-subsidized group therapy program, and later, as my financial situation improved, I worked with private mental health therapists. If you lack resources and access, some kinds of mental health support may be less available to you. Nonetheless, if you need help and healing, I encourage you to seek out and take advantage of the resources that you do have access to.

It can be difficult to know when and how to seek help. Think of it as triage in this order of priorities:

1. Threats to life.
2. Threats of bodily harm.
3. Life dysfunction and misery.

Let's discuss threats to life. If you or someone you know has suicidal or homicidal thoughts, seek professional care.

Suicidal thoughts can take many forms: maybe you are actively thinking about or planning how to kill yourself; maybe you feel trapped in a painful situation and can't think of any other way out; maybe you think everyone else would be better off if you weren't here; maybe your brain flashes pictures of you driving into a tree when you get behind the wheel; maybe you feel numb and you've been thinking there's no point in living if this is all there is; or maybe you believe there is something dangerous, evil, or wrong with you that can only be cured by death.

Homicidal thoughts also take many forms. Maybe you think ending another person's life is the only way out of a painful situation; maybe you think you can't live without that person; maybe you think you are entitled to punish them for how they treated you; maybe your brain is flashing images at you of killing or injuring them; maybe you believe they are yours to do with as you see fit; or maybe you believe there is something dangerous, evil, or wrong with them that can only be cured by death.

All of these thoughts are indications that professional help is in order. In the United States, you can call suicide hotlines or go to an emergency room for an assessment. If you call 911, ask for mental health or medical intervention services. The National Suicide Prevention Lifeline is available 24 hours a day in English and Spanish at 800-273-8255. We also have a new Suicide and Crisis Lifeline that can be accessed by dialing 988.

Keep in mind that accessing these services might mean spending some time in an inpatient setting, and that may be imposed on you against your will. The people you are seeking help from have the authority (and legal responsibility) to confine you if they determine you are a risk to yourself or others. This is usually short-term (three to 14 days) so plan ahead, if you can, regarding your housing, pets, job, and children.

I don't want to discourage anyone from seeking emergency help if it is needed. But I also want to encourage caution when contacting authorities for that help. In many places the police are still the people who respond to these calls for help. This can lead to bodily harm and sometimes death because police may not be adequately trained in de-escalation or how to respond to a person having a mental health crisis.

Also keep in mind that hospitals, agencies, and even private therapists may not be knowledgeable or affirming of some of the things that are central to your identity or relationships. They may not know much about ethical non-monogamy, LGBTQIA2+ identities, or kink and BDSM. Many people have been harmed by the lack of expertise and support for their lives, identities, and family structures they have experienced in these settings. If you need to seek emergency help, be prepared to either advocate for yourself or a loved one, or cope with the lack of expertise you may experience.

The next level of severity as you decide whether to seek professional help is if you are not overtly suicidal or homicidal, but are doing things that could harm yourself or others. These behaviors include injuring your body with burning, cutting, or punching yourself; neglecting your body by not eating, bathing, or taking medication you need to stay healthy; and risky behaviors that could threaten your life, health, or safety, such as running out into traffic, severe substance abuse, driving in a very risky way, or engaging in very risky sexual behaviors.

Certain inpatient settings can be very helpful for this level of severity. In the United States, cities and counties usually provide options for low-income people, such as detox centers for substance abuse issues, eating disorder inpatient programs, and more. Depending on your location, they may be easy to access or very difficult to access based on available beds, your access to insurance, or the expectation of a financial contribution from the patient.[5]

If inpatient programs are not accessible or would not be helpful, in the United States most cities and counties operate outpatient mental health services for low-income and indigent people. They are sometimes called "community services boards," and they provide individual and group therapy programs at very low or no cost. (This is probably what I accessed when I was young.)

If you are not in a life-or-death emergency situation, it's important to take the time to try to find therapists, agencies, or hospitals that will be as supportive as possible of the elements of your identity that are important to you. Look for local, national, or international lists.[6] You can also search for individual therapists in your area using a search word such as "polyamory" or "trans-affirming" and then reach out to those therapists. If you can't work with a private therapist, you can still contact them and ask which agencies, hospitals, or low-income options would be most affirming for you. Most private therapists are happy to help with this information if they can.

---

5 The United States does not have a publicly funded healthcare system. Most people in the US pay for expensive medical care through private health insurance. People who do not have private insurance must either pay with personal funds, access limited public resources, or wait until their condition is life-threatening and private facilities are required to treat them without upfront payment. Or they simply can't access the care they need.

6 Here are a few that may help:
https://www.kapprofessionals.org/
https://www.seculartherapy.org/
https://openingup.net/open-list/
https://www.polyfriendly.org/categories/psychotherapists-licensed-or-registered/
https://nqttcn.com/en/
https://www.psychologytoday.com/

Now that we (in the United States) have the Affordable Care Act, a social worker at any of the agencies mentioned just now can probably help you sign up for health insurance. This opens up access to thousands of private therapists who take insurance. If you live in a rural area or transportation is an issue, many therapists and organizations have embraced telehealth, so you might be able to access care by phone or online.

If you access care through an agency or hospital, a psychiatric evaluation is usually one of the services they provide. A psychiatrist is a medical doctor who is able to recommend and prescribe medications. Mental health therapists don't usually have that ability. If you are seeing a private therapist, ask if they think you would benefit from seeing a psychiatrist, too.

If you are struggling with basic functionality, such as getting yourself to go to work or keeping a job, or if you're unable to function due to panic attacks or can't leave the house due to fears or obsessive thoughts, professional mental health care might be necessary to help you improve, and it would certainly be helpful.

Some private therapists don't take insurance. If you are reaching out to one of them, and their fee is not affordable for you, it never hurts to ask if they can allow you to pay a reduced rate. Most private therapists allow for a handful of clients to pay a reduced fee. Our ethics codes encourage us to do so.

With all of that said, self-help resources can also be very beneficial. As they say in Alcoholics Anonymous, "The program works, if you work it." The same is true for therapy. The amount of energy you put into the process will impact the extent of the positive results you get out of it.

Rather than only going into the therapy office for an hour every week or two, read self-help books and attend self-help groups if you can. Ask your therapist for supplemental reading material. Think about your therapy sessions during the time in between and journal about insights, problems, dreams, and whatever else seems pertinent. Practice the skills you learn in therapy or through other sources. A combination of professional guidance and your own efforts typically gets the best results.

Finally, many people will do just fine using only self-help resources. If you are mostly functional in life, you've got pretty good coping skills, you're fairly resilient when life throws a monkey wrench at you, and you don't engage in life- or safety-threatening behaviors, you may find that reading or participating in self-help resources is all you really need for your continued personal growth.

How is this book organized?

Here's the breakdown of what you can expect.

Part 1: Cultivating connection

In chapter 1, I paint a picture of the spirit of healthy relationships and explain our basic attachment needs to give you an idea of what that fine balance looks like. Chapter 2 goes deeper into our neurobiology and how it can complicate our responses in relationship conflicts. Chapters 3 and 4 teach real tools for healing rifts due to arguments and creating co-regulation and connection in our relationships.

Part 2: Fostering autonomy

It's important to be flexible and giving, but it's equally important to not give away too much. In chapter 5, I outline what I believe are our basic human rights when in relationships. And in chapters 6 and 7 we look at common obstacles within ourselves and coming from others that can make standing up for our rights more challenging.

Part 3: Working together

I explain the essential elements of healthy relationship agreements in chapter 8. Chapter 9 provides a personal responsibility flow chart for determining what individual work each person needs to do and how to determine who should work on what. It is so important that we take responsibility for ourselves, identify what issues we need to work on, and do our own work. Chapter 10 revisits attachment theory and looks at how to use the tools taught in this book to create earned secure attachment in a way that is sensitive to the mental health issues we or our partners might have. It also teaches the seven essential elements to maintain secure attachment and explains that this is an ongoing practice within relationships. The conclusion reviews what we've learned and how to apply these concepts and skills.

I hope you find this book helpful in creating loving, lasting relationships and in fostering your own individual growth. I also hope it gives you the confidence and strength to know when and how to advocate for yourself, and when and how to work together as a team with the people close to you.

Part 1

Cultivating Connection

CHAPTER 1

The Spirit of Healthy Relationships

Human beings are social creatures hardwired to connect and bond with others, so healthy relationships are truly one of the keys to our happiness. Because relationships are so important and so central to human happiness, they are also one of our greatest sources of pain when they go wrong, or when we struggle to develop them in the first place.

How to achieve happy, healthy, stable relationships is often one of the great mysteries for many people. It just sort of happens, or it doesn't. When it does, we plod along thinking everything is going great—until it's not. Then we have a mess to go back and untangle, and we are often at a loss as to how to figure it out and repair it.

Often, we turn to books and articles for relationship advice. But there's so much of it available that we can easily become overwhelmed trying to read it all. What I've noticed is that much of it is written in the form of individual examples. "When this happens, do this. When someone says this, it's unhealthy. But in this *other* circumstance, the exact same thing *is* healthy."

When I'm working with clients in relationship counseling, they often ask me to recommend reading material. I've found it frustrating that much of the reading material written for the general public seems to be written in the form of, "Let's provide lots of examples and then you'll know what's healthy when you see it."

I wanted to be able to explain to my clients *why* something was healthy, or why it wasn't. If words or behaviors are healthy in this circumstance, but not in that circumstance… *why*?

Reading material for therapists is sometimes written in a heavy academic style, and it requires considerable background knowledge in psychology.

For the average reader, this means slogging through information they don't need. Also, very few resources, both academic works and material for the general public, are written with non-monogamous people, kinky people, or LGBTQIA2+ people in mind.[7]

You'll know what's healthy when you see it?

Not really. When we look at other people's relationships, we have to remember that we are only seeing the outside experience, or what some people call "the front stage."

Using the analogy of theater, the front stage is the final, perfected presentation designed to be viewed by the audience. The backstage, in contrast, is the messy, often chaotic lived experience of the actors in the play: stagehands moving pieces of scenery, actors running about half-dressed looking for important bits of costume, assistants trying to get people to their proper mark at the right time, and others whispering forgotten lines to the people on stage.

Many of us have an unhelpful habit of comparing our messy backstage to other people's neat and tidy front stage presentations.

When out in public, with friends and family, or posting on social media, people in relationships tend to be on their best behavior. (Sometimes even during therapy, the time when they should be the most open and honest about their issues!) They don't usually display their arguments (or the severity of them), hurt feelings, raised voices, selfish acts, overreactions, moments of thoughtlessness, or power plays for the world to see.

No relationship is perfect; everyone makes mistakes. But if we don't have a lot of exposure to healthy relationships, we won't really know if our current relationship has an acceptable or unacceptable amount or type of arguing.

In this book, I give you a view of the messy backstage of relationships and explain how to manage them as well as possible so that you can move toward healthy, happy resolutions of conflicts and disagreements.

---

7 LGBTQIA2+ stands for lesbian, gay, bisexual, transgender, queer, intersex, asexual, Two-Spirit, and more.

You'll know it when you live it

I believe you'll know what's healthy when you live it. When you experience it. And if both or all people involved are willing and able to do the work, you'll get to experience what it feels like to be in a happy, healthy relationship. Until you've had this experience, it's really hard to know when what you're living isn't it.

I say this from personal experience. I came from a family that did not model healthy relationships or healthy communication or interaction skills. When I was younger, and before I became a therapist, I tried repeatedly to turn the romantic relationships I was in into happy, healthy, stable relationships, and I couldn't understand why I failed, over and over. Then, while I was in training to become a therapist, at 45 years old, I met a person (my current partner) who was willing and able to do the work and it's the happiest, healthiest relationship I've ever been in.

Due to the combination of my therapist training and this relationship, I learned several really important things:

1. I already had the skills and capacities to do my half of a healthy, happy relationship. I just kept pairing up with other people who didn't. Which means I lacked the ability to assess when a relationship was not measuring up, and when it should end.
2. Since I lacked confirmation that I had healthy relationship skills and expectations, I was easily manipulated and pressured by unhealthy people to accept their unhealthy behavior as normal relationship conflict.
3. I can only do my half of a relationship. No amount of effort can make the other person do their part if they don't want to or are unable to.
4. When I experienced another person (my current partner) responding to me or to a difficult moment in our relationship with love, kindness, respect, and generosity, I finally understood how the balance of healthy individuals and a healthy relationship is created and sustained.

Since then, I have studied relationship research and literature so that I could teach my clients helpful techniques to repair and improve their relationships (when possible).

What does healthy look like backstage?

All relationships have their difficult moments. What does it look like back-stage when a difficult moment happens in a healthy relationship? How do individuals respond to each other when emotions are high and they're having a conflict? Here's an example.

Sarah was the outdoorsy type. She and Jenny had been dating for a couple of years and they were very much in love. Jenny had a long-term nesting partner of eight years, and Sarah was a relationship anarchist. On their weekly date, they were walking a trail that ran parallel to a river. Trees and shrubs were blocking their view of the river. Then they came to a pile of boulders. Sarah believed she could climb over the boulders to get a beautiful view of the river

As she started to climb, Jenny told her to not do that. Sarah, who didn't like being told what to do, responded, "It will be a beautiful view." And she continued climbing. Jenny's voice became louder, and she ordered Sarah to stop.

Sarah had never seen this behavior in Jenny before. She felt immediately angry and didn't want to set a precedent in their relationship where Jenny felt she could order her around. But since the behavior was so out of character for Jenny, Sarah also didn't want to jump to conclusions.

Sarah took some deep breaths, climbed down to Jenny's level, sat on a rock, steadied her voice, and asked, "What's going on?"

"You can't climb those rocks! You'll get hurt!" Jenny said.

"I have confidence I can climb these rocks without getting hurt," Sarah replied.

"Well, I don't!" Jenny countered.

Resisting another wave of anger and continuing to keep her voice as calm as possible, Sarah said, "I don't think it's fair that I should have to give up something I enjoy because you don't have confidence in me. And I don't like being ordered about. You've never spoken to me this way… What's going on?"

Jenny stood silently, looking down.

Sarah softened her voice, "Honey, I just want to know what you're feeling."

"I don't know," Jenny said, looking away.

It was then that Sarah noticed a slight tremor in Jenny's arm.

"I see you're shaking. Is that anger, or fear?"

"Fear!" Jenny said, making eye contact again. The look on her face said, "How could you not know that?"

"What are you afraid of?"

"That you would get hurt!"

They seemed to be at an impasse, then Jenny continued, "It's not that I don't have confidence in you. It's that I don't have confidence in myself. If something did happen to you, I don't think I could climb those rocks. I wouldn't be able to get to you. I wouldn't be able to help."

Sarah reflected on what Jenny had said. She tried to imagine being Jenny and the feelings of fear and helplessness if something had happened and she couldn't get to her partner. She knew she had a right to make her own decisions about risk, but maybe she didn't have the right to expose Jenny to seeing her climb the rocks.

"Okay, I won't climb these rocks right now. I want to be clear that I reserve the right to choose to climb rocks if I want to. But I'll agree to not do it in front of you, so you don't have to experience this fear. Does that work for you?"

Jenny's shoulders immediately relaxed. "Yes, thank you."

"I will also try to remember that when you use this tone, it's because you're afraid. But I'd like you to understand that I really don't like it. It reminds me of my mother. So I'd like you to work on telling me what you feel and asking for what you want, rather than using that tone with me. Deal?"

"Yes. Thank you."

They hugged and kissed. They reassured each other and expressed their love. They continued on and enjoyed the pleasant day.

How do people achieve this beautiful picture of relationship interactions even in the face of conflict? How did Sarah know to take deep breaths and ask questions rather than lash out at Jenny? How did Jenny know to explain herself rather than simply get more demanding? Why did Sarah explicitly remind Jenny that she reserved the right to climb rocks if she wants to, but then *ask* Jenny to work on changing her tone? Why did Jenny thank Sarah rather than pressure Sarah to agree that she should not climb the rocks or even want to climb the rocks?

Happy, healthy, egalitarian relationships are built upon some underlying principles that guide people's daily interactions. A desire to value and embody these principles is what I call the spirit of healthy relationships. They are:

1. Each person respects the rights and autonomy of each other person.
2. The interactions between the people in the relationship demonstrate respect, kindness, and compassion.
3. Mind reading (or expecting others to mind read) is not helpful. Each person agrees that they can't know another person's thoughts, feelings, or motives unless they ask them.
4. Each person can be trusted to do their (imperfect) best to take responsibility for their own thoughts, feelings, and actions, and for resolving their own painful emotions.
5. The people communicate with each other about their struggles, and even when it is not their responsibility to solve a problem, they each offer to help the other wherever they can offer that help authentically and willingly.
6. When asking for help with painful emotions, or when asking for accommodations, they each acknowledge this help would be a gift, and they express appreciation for it.
7. When people make relationship agreements, they are very invested in making sure each person is agreeing voluntarily, with informed consent, and not feeling pressured or coerced in any way.
8. All relationship agreements are unanimous.
9. When people make relationship agreements or agree to accommodations, they can be trusted to do their (imperfect) best to live up to those agreements.
10. If any relationship agreement is no longer working for someone, they can be trusted to initiate a renegotiation.
11. The people in the relationship have fostered an environment where each person is able to feel safe enough to communicate openly and honestly about their feelings, motives, and actions. This safety is created through engagement, listening, validation, affection, consistency, acceptance, patience, and refraining from criticism, judgment, condescension, paternalism, invalidation, neglect, and contempt.

12. The people in the relationship do their best to approach difficulties (emotional and material) with an attitude of teamwork. They see it this way: "We are a team, and solving this problem involves all of us. We will all benefit. And the solution must take all of our needs and wants into account."

13. They recognize that power differences are easily created in relationships. If they wish to have an egalitarian relationship, they seek to be aware of power differences and actively take steps to re-equalize power. If they are seeking to create an intentional power dynamic, they begin as equals, voluntarily consenting and continually re-consenting. They understand that having power or dominance is a responsibility, as is providing service or being submissive. These are relationship agreements like any other and can be renegotiated.

As we go through the book, I'll teach you specific methods for how to enact these principles in our behavior, how to identify the obstacles that may arise, and what to do to resolve those obstacles.

Attachment theory

A great way to understand the interplay of how healthy individuals promote healthy relationships, and healthy relationships promote healthy individuals is through attachment theory.

There's considerable debate regarding whether attachment theory applies universally to all humans. It's very likely that this model is only a useful descriptor for the psychology of children and adults raised in Western, industrialized societies.[8] Since I assume my readers are most likely from this background, I believe the theory will be very helpful in understanding how we bond in relationships. However, if a person is from a non-Western, non-industrialized background, or is a first or second-generation immigrant from a non-Western, non-industrialized background, please keep this in mind if the model doesn't appear to fit or feel useful.

---

8 Heidi Keller, 2018. Universality claim of attachment theory: Children's socioemotional development across cultures. PNAS (*Proceedings of the National Academy of Sciences of the United States of America*) 115 (45), p. 11414–11419. https://www.pnas.org/doi/10.1073/pnas.1720325115

Attachment theory was created by John Bowlby and Mary Ainsworth,[9] and explains how our interaction patterns with our earliest caregivers shape the foundational patterns of how we see ourselves, interact within our closest relationships, and view the world at large. For our discussion of adult relationships, it's important to understand the child's patterns, what they do and why, because we often replay these patterns in our adult relationships.

Mary Ainsworth's research shows that babies' behavioral patterns as they interact with their caregivers are shaped by how their caregivers interact with them. When the caregiver is good at picking up on the baby's distress signals and at interpreting what the baby needs, responds quickly and dependably, and shows joy and affection in their interactions with the baby, the baby tends to develop secure attachment and optimal mental and emotional potential.

Even as infants, we as individuals are shaped by the quality of our relationships with others. Children and adults with secure attachment styles score higher in every area of mental and emotional development, such as:

- optimal brain development
- learning and memory
- ego resilience
- self-esteem
- ability to manage stress
- ability to form healthy interdependent relationships and social friendships
- ability to self-regulate their emotions (calm themselves)
- ability to enjoy themselves and enjoy life.

When caregivers are inconsistent, non-responsive, excessively preoccupied, angry, resentful, punishing, frightening, anxious, overbearing, abusive, or neglectful, children develop one of the non-secure attachment styles.

Mary Ainsworth originally theorized only two non-secure attachment styles: avoidant and ambivalent. In her Baltimore longitudinal study from 1963 to 1967, she found the distribution of attachment patterns among her subjects to be 66% secure, 22% insecure avoidant, and 12% ambivalent

9 Inge Bretherton, 1992. "The Origins of Attachment Theory: John Bowlby and Mary Ainsworth." *Developmental Psychology* 28, p. 759–775. http://www.psychology.sunysb.edu/attachment/online/inge_origins.pdf

attachment.[10] She admitted that she felt some of the children in her studies didn't fit well into either category.

Mary Main later developed a third non-secure category that she called disorganized, which better explained those children who didn't fit well into the other non-secure categories.[11]

To summarize:

Children with secure attachment are typically happy and explorative. They tend to feel safe with their caregivers and seek out their caregivers when distressed. The caregivers tend to be attuned to the child's emotional states and respond sensitively, quickly, and consistently to the child's needs. The child tends to trust that their needs will be met.

Children with avoidant attachment tend to be very independent and explorative, but do not seek out their caregivers when they are distressed. Their caregivers tend to be distant, disengaged, insensitive, or rejecting. The child does not appear to trust that their needs will be met.

Children with ambivalent attachment tend to be clingy and dependent toward the caregiver, but are not easily soothed by the caregiver when distressed. The caregivers tend to be inconsistent in meeting the child's needs, thus the child learns that sometimes their needs with be met and sometimes they won't.

Children with disorganized attachment tend to be the most distressed of all the attachment styles. They demonstrate both strong dependence and strong avoidance toward their caregivers, and sometimes appear disoriented and dazed after experiencing distress. They appear to have no organized strategy for getting their needs met. Their caregivers tend to be both abusive and the child's only source of comfort.

Ideally, when a child is distressed, the caregivers comfort and soothe the child, helping them return to an emotional state of comfort and safety. If these interactions go well, this is where children learn to:

- self-soothe
- trust people

---

10 Mary D. Salter Ainsworth, Mary C. Blehar, Everett Waters, and Sally N. Wall, 2015. *Patterns of Attachment: A Psychological Study of the Strange Situation*. Psychology Press.

11 Mary Main and Judith Solomon, 1986. "Discovery of an insecure-disorganized/disoriented attachment pattern." In T. B. Brazelton and M. W. Yogman (Eds.), *Affective Development in Infancy*, p. 95–124. Ablex Publishing. https://psycnet.apa.org/record/1986-97821-005

- feel safe
- value themselves, their needs, their feelings
- validate their own perceptions and experiences
- value the fulfillment and benefits that come from relationships with others
- trust the world in general.

By soothing us, our caregivers teach us how soothing is done. By valuing us and our feelings enough to respond with love and affection when we are distressed, they help us learn to value ourselves and our own feelings. By showing that they trust that if we are crying out, there must be something wrong, they validate our perceptions and teach us to validate ourselves. And by showing up this way consistently, they teach us that people can (in general) be trusted and the world (in general) is a safe place.

Two other concepts are important to understanding secure attachment: the *safe haven* and the *secure base*.

By responding to the child's needs with acceptance, love, and affection, the caregiver becomes a safe haven for the child. By having a safe haven consistently, the child learns they can go out and explore the world, knowing the caregiver will still be there and the relationship will be unchanged when they need or want to return. This is what's called the secure base.

Jessica Fern put it this way in the book *Polysecure*:

> When safety [a safe haven] is established with our attachment figures and we have an internalized felt sense that we can turn towards them and lean on them when needed, we are freed up to securely turn away from them and engage in the world, whether with them by our side or on our own. A secure base provides the platform from which we can move out in the larger world, explore and take risks. This exploration facilitates our sense of personal competence and healthy autonomy.[12]

---

12 Jessica Fern, 2020. *Polysecure: Attachment, Trauma and Consensual Non-monogamy.* Thorntree Press.

Some of the behaviors and attitudes the caregiver will need to show in order to create a safe haven and secure base for the child are physical touch and soothing, joy in spending time with and interacting with the child, attentiveness, attunement to the child's emotional state (this includes the caregiver appropriately shifting their own emotional state as the child's emotional state changes), and being mentally, emotionally, and physically present.

Attunement doesn't mean providing an exact mirror of the child's emotional state. Simple mirroring is fine when the child is happy, safe, or calm. But when the child is upset, in pain, feeling fear or any other form of distress, the caregiver must shift their state to concern, while maintaining emotional equilibrium, combined with validating the child's experience, pain, or distress as justified given the circumstances. By maintaining a degree of equilibrium, while validating the child's experience and showing concern, the caregiver creates a safe container for the child's distress. This communicates that it's safe for the child to be distressed to the degree of losing awareness of their environment or control of themselves, because they know their caregiver is in control and will keep them safe.

In the book *Raising a Secure Child*, the authors describe the ebb and flow of interactions between the child and caregiver as a circle.[13] For an ambulatory child, we can envision this as a literal circle of movement. The child comes to the caregiver to experience acceptance and attunement, to experience the safe haven, and fill their emotional gas tank, so to speak. When it's full enough to induce feelings of safety, they feel free to go out and experience things away from the caregiver. This fulfills their need to experience autonomy and develop self-mastery. If they continue to feel safe, their fuel lasts longer. If they experience something frightening or painful, their tank empties more quickly. As their emotional tank empties, they circle back to the caregiver to experience more acceptance and attunement in order to refuel. As they explain,

> The Circle of Security shows that little children can be viewed as constantly "going out and coming in." ... exploring, then seeking

---

13 Kent Hoffman, Glen Cooper, and Bert Powell, with Christine M. Benton, 2017. *Raising a Secure Child: How Circle of Security Parenting Can Help You Nurture Your Child's Attachment, Emotional Resilience, and Freedom to Explore.* Guilford Press.

comfort or reassurance or safety and, once they've filled their emotional cup, running out to explore again.[14]

For non-ambulatory children, the circle is more figurative. They call out to the caregiver, or use other proximity-seeking behaviors such as reaching for the caregiver, in order to bring the caregiver to them. They fill their emotional fuel tank with touch, attentiveness, cooing, getting their needs met, and more, and then they feel safe to disengage from the caregiver and explore the larger world with their eyes, hands, and bodies, to play with toys, or to otherwise shift their attention and focus away from the caregiver. When they're ready to refuel, they call out and bring the caregiver back to them.

Attunement to the child's emotional state and current need must include an awareness of the child's need for autonomy, exploration, and opportunities for self-mastery as well as their need for comfort, reassurance, and safety. When the child is ready to explore, the attuned caregiver will also feel safe allowing this temporary disconnection and exploration. They will encourage the child and express confidence in the child's budding self-mastery. They will exhibit a "go have fun, you can do it" attitude.

This is why being mentally and emotionally present and attuned to the child's needs is so important. The child needs the caregiver to notice when they are seeking proximity and refueling of their emotional tank. They also need the caregiver to notice and acknowledge their need to separate, explore, and experience self-mastery. And the child needs to know that the caregiver will be watching, aware, and the safe relationship will still be there, unchanged, when they return.

Given all this responsibility and power, caregivers can fear that they have to be completely and perfectly available and attuned at all times or risk damaging their child. But no one can do that. Mistakes, misattunement, and ruptures in the relationship are inevitable. Therefore, caregivers need to relax and accept their own imperfections, and know what to do when misattunement happens and how to repair ruptures to the relationship.

---

14 Ibid

Dr. Diana Divecha, a developmental psychologist and assistant clinical professor at the Yale Child Study Center and Yale Center for Emotional Intelligence, wrote in her review of *Raising a Secure Child*:

> No one can be attuned to another person at all times, though. In fact, the authors assert that the myth of "complete availability" actually undermines a child's development. Ruptures, small and large, happen all the time in the fabric of human relationships, and so it becomes important that repairs, small and large, become second nature to parents. Caregivers may be relieved to know that children are not keeping a parenting score, but rather assessing whether the relationship is safe and secure overall. Good enough [parenting] is truly good enough.[15]

With this in mind, the caregiver also needs to notice when ruptures happen, identify the child's underlying emotional need, respond to that need, and repair the ruptures.

Childhood attachment styles are not written in stone. They are impacted by our relationships with adults other than our primary caregivers during our childhood and they continue to be impacted by our many relationships with our peers as we grow up. Then we take that attachment style into adulthood and it becomes the template that shapes how we interact in our friendships, in organizations, and in our romantic relationships.

John Bowlby theorized that the attachment system impacted people "from the cradle to the grave." But most of his work and most of the research on the attachment system focused on caregivers and children. Finally, in the mid-1980s, other researchers began to publish work about attachment patterns in adult romantic relationships.

According to R. Chris Fraley,[16] a researcher and professor of psychology at the University of Illinois, the adult attachment system works in very similar ways to the caregiver-infant attachment system. When we are securely attached, we turn toward our partner for comfort and soothing and we give

---

15 Diana Divecha, 2017. "How to cultivate a secure attachment with your child." *Greater Good Magazine*, February 3. https://greatergood.berkeley.edu/article/item/how_to_cultivate_a_secure_attachment_with_your_child

16 R. Chris Fraley, 2018. "Adult attachment theory and research: A brief overview." http://labs.psychology.illinois.edu/~rcfraley/attachment.htm

comfort and soothing when they are distressed. When we know our relationship with them is secure, we feel able to go out and explore the world, knowing we can depend on them and the relationship to be there and be unchanged when we return. Part of that security is based in knowing you can repair ruptures if they happen. And we also look for our partners to be emotionally attuned to us, as we seek to be attuned to them.

Subsequent research has found that adult attachment is best understood as an interplay between two attachment-related variables: attachment-related anxiety and attachment-related avoidance. Fraley explains it this way:

> People who score high on [attachment-related anxiety] tend to worry whether their partner is available, responsive, attentive, etc. People who score on the low end of this variable are more secure in the perceived responsiveness of their partners. The other critical variable is called attachment-related avoidance. People on the high end of this dimension prefer not to rely on others or open up to others. People on the low end of this dimension are more comfortable being intimate with others and are more secure depending upon and having others depend upon them. A prototypical secure adult is low on both of these dimensions.

This graph[17] helps explain the two dimensions and how they relate to the four most common adult attachment styles:[18]

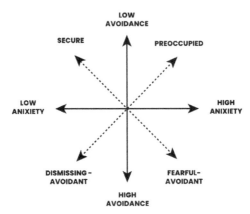

17 Ibid.
18 Reproduced with permission from R. Chris Fraley, University of Illinois.

The four most common adult attachment styles are slightly different from the childhood attachment styles. They are:

- Secure
- Preoccupied (also known as anxious-preoccupied)
- Fearful-avoidant (also known as unresolved disorganized)
- Dismissing-avoidant

A securely attached adult is low in relationship anxiety (they tend to feel secure) and low in avoidance (they seek comfort in relationships). An adult with the preoccupied attachment style is low in avoidance (they seek comfort in relationships), but high in anxiety (they fear their partner won't be there or will respond with rejection).

An adult with the fearful-avoidant (or unresolved disorganized) attachment style is high in anxiety and high in avoidance. They believe they want a relationship, but they avoid relationships because they assume rejection, or they may sabotage a relationship they are in due to their high anxiety. This group tends to feel most comfortable loving someone from afar, or loving someone who is unavailable. When they are in a relationship, that's when the unresolved disorganized attachment behaviors are more readily observed; they don't appear to have a coherent strategy for getting their needs met in times of distress. They will sometimes respond with anger, sometimes with passivity, and sometimes with fear and creating distance.

Disorganized attachment is the result of abusive, manipulative, isolating relationships. If you have experienced this sort of damaging relationship in your childhood, an unresolved disorganized attachment style might be the baseline pattern you bring with you into your current relationships. It can also be developed in adulthood due to abusive, terrifying, controlling, highly manipulative relationships or environments such as cults.[19] I revisit adult-onset unresolved disorganized attachment in chapter 10.

Lastly, an adult with the dismissing-avoidant attachment style (high in avoidance and low in anxiety) is what we think of as the stereotypical lone wolf; they prefer to not depend on or seek out relationships or to have

---

19 Alexandra Stein, 2016. *Terror, Love, and Brainwashing: Attachment in Cults and Totalitarian Systems.* Routledge.

others depend on them. When they do have relationships, they're skilled at suppressing and covering up evidence of their distress or pain.

The current attachment style we have in any given relationship is a combination of who each person is in their relationships (their baseline attachment pattern) and how the two people interact. Polyamorous people may be more securely attached in one relationship and more anxious-preoccupied in another. A person with an unresolved disorganized baseline attachment style might find they display very different attachment strategies in each of their relationships.

Though the distribution of attachment styles among adults is similar to those found in infants and children,[20] this doesn't mean that the attachment style we develop as children is indelible. The research does not show a direct correlation between our childhood attachment styles and our adult attachment styles. The research shows only a small to moderate overlap between childhood attachment patterns and adult attachment patterns. Though further research is required, there is reason to believe that just as our additional relationships in childhood continue to shape our attachment styles beyond infancy, our adult relationships continue to shape and may even overwrite our baseline attachment styles.

In other words, an insecurely attached person can become securely attached in a relationship that is nurturing, responsive, and affectionate, and in which interactions are primarily ethical. And a securely attached person can become less securely attached when in a relationship that's neglectful or abusive, or when the interactions within the relationship tend to be unethical.

Interestingly enough, when interviewed most adults will describe the characteristics of secure relationships as the most desirable characteristics. Given that information, you'd think we would all hold out for secure, stable relationships and partners with secure attachment patterns. But we don't. In fact, Fraley says that according to some evidence, people end up in relationships with people who confirm their pre-existing understandings of how attachment-based relationships work.[21]

This is where we frequently see people with the anxious-preoccupied attachment style pair up with people who have one of the avoidant

---

20 Fraley, 2018.
21 Ibid.

attachment styles. For both of them, their partner confirms their existing beliefs and fears about attached relationships.

For the anxious-preoccupied person, when things get rocky in the relationship, their avoidant partner seeks distance and escape. This triggers their fear of abandonment and confirms for them that their relationship is not a safe haven. They cannot expect their partner to respond positively and soothingly to their pain, and they can't count on their partner to be consistently available.

For the avoidant partner, when things get stressful in the relationship, they seek distance because that calms them and they feel safer. When they return, they see an angry, upset, distressed partner who may be hurling judgements and accusations at them. This confirms for them that their relationship is not a secure base. When they try to return from their "time-out," they are distressed to find the relationship and their partner have changed.

Whether as children or as adults, we're hardwired to be shaped and changed by our interactions with others. This is why I believe so strongly that healthy relationships are a vital part of creating and supporting healthy individuals and vice versa. Jessica Fern puts it this way in *Polysecure*:

> In many ways, we can see attachment as a nice feedback loop in which relationships shape the individual and individuals then shape their relationships, with relationships further reshaping the individual and so on repeatedly.

The one ingredient in this discussion that's still missing is the innate temperament of the individual. We are not just blank slates when we come into the world, and we are not completely shaped by our experiences. Two babies in the same environment will respond differently depending on their inborn nature.

Some people are born with very sensitive nervous systems, like wires with the insulation scraped away—raw and exposed. Others are born with resilient, durable nervous systems. To illustrate this, think of the happy, easy baby that laughs and coos at everything and bounces back quickly from small shocks or injuries. Compare that to the tense, nervous, sensitive baby that cries quickly and inconsolably with every loud noise or experience of physical discomfort.

Our brains and nervous systems are highly adaptable. We are so adaptable that the stress experienced by our parents and earlier ancestors can trigger adaptations that prepare us for a stressful environment, even before we are born. Research has shown that parents who have experienced trauma or high stress have babies with more sensitive and fragile emotional nervous systems.[22]

Because of this, as well as natural genetic variation, I like to say that each child is unique and is born with an innate temperament. Caregivers have the luxury of being able to make more mistakes with the "easy babies" without it resulting in attachment injuries, while caregivers with reactive babies may get attachment injuries with far fewer mistakes.

I think of the building blocks of attachment in this way: First we have human beings as a species. We are highly intelligent, very social creatures whose brains and nervous systems evolved primarily in a Stone Age environment where we needed to be able to depend on each other to protect the group and our most vulnerable members (including babies and young children) from the elements and from predators. Therefore, we are hardwired for attachment and bonding with other humans.

Second is the baby's innate temperament. This is a combination of their natural genetic variation and the parents' and ancestors' experiences. This will determine how many mistakes and how much environmental stress the baby can endure before attachment injuries occur.

Third is the child's attachment experiences. This involves how kind, loving, caring, attentive, and consistent the caregivers are, as well as environmental stressors that can impact the attentiveness and reliability of their caregivers.

And then there are the child's ongoing experiences with other adults and with peers, as well as their relationships with others as an adult, which all continue to shape their attachment system. There's probably also a cultural element that is beyond my expertise or the scope of this book that gives the child scripts for how they might interpret the meaning of their attachment experiences or may negate the use of attachment theory altogether.

What does healthy mean for an individual?

When I was young, it was common to hear people in the media, politics and religion lament the rising divorce rate and the increase in single-parent

---

22 Mark Wolynn, 2016. *It Didn't Start with You: How Inherited Family Trauma Shapes Who We Are and How to End the Cycle.* Penguin Books.

households. These talking heads often said, "Children need a father!" Even when I was a child, my response was, "No they don't. They need a *good* father." (Or good mother, or good caregiver.)

I believed then, and I believe now, that children need a good, loving, stable caregiver (or two, or several) who will help them develop healthy self-esteem, self-respect, and self-compassion. Children are harmed by abusive, immature, neglectful caregivers; such people contribute to mental and emotional damage in those children.

Likewise, I believe that good, healthy, stable, loving adult relationships contribute to the healthy self-esteem, self-respect, and self-compassion for the adults in those relationships. What is healthy for the individual and what is healthy for the relationship work together, symbiotically.

Unhealthy, damaged individuals can create unhealthy relationships, and unhealthy, damaging, abusive and neglectful relationships can cause damage to an otherwise healthy individual.

When I say that something is "healthy" for an individual, what I mean is that it contributes to our self-esteem, self-compassion, and self-respect, and to our ability to be true to who we inherently are, to know ourselves and our values, to live consistently with those values, and to feel confidently at peace with who we are.

To find, develop, and own our individual identity, it's important to feel free to explore our interests and values, and to not fear we will be judged or rejected as we explore.

Notice how this links symbiotically with having healthy, loving, supportive relationships: to feel free to explore our interests and values, we benefit greatly from having encouraging, accepting partners who do not judge us or reject us as we explore.

Self-respect is similar to what we do when we respect others. Self-respect involves respecting our own rights and our own dignity; not allowing others to violate our rights or our dignity is an important part of creating and protecting our self-respect. Self-respect also includes making a choice to value ourselves, our preferences, and the decisions we make as good and valid.

For example, if I have chosen teaching as my career, but I refer to teaching as a less than optimal choice—such as if I say, "Those who can, do. Those who can't, teach"—then I am disrespecting myself and a choice I made that is central to who I am.

Self-compassion is similar to feeling compassion toward others. It's the ability to give ourselves grace for our imperfections while retaining the ability to think and feel positively toward ourselves. It means acknowledging and being gentle with ourselves when we're suffering. It means learning to validate our own feelings, experiences, and perspectives. And it means forgiving ourselves when we fail at a goal or fail to live up to our values or to a relationship agreement.

This isn't meant to be a blanket excuse for not trying. To also develop self-esteem, we need to know we tried to do well and balance that with compassion for being imperfect at those things we try to do.

Dr. Kristin Neff's research suggests that self-compassion may be more valuable to happiness than self-esteem, though I believe self-esteem also has value and is worth cultivating side by side with self-respect and self-compassion.[23]

There's a great deal of research on the factors that contribute to strong self-esteem, and those factors are not always what feels good in the moment. Setting goals that are difficult and achieving them builds our self-confidence and our self-efficacy (our belief that we can achieve what we set our minds to do), and thus builds our self-esteem.

Sometimes, it's painful to communicate with others about tough topics, to set and defend our appropriate boundaries, or to learn to live up to our responsibilities, but ultimately all these things raise our self-esteem and our self-respect.

Communicating with others on tough topics and living up to our responsibilities and agreements are two practices that are central to treating others ethically. Knowing that we tend to treat others ethically is also important to our self-esteem, and this in turn helps us foster healthy, strong, secure relationships.

Once again, what is healthy for individuals works hand-in-hand with what is healthy for our relationships.

---

23 Kristin Neff, 2022. Definition of self-compassion. https://self-compassion.org/the-three-elements-of-self-compassion-2/

What does healthy mean for a relationship?

Healthy relationships are as unique as the individuals in them, but they have some qualities in common:

- The people in the relationship hold each other in high regard.
- They give and receive acceptance and affection.
- They create an atmosphere of safety and security in the relationship.
- Because of that safety and security, they can also share humor, and they can expect an experience of teamwork and cooperation in the relationship.

Overall, each member can say that the relationship makes their life better, more peaceful, easier, and happier, and that because of the relationship, they are more confident as an individual and they feel more secure in the world.

We can tell a practice is healthy for a relationship when it:

- is healthy for all the individuals in the relationship.
- increases the trust, safety, intimacy, and bonding in the relationship.
- increases each person's compassion for themselves and for each other.
- makes space for each person to be true to who they are inherently.
- reduces conflict in the relationship overall (though this may require facing a conflict in the present).
- embraces truth and ethics, and encourages open, honest communication.

Having self-compassion helps us accept that our partners are also imperfect and may struggle with unpleasant feelings or thoughts. When we respond to their mistakes and shortcomings with compassion, understanding, and forgiveness, this increases their feelings of safety and acceptance in the relationship.

To create safety and security in a relationship, we need to express acceptance and show that we hold the other person in high regard. Being fairly consistent in doing both of these things is an important factor in keeping love alive.

Because love is an emotion that leaves us feeling vulnerable, love relationships need safety and security. The deeper the love, the more vulnerable we feel, and the more vulnerable we feel, the more we need that safety and security.

Sometimes people have a pattern of sabotaging love relationships because they experience vulnerability but don't know how to create the safety needed to help them hold and tolerate that vulnerability. Without safety, vulnerability can be uncomfortable, painful, even terrifying.

Some people hate roller coasters. They don't feel safe, so the experience is terrifying. But the people who enjoy roller coasters are able to enjoy the experience because they feel safe. Feeling safe transforms the fear into excitement and fun.

The same is true for love.

It's important that we create this safety for ourselves in a way that also creates safety for our partners.

When Jenny ordered Sarah to not climb the rocks, it was because Jenny was scared. She was afraid she would lose her partner. She needed to regain a feeling of safety and she made the mistake of trying to get that safety in a way that non-consensually restricted Sarah's choices. This, in turn, threatened to damage Sarah's sense of safety and security in the relationship. Due to Sarah's history, she felt unsafe with a person who would order her about. Luckily, they were able to talk this through in a way that resulted in consensual agreements and mended the potential rift in the relationship.

When we make the mistake of trying to create safety for ourselves in a way that non-consensually restricts our partners, we may increase our safety, but we damage their safety in the relationship. If any one person in a relationship feels their trust and safety is damaged, the whole relationship loses something important and valuable.

This is also true in relation to metamours.[24] If Jenny's long-term nesting partner was struggling with insecurity and tried to create security for herself by pressuring Jenny to restrict her relationship with Sarah, it would not only damage Jenny's feelings of safety in her relationship with her nesting partner, but if Jenny complied with those restrictions without getting authentic consent from Sarah, it would damage her relationship with Sarah as well.

Even in a consensual power dynamic, where we might eagerly seek a relationship where someone takes control and the other submits to that control, each person needs to feel safe. The dominant needs to feel safe

---

24 A metamour is your partner's other partner.

accepting that responsibility, and the submissive needs to feel safe in trusting the dominant's choices and judgment.

A word of caution about "healthy"

All the concepts I teach in this book—rights, boundaries, agreements, and more—can be misused and weaponized. We need to pay equal attention to *how* we apply these concepts, *how* we speak about them, and *how* we conduct our negotiations. We need to make sure we do all these things in the spirit of healthy relationship interactions.

As I hope to make clear in the following chapters, resolving conflicts in healthy ways, using healthy methods and techniques, is every bit as important as learning concepts such as rights and boundaries.

CHAPTER 2

Why Arguments Are So Upsetting and What to Do About It

Different relationships fulfill different kinds of needs and different depths of needs. Whether a relationship is professional, parental, platonic, or romantic, the way we tend to and care for each other's feelings is of central importance to creating and maintaining that relationship's trust, safety, and enjoyability.

Trust and intimacy are built on exposing information or feelings that are of increasing levels of sensitivity (meaning things we fear we could be judged or rejected for) and getting acceptance and compassion in response from the other person.

Let's use an example of a relatively impersonal relationship with a work supervisor. Imagine you have been assigned to give a presentation and you're nervous about speaking in front of a group of superiors. Your supervisor visits your workspace and asks if you're prepared. You seem out of sorts.

What if your supervisor says something lacking compassion, such as, "You'd better get yourself together. The meeting is today." A response such as this will leave you feeling alone in handling your fear. Will you feel any closeness in your relationship with your supervisor? Most likely not.

How different does it feel to imagine your supervisor saying, "You seem a bit out of sorts. Tell me what's going on." And after you admit to being nervous, they say, "Sit down with me. Take some deep breaths. I rarely tell people this, but I get nervous before presentations, too. It helps me to think of all the good presentations I've done. Let's review some of yours.

Remember that toast you made at the holiday party? That was wonderful. And the time you led your team meeting? You did great. Remember how confident and relaxed your voice sounded? I know this is a little different. These people are 'higher-ups' but if you think of them as equals, it might help you. How are you feeling now?"

This response shows an interest in how you're feeling. It shows compassion for any pain or discomfort you may be feeling. By admitting that they also feel nervous before presentations, they seek to normalize your nervousness, and thus show acceptance for it. And it shows this person is willing to spend time and effort helping you feel better.

If this is the first time this supervisor has shown an interest in your feelings, it would likely feel like a transformative moment in the relationship. You might suddenly feel "seen" by this supervisor. Rather than simply being a cog in the corporate machine, you might suddenly feel human to your supervisor, a person they actually care about.

Because they showed that they cared about how you felt, you feel safer with this person, valued, and important. And you'll remember this moment in the relationship as one when you became closer. You might start thinking of this supervisor as a potential friend, or begin to hope this could become a mentoring relationship.

In the language of polyvagal theory (see the Introduction chapter), when you feel someone "gets you," when they notice your emotions and engage with them, and you feel connected and understood, that's attunement.

Caring about another person's feelings and believing they care about your feelings are key ingredients in building safety and trust. To feel that safety and trust, we need to know the person holds us in high esteem and that they value our friendship or intimacy. These things help us to identify a relationship as worthwhile.

In another example, imagine you have a friend who doesn't know you're polyamorous. Think of how vulnerable you might feel if you are about to come out to this friend, especially if what they think of you matters to you. Coming out to anyone opens you up to possible judgment or rejection. It makes you vulnerable, which explains why people tend to feel nervous in these moments.

If this friend responds with acceptance, you might feel relief wash over you and you would realize your fears of rejection and judgment won't be coming true. After this coming out and acceptance, you feel closer to that friend than you did before. And the friendship becomes elevated to a higher or more intimate level because of it.

The closer a relationship is, the more sensitive and vulnerable our feelings can become. We tend to be the most vulnerable to hurt in the relationships that are the most important to us: our life partners, other partners, crushes, metamours, best friends, parents, siblings, and children. Some of these relationships will be attachment-bonded relationships, and the depth of our interconnectedness increases our vulnerability even further.

The more casual or distant the relationship, the less vulnerable or sensitive our feelings usually are. In these relationships, it's easier to dismiss a negative judgment or a rejection.

When a relationship is important to us, our desire to keep the attunement and stay on good terms, as well as our fear of a rupture to an attachment bond, means that arguments can be frightening. Many people feel pressured to say whatever will quickly repair the rift and return the people involved to connection and attunement.

Not all disagreements are arguments. Often, one person is asking for something: a change, an accommodation, or to renegotiate a prior agreement. And if we can, we typically want to say yes. But if the request feels threatening, our own vulnerable feelings of jealousy, anger, fear, and loneliness can sometimes make that yes difficult, if not impossible, to get to authentically.

Getting to an authentic yes

If we can get to a yes, it's important for it to be authentic in order to avoid creating other problems in the relationship. And it's important to be strong enough to say no when that's the authentic, truthful answer. Saying yes when we don't really feel sure of it can lead to resentment, feeling distant or estranged, and sometimes rebelling against or breaking relationship agreements.

Getting to yes authentically means knowing *how* to approach and resolve our own feelings of fear, anger, and jealousy in a healthy manner. We're going to learn how to communicate in a way that tends to those feelings kindly, expresses content effectively, and ensures that everyone feels that their feelings matter. This chapter covers the first step in that process which is how to soothe our distress so that we can continue to engage constructively and cooperatively with our partners, metamours, and others on difficult topics.[25]

What happens in arguments?

Not every disagreement becomes a painful argument. If they agree on the basic facts, two or more people in disagreement can often resolve it in a way that's peaceful, collaborative, and respectful.

We have all felt the painful moment when a peaceful disagreement crosses an invisible line and becomes an argument. It's not the moment you feel a painful emotion activated in yourself or you sense a painful emotion has been activated in the other person. It's the moment after that, when one person reacts to that painful emotion in a way that is hurtful, and the second person reacts to that reaction in a hurtful way, and so on.

Take the example of Sarah and Jenny in the previous chapter. They almost argued. They stopped just short of an argument. Jenny had already reacted to her fear and spoke to Sarah in a way Sarah experienced as hurtful. But Sarah resisted responding in kind. She took some deep breaths, calmed her voice, and asked non-judgmental questions.

In arguments, we are often trying to resolve painful feelings such as jealousy, anger, fear, and loneliness. But when we lash out or withdraw in reaction to those feelings, we're being ineffective in our attempts to resolve them and ineffective in communicating what we need, and we're taking the first step toward transforming a disagreement into an argument.

When this happens, the other person has difficulty actually listening and hearing what's bothering us, and what we are trying to say we need, because we are expressing ourselves in a hurtful way.

When we communicate in a hurtful way, we are not only communicating the content of our words. We are also communicating a disregard for the feelings of the person to whom we are speaking harshly. Therefore, regardless of the truth of what we're saying, we're damaging the relationship by *how* we're saying it.

When our partner says or does something that gives us the impression that our feelings are not being well cared for, or we are no longer being held

---

25 In order to avoid cumbersome language, I may speak of arguments, agreements, and using communication skills with partners. But I also mean any other adult you may be interacting with, such as metamours, friends, co-workers, family members, and more.

SANDER T. JONES, LCSW, LISW-CP, CCH

in high esteem, this triggers a fear that the relationship is in danger. Since relationships are very important to our happiness and survival, this can be very upsetting.

The expression that turns a discussion into an argument can be verbal or nonverbal. We've probably all experienced how an eye roll, an exasperated sigh, a "talk to the hand" gesture (or other hand gestures), or the other person leaving the room while we're still talking can escalate the emotionality of an interaction.

Likewise, verbal and tonal expressions can escalate an interaction. Taking on a mocking tone, or an intellectualized monotone, or using phrases such as "What the fuck?", "How could you?" or "What were you thinking!" or judgmental expressions such as "That's just stupid" can quickly turn a collaborative discussion into a heated argument.

When a conflict gets heated or upsetting, if we express our emotions— anger, hurt, anxiety, loneliness and fear—in a hurtful manner, such as by lashing out, mocking, judging, or withdrawing, this is when the person we're speaking with may begin to believe that their feelings don't matter to us.

This is the damage we risk when we argue poorly. We risk damaging the relationship because we or our partners may walk away from the disagreement believing that our feelings have been disregarded or attacked. When this happens, we feel our partner has shifted from team member to adversary, we feel personally attacked or abandoned (and so does our partner), the safety and trust in the relationship is damaged, and the bond between the two people is weakened.

Example: The dishes

Brian and Samantha are about to go to bed. They both worked that day and they're both working tomorrow. Brian made dinner. He has an expectation that since he made dinner, Samantha will wash the dishes. He looks at the sink as they are both headed for bed, and says...

Brian: You didn't do the dishes.

Samantha: I wasn't planning to do them.

Brian: But I cooked and they need to be done before we go to bed.

Samantha: Argh! Why can't they wait until morning? (She's beginning to sound exasperated.)

Brian: Leaving dishes overnight invites roaches and ants! (He's beginning to sound angry.)

Samantha: But I'm tired at night! Isn't that more important? (Now she's also sounding angry.)

Brian: (clearly angry now) You think I'm not tired? I did the day-time dishes and prepared dinner before you got home. And I have to get up for work at 4 a.m. and see bugs in the sink!

Samantha: (also clearly angry now) At least you *get* to come home in the afternoon and cook. I work 12-hour shifts plus commuting… When I work, I'm gone 15 hours in a day, and I'm tired!

What do we *do* about this? These arguments can be surprisingly upsetting. The argument, on the surface, is about the dishes. However, there's also a second, hidden argument, beneath the surface, about the relationship and whether each partner cares about the other's feelings.

Why do people get so upset during arguments?

During an argument, one person, or both of them, may feel intense fear, hurt, or anger—over something as insignificant as who will do the dishes! Why? Because if during an argument, one or both people get the impression that the other person doesn't care about their feelings, it feels threatening to the relationship. It feels like the quality and depth of the relationship are at risk. If their partner doesn't actually care about their feelings, that means the relationship might be degrading. The love could be waning. The attachment bond may be fracturing. The goodwill and mutual caring that they were able to count on before now might be dying!

Therefore, subconsciously, each person is fighting for the relationship.

The three Fs: fight, flight, and freeze

I can imagine that as I've been writing about not lashing out or withdrawing during arguments, that many readers have been thinking, "Sure, that would be great, but I don't feel like I have control over whether I lash out or withdraw. It just happens."

Yes. I know. And I understand. That automatic, out-of-control experience is the fight-flight-freeze response, or the 3F response. I touched on it in the introduction. Now I'm going to explain a bit more about what it is, why it happens, how to recognize it, and what to do about it.

When we are very upset, we might find ourselves experiencing the fight-flight-freeze response. It can feel similar to panic and is a survival mechanism hardwired into humans. All mammals, reptiles, and even fish display a version of this survival mechanism.

The amygdala is the threat perception and response center of the brain. It is believed to have some genetically encoded threat information—such as when an infant can't get the attention of a caregiver, or we are looking at a room full of angry faces, or when we jump back and then look down only to realize that what we thought was a snake was just a garden hose. The amygdala also learns about threats, correctly and incorrectly, through life experience, such as when we experience trauma, develop phobias, or simply learn that falling from a height can be life-threatening.

One of the frustrating things about the 3F response is that it is automatic. We often don't feel we have any choice over which response we have. Sometimes this leaves people feeling embarrassed or angry with themselves that they ran or froze when they wish they had fought instead.

We don't have conscious control over what the amygdala decides is a threat or over the response the amygdala initiates when it perceives a threat. Polyvagal theory calls this neuroception, because it's a kind of perception experienced by our nervous system, but it's below our level of conscious awareness and happens outside of our ability to consciously impact it with our thoughts.

Neuroception can be altered through exposure, repetition, and methods designed to reprogram the subconscious. These methods can take considerable time and effort to implement. For now, I'd like to focus on helping you understand your own and your partners' reactions and what techniques you can readily implement.

When the amygdala perceives a threat, it initiates a process that triggers the release of adrenaline into the bloodstream, providing a burst of energy that we can use to either fight the threat or run away from the threat. When the amygdala perceives the threat to be too great to fight or too unavoidable to run from, the most ancient response system takes over and we freeze or play dead in the hope of avoiding the threat. Here's a little more about each of these.

Fight: When we can't run, when we perceive we have a fighting chance, when life experience has conditioned us to, or when the social cost of not fighting is severe, we might respond with aggression.

Flight: When an escape route is available, and when the threat appears too big or too powerful to fight, we might respond by running away.

Freeze: When we don't have an escape route and the threat appears too big or powerful to fight, we might respond by freezing in place. We may be unable to speak or move when this happens.

We are able to track these three responses—fight, flight, and freeze—as part of our physiological threat response in the body. Some therapists and theorists have offered up additional threat responses that resonate with many people. I've listed a few of them as follows, taken from the Enlightened Solutions website.[26] But keep in mind, as far as we know, these are not distinctly different threat responses with their own neural pathways. They are most likely learned, conditioned variations of fight, flight, or freeze.

Flood: When faced with a threat, if a person "breaks into hysterics" or gets "overly emotional," this is called the flooding effect, "where we are flooded with emotions which need to be released."

---

26 Enlightened Solutions, n.d. "There are more F's to fight, flight, or freeze." https://www.enlightenedsolutions.com/there-are-more-fs-to-fight-flight-or-freeze/#:~:text=For%20someone%20facing%20a%20threat,known%20response%20to%20a%20threat

Fatigue: "When the body and the brain are so overwhelmed by stress, [or] the response to fear, the body can shut down. Fatigue is total exhaustion of mind and body. Some people become very sleepy in the face of a threat and feel like the only thing they can do is sleep."

Fawn: "For someone facing a threat, to fawn is to strategically, or perhaps subconsciously, submit to the threat and the demands of the threat … in order to avoid hurt, pain, more fear, or other consequences."

Fawning appears to be unique to social animals. Dogs and wolves will roll over, expose their belly and lick the underside of the muzzle of a more dominant animal. Gorillas will prostrate themselves and act submissive to placate a threatening dominant gorilla. And humans—you guessed it—will try to placate an aggressive human with fawning words, exaggerated apologies, offering to give them whatever they want, and submissive body language (especially if we have a trauma history).

I would like to offer up another option I have seen in practice: frustrate.

Frustrate: The opposite of fawn. When a person feels threatened, they throw every possible uncooperative, disagreeing statement at the other person and the topic while in a state of semi-panic or emotional distress.

In the ADD (attention deficit disorder) magazine *ADDitude*, Monica Hassall and Barbara Hunter introduce another F response: fib.

Fib: "When faced with a threat of attack, rejection, or punishment, a person may lie to avert a present danger or threat, at least for the time being. The escape from fear, embarrassment, judgment, guilt, or shame provides a brief but powerful sense of reward (or escape/victory)."[27]

---

27 Monica Hassall and Barbara Hunter, 2022. "Fight, flight, freeze… or fib?" *ADDitude*, July 25. https://www.additudemag.com/why-lie-adhd-fight-flight-freeze/

Additionally, they say something brilliant regarding the physiology of the fight-flight-freeze response:

> As neuroscience research itself continues to evolve, it appears to support these observed behaviors related to stress. However, neuroscience also encourages us to study the development of the neocortex (the outermost layer of the brain), which is an additional avenue for processing thoughts and a new line of self-defense achieved through language. With complex and advanced language (not available to our primitive ancestors), we have the ability to verbalize both factual and/or fictitious reasoning instantaneously at point of performance, most notably in times of stress and threat.[28]

I think this passage is brilliant because it expands our mental image of the fight and flight response to include both physical fighting or fleeing and verbal fighting or fleeing. Of course, humans fight with words! And we can use words to flee or avoid conflict as well.

The freeze response is different. Freeze includes immobilization, dissociation, or both. Language is usually not accessible for a person in the freeze response.

A brief description of the physiology of the 3F response

In the introduction, I gave you a very brief sketch of how polyvagal physiology works. Here, I'll reiterate some of that, take it a bit deeper, and explain how you can apply this information to your everyday life and relationships.

Polyvagal theory was created by Stephen Porges, a neurophysiologist. Deb Dana is a clinician who has worked closely with Steven Porges and has written extensively on how to apply polyvagal theory to clinical practice, particularly with trauma clients. My explanations draw heavily on her work.[29]

The autonomic nervous system is the part of the nervous system that regulates a wide variety of automatic bodily functions that take place outside of our conscious thought or control, such as heart rate, digestion, and

---

28 Ibid.
29 Dana, 2018.

the fight-flight-freeze response. It has two branches: the sympathetic and parasympathetic nervous systems. The parasympathetic nervous system includes the vagus nerve, which divides further into two pathways: the ventral vagus and the dorsal vagus. Polyvagal theory arose out of the physical study of the ventral and dorsal vagal nerves.

Imagine that a person spends most of their time feeling safe and at peace. They have the capacity to feel curious and creative, and they feel open to engaging socially with others. Their heart rate and breathing are slow and calm. In polyvagal theory, this state is called "safe and social" and is regulated by the ventral branch of the vagus nerve, which begins at the brain stem and interfaces with nerves in the face, eyes, ears, mouth, throat, heart and lungs.

The ventral branch of the vagus nerve engages the bodily functions and sensations above the diaphragm. The ventral vagal branch is the newest addition, evolutionarily speaking, and is common only to mammals.

If this person's amygdala neurocepts a threat and they are activated into the fight or flight response, the sympathetic branch of the autonomic nervous system that runs down the middle of the spinal cord takes over, adrenaline in dumped into the bloodstream, the heart rate and breathing rate increase, and the body is revved up and prepared to move, to take action, to fight or flee in service of survival.

If the threat is overwhelming, or there is no escape, the freeze response is activated. This is the oldest survival response, evolutionarily speaking, and is controlled by the dorsal branch of the vagus nerve that runs down from the brain stem into the belly, below the diaphragm. Mammals, reptiles and even fish have a dorsal vagal nerve that activates a freeze response. When this is activated, our bodily systems freeze up. Our faces go blank, we lose access to speech, executive brain functions go offline, and we turn inward, often dissociating from some aspect of our experience. This can be for a brief moment, or go on for an extended time.

In polyvagal theory they call this "moving down the polyvagal ladder." Safe and social is at the top of the ladder where the ventral vagal branch engages the body from the face to the heart area. The middle of the ladder is the fight-or-flight response controlled by the spinal cord in the trunk of the body. And the bottom of the ladder is the freeze response, orchestrated by the dorsal vagal nerve and engaging the body below the diaphragm.

Each part of the fight-flight-freeze response has its own neural pathway, and so does the state of feeling safe and socially engaged. As I mentioned, only fight, flight, and freeze are currently recognized as distinct neurologically based phenomena. The additional variations (fawn, flood, fib, frustrate) are useful descriptors and many people can relate strongly with these patterns. My opinion is that they are variations of fight and flight that include the use of language. Fawn and fib are ways of fleeing conflict using words. Flood can be either fleeing or fighting with words. And frustrate is a way of fighting with words.

After we have experienced the effects of the 3F response and we begin the process of calming down and returning to the safe and social mode, it is common to feel tired, sleepy, or exhausted. Recovery time varies considerably. Typically, recovery time is 20 to 60 minutes, but some people may feel exhausted for one to two days. I believe this is what the fatigue response refers to.

The fight-flight-freeze response is not an all-or-nothing experience. Sometimes it escalates quickly, going from "I'm totally calm" to "I'm in a panic!" or "I'm enraged!" Most of the time, however, it's not like that at all. Most of the time it's more like a dimmer dial. You can be a little activated, like when you are kind of nervous about something. You can be highly activated, such as when you have a near-miss accident on the highway. Or you can be completely activated, which is more like a panic state.

Anger is also experienced in this graduated way. You can be slightly irritated. You can be pretty angry. And you can be in a blind rage.

When the fight-flight-freeze response happens, and adrenaline and cortisol flood the body, you may notice physiological symptoms: the heart rate increases, the bladder relaxes, you may get tunnel vision, or you may experience hearing loss, a change in hearing sensitivity, or ringing in the ears. You may experience dry mouth, dilated pupils, physical shaking, or flushed skin, or the blood may drain from your face.

Action item: Identify symptoms that you experience or that each of your partners displays that will help you know when you or your partners are in fight-flight-freeze response. Does your mouth get dry? Do your ears ring? Do your partner's pupils dilate? Do you launch into fawning behavior and words? Does one of your partners freeze up? Does another partner verbally attack? Take notes and talk about what you are each feeling in those moments.

The 3F response also includes physiological symptoms that you are unlikely to notice, such as your digestion slowing down. As well, it has a profound impact on brain functions. Some of these hidden effects on the brain are very important to understand because they can greatly impact what happens during an argument with a loved one.

During the 3F response, the executive functions of the brain reduce or shut down. Cognitive skills and abilities, memory, decision-making, and empathy are some of the executive functions of the brain that become impaired or stop working during the fight-flight-freeze response.

You may wonder why we would develop an emergency response system that shuts down important brain functions. Since this is a survival mechanism, we can ask, "How would this help an individual human or animal survive an emergency situation?"

In an emergency, such as an attack by a predator, the cognitive brain and executive functions are too slow. If we had to wait for the cognitive brain to assess—"The big animal with stripes is moving toward me... Oh no! That's a tiger!"—we'd get eaten. If you have ever experienced a moment like this, the body seems to turn and run, on its own, and several seconds later the cognitive brain catches up and says, "Oh no! That's a tiger!"

Why would empathy shut down? It's controlled by the executive function part of the brain (prefrontal cortex). Maybe it gets shut down because everything in that location of the brain is getting shut down. Or maybe it's because if empathy stayed functional, the person would be more likely to stay and help other people under attack, thus increasing the likelihood they themselves would get killed or injured. Either way, I believe this is why, when people do stay and help others under attack, we elevate those people to hero status. We recognize that this automatic survival mechanism is difficult to override.

Another way to think of it (probably more accurate) is that the ancient fight-flight-freeze mechanism existed long before we developed the more advanced systems of individual identity, complex thought, language, group cohesion, and social engagement. In this way, being human is a lot like being an advanced mind living within or riding upon a primitive, beast-like animal. (Or, if you're a science fiction fan, it's much like the Goa'uld in the TV series *Stargate SG-1*. However, imagine that the Goa'uld parasite has language and complex thought and the host it lives within does not.)

When it comes to a survival moment, the beast takes over and acts without bothering to engage the advanced part of the brain. It doesn't need to. The links between the amygdala, hypothalamus, sympathetic nervous system, vagus nerve, and adrenal glands existed long before we evolved the more advanced parts of the brain, where we make conscious decisions.

While this may seem like I've gone off on a tangent, I bring up this topic to help you understand what may be happening in your arguments. If either you or your partner (or partners) are activated into the fight-flight-freeze response, you may experience your reactions as out of your conscious control. This can be why you and your partner (or partners) have struggled to change the damaging patterns that may play out when you have arguments, because regardless of how much you may want to make better choices, you may not feel able to.

Action item: Reflect on what tends to upset you or activate your 3F response. Ask your partners to do the same. Discuss, when you are all calm, how you might disarm these triggers. One way to show we care about the other person's feelings is to agree to avoid doing or saying the thing that activates or triggers the other person. Sometimes a trigger can be disarmed by explaining what your intention is when you do the triggering behavior. Your intention may be different from what it means to the other person and hearing your true intent can remove the upsetting element.

Sometimes asking a partner to avoid doing a triggering behavior is not appropriate to our value system, or that partner is unwilling to stop doing that behavior. I address this circumstance in chapters 8 and 9.

When executive brain functions shut down

Here are some common patterns and problems in relationship arguments that are related to the fight-flight-freeze response.

Saying hurtful things we regret later

We all think harsh and judgmental thoughts from time to time. Thinking these thoughts doesn't mean we are bad people, nor does it mean we don't love the person we are thinking harsh thoughts about.

Typically, we also have contradicting thoughts that are kind and non-judgmental. This mixture, or ambivalence, is often present because of empathy. Empathy is the ability to imagine being the other person and feeling care and concern for their experience. This allows us to imagine explanations for their behavior that are more understanding and non-judgmental.

Empathy is also the filter that keeps us from speaking harsh, judgmental thoughts we believe will hurt others. When empathy shuts down during the fight-flight-freeze response, this filter goes offline. Suddenly, those hurtful things feel like the right thing to say. They may sound like the hard truth this person needs to face, or we may know the words will hurt them and we are landing a blow during a fight with words.

This also explains hurtful behavior we might do during the fight-flight-freeze response, such as throwing things, damaging property, and more.

Action item: The first part of this exercise is a solo task. Review past arguments where you said something hurtful to a partner. Do you regret what you said, or how you said it, or maybe when it was said? Reflect on how you felt while you were saying the hurtful thing. Reflect on the time before you said the hurtful thing. Were you in the 3F response? Can you pinpoint when you became activated into the 3F response? If you have a partner who is also doing this exercise, see if you can come together and express regret for the times you each said hurtful things. Apologize if it feels appropriate. Resist the urge for either of you to ask about hurtful statements the speaker did not present. Those are covered in chapter 4, where we learn the Imago exercise.

Becoming intellectual and condescending

This is also related to the shutdown of empathy during the 3F response. To be condescending is to take a position that someone isn't as intelligent or responsible as we are, which is a harsh judgment. Sometimes intellectualizing goes hand in hand with a mocking tone of voice, or to talk to someone as if they are stupid. Intellectualizing is a form of emotional withdrawal. The person experiencing this will often say it feels like a switch is flipped and their emotions shut off.

This incarnation of the fight-flight-freeze response is an attempt to shut down all emotions so the person can prevent a panic response and try to retain access to their cognitive brain functions. Often these people have confidence that their thinking brain is one of their best tools, and they use it to think their way out of emergency situations.

> **Action item:** Reflect on whether you or your partner succumb to intellectualizing or condescension during arguments. Can you pinpoint at what moment the person becomes activated and switches to this communication style? Can you identify other symptoms of the 3F response? Discuss your perceptions of this communication style from each person's perspective. What is the speaker's intent, and how is the speaker perceived by others when this happens?

Fawning

The fawning response is closely related to intellectualizing. When we are fawning, the part of the cognitive brain that stays functional is focused on emotionally reading the other person and accessing what we know of them. We use this information to figure out what words or behaviors will appease and calm the other person.

When fawning, we shut down self-empathy and awareness of the longer-term consequences of what we are saying, and instead we say anything that might placate or pacify the other person.

Fawning can happen when we perceive the other person as an attacker and we are trying to deescalate an attack. It can also happen when we perceive abandonment, such as when the other person is withdrawing or leaving. When we fear abandonment, we fawn by saying anything we think will keep that person from leaving.

When fawning, we may agree to things, compromise on things, or give away things we don't really want to. We may feel ashamed later and disappointed in ourselves that we didn't stand up for what we truly wanted. Or we may feel pressured to live up to the agreements we made, even though we made the agreements under duress.

The person on the receiving end of the fawning behavior may have no idea that we felt distressed. They may feel betrayed later or lied to when they learn that we didn't really want the agreement we made or that we didn't mean the words we said while fawning.

Action item: Reflect on whether you or a partner succumb to fawning during arguments. Can you pinpoint at what moment the person becomes activated and begins to fawn? Discuss your perceptions of this communication style from each person's perspective. What is the speaker's intent, and how is the speaker perceived by others when this happens?

Action item: If you find that relationship agreements have been made while anyone was fawning, I suggest you adopt a new habit of writing down anything that is decided and both approve the language with initials, signatures, or personal marks. Then commit to reviewing what was written within 24 hours. Discuss how you can each review this material without re-triggering fawning behavior. The goal is to give the person who fawns an environment safe enough they can admit when they don't really want a particular agreement, if that happens to be their truth.

Shutting down or withdrawing

Shutting down and withdrawing—inwardly, as opposed to withdrawing by physically leaving—is a manifestation of the freeze response. A person may freeze up and their mind goes blank. Or they may physically freeze while their mind races. In the first scenario they can't access any thoughts. In the second, they can't access words. Sometimes both happen at once. They may feel intense emotions during shutdown, such as profound sadness, pain, fear, or anger, or they may feel nothing at all.

If the partner of the person shutting down has a fear of abandonment, the withdrawal of their partner can activate them into attacking or fawning in an attempt to get the withdrawing partner to re-engage.

This self-perpetuating cycle has been called many things in relationship literature: the approach-avoidance dance, the push-pull relationship pattern, the cling-pull away pattern, and the distancer-pursuer pattern, to name a few.

> **Action item:** Reflect on whether you or your partners experience the freeze response during arguments or disagreements. Can you pinpoint at what moment the person becomes activated and begins to withdraw or shut down? Discuss your perceptions of this behavior from each person's perspective. What does each person need in that moment to feel better? You may find you need opposite things. It's okay. We'll discuss solutions in chapters 4 through 8.

Running or leaving

To physically leave during arguments is a manifestation of flight. If you are leaving as the flight part of the 3F response, you might be thinking corresponding thoughts such as, "I can't take this anymore," "I'm suffocating," "I can't handle this," or "I've got to get out of here."

A person can also metaphorically run. This is when a person breaks up or ends the relationship simply because they are upset in the moment.

Sometimes people physically leave during arguments as a way of stonewalling their partner. It's a way of putting pressure on the partner to give in. They might say, "I'll come back when you can be rational." And rational means, "When you agree with me and what I want."

On the other hand, sometimes people physically leave during an argument because this is how they know how to calm themselves down, to restrict themselves from saying things they might regret later, or to calm both people down and de-escalate the situation.

It's important to understand the runner's motives. Their motives might not be to frighten or abandon their partner. Their motives might be to protect their partner from the damaging things they fear they would do or say if they stayed present.

And, again, if the partner of the runner has a strong fear of abandonment, this can trigger them into a panic, increasing their clinging, verbal fighting, or fawning behaviors.

> **Action item:** Reflect on whether you or a partner physically or metaphorically leave during arguments. Can you pinpoint at what moment the person becomes activated into the flight response? Discuss your perceptions of this behavior from each person's perspective. What is the runner's intent, and how are they perceived by others when this happens?

Memory issues

Sometimes people don't remember everything that was said or everything that happened during an argument. This happens due to memory impairment caused by the fight-flight-freeze response.

This can be very frustrating if you think you and a partner have resolved an issue during an argument and later you find out your partner has no memory of that resolution.

Action item: If this tends to happen in your relationship, I suggest you both write down what was decided and both approve the language with initials, signatures, or personal marks. Then commit to reviewing what was written within 24 hours to make sure you both still agree, and to make sure you are both aware this agreement is in place.

Thinking and reasoning impairment

In arguments with others, we have a problem we're trying to resolve. It could be regarding what action to take, or how to think or feel about an issue. We may need to negotiate a compromise or brainstorm new solutions. Either way, resolving any disagreement will require access to the full and best abilities of our thinking and reasoning brain functions.

When either or both people are in the fight-flight-freeze response, the thinking and reasoning functions of the brain can be partly or fully offline. Therefore, it's a terrible time to try to negotiate compromises or brainstorm solutions.

Perception is also affected by the 3F response. Allies can be perceived as adversaries. Safe situations can feel dangerous. Our ability to think flexibly, see things from a different perspective, and balance what we know with what we feel is impaired. We may not be able to balance what we know about a partner ("they would never hurt me") with what we feel ("I feel attacked").

Action item: Reflect on yourself and your partners and whether the fight-flight-freeze response is activated in you or your partners during arguments. What forms of impairment have you experienced? What forms have you seen in your partners? List and describe them. Discuss these patterns with your partners.

What to do? Call for a timeout!

Continuing to talk or argue when one or more people are in the 3F response is at best risky and at worst damaging. When the executive functions of the brain (empathy, memory, reasoning and decision-making skills) are impaired or completely shut down, you are less likely:

- to be willing or able to understand and feel compassion for the other person's experience
- to retain your focus and actually listen to the other person
- to think of creative solutions to the surface-level problem
- to remember the details of what solutions you made
- to be able to work collaboratively with the other person to resolve the matter.

As you will see in the following chapters, executive function skills are exactly what you need to resolve arguments in a way that strengthens and improves a relationship rather than degrading it or tearing it down.

I recommend learning how to recognize when either you or the other person are activated or upset, name it, and call for a timeout. Make an agreement with your partner or partners (or metamours, friends, roommates, coworkers, or extended family members) to notice the 3F response and gently call a timeout.

Keep in mind that some people will strongly resist allowing for timeouts. Sometimes this is because their fear of abandonment is triggered. We will discuss shortly how to soothe that fear so you can still call for a timeout.

Other times it's because they know power over the other person can be easily created in these intense emotional moments. If my goal is to win the argument, rather than to create a mutually respectful egalitarian relationship, then I won't want a de-escalation of emotions at that time.

If the other person knows your fear of abandonment is triggered when they withdraw and become cold, that's power they can use to pressure you into giving them what they want. If they see a pattern of fawning when they raise their voice and act threateningly, they might use it to get you to agree to restrictions you wouldn't otherwise agree to. If when they start to cry or panic or otherwise appear to have a meltdown, they can count on that being so upsetting for you that you back down from what you want, they might want to escalate the emotionality of an argument so that they can exercise that power and win.

Exercising non-consensual power over another person is unethical and damages their feelings of safety in the relationship and their ability to trust you as an individual. You can't use non-consensual power over another adult person and have a healthy, intimate, trusting relationship.

If our goal is to have an ethical, egalitarian, mutually respectful or deeply trusting, intimate relationship, we need to learn to recognize these moments where power can be easily created and abused and learn to step back from that precipice. Calling for a timeout and seeking to de-escalate an argument is one way of voluntarily stepping away from an opportunity to create and abuse power. It's also a great way of refusing to allow someone else to create and abuse power over us.

When calling for a timeout, you will need to discuss with each person exactly how to do it so that it has the desired effect of de-escalating (rather than escalating) the conflict. It's important to talk with the other person in advance so they know what you're doing when you call a timeout and why you're doing it.

You are calling for a timeout to avoid escalating the conflict and to give you each an opportunity to calm yourselves so you can return to the discussion with full access to your executive brain functions.

Talk with each person and agree on what language to use. Done poorly, calling for a timeout can be additionally upsetting to one or both people. Some examples of poorly declared timeouts are:

- Exclaiming, "That's it. I'm done!" and leaving the room or building.
- "Will you just stop talking, already?!"
- "You never listen! I'm not talking about this anymore!"
- Putting your hands over your ears, closing your eyes and saying "La, la, la, I can't hear you!"

Agree on what language or hand gestures to use. If, when upset, one person has a tendency to freeze and not be able to speak, agree on a gesture for calling a timeout, such as the time-out hand signal used in American football, or holding up a hand in the "stop" gesture. If you can speak, name what you feel and gently call for a timeout. It might sound like this:

- "I'm starting to feel upset. I need a few minutes to calm down so that I can really hear what you're saying."
- "I can't seem to think right now. I need a few minutes to gather my thoughts."
- "I think we are in our destructive pattern again. Rather than repeat it, let's take a timeout and try to talk about this again when we're both calm."
- "Remember when we agreed to call timeouts when either of us is upset? I'd like to call a timeout."

During the timeout, engage in calming yourselves so that you can return to the discussion with your wonderful executive brain functions fully available for your use.

Action item: Talk with each of your partners, or other people you may have arguments with, and identify when during a disagreement someone gets activated into the 3F response. See if you can agree to call for a timeout at these times. Discuss how to call for a timeout, such as what language or hand gestures are to be used.

What you will do in relation to each other during the timeout

It's very important that you discuss how the two of you (or three or four) will interact during the time out. Our goal is to create an environment where both or all the people are able to calm and soothe themselves so that the 3F response passes and everyone can return to the discussion with their executive brain functions in full working order.

During the 3F response, adrenaline is released first. It takes a minimum of 20 minutes for it to be flushed from the bloodstream. If we perceive the threat to be ongoing, cortisol is released. Cortisol (the chronic stress hormone) keeps a person revved up and prepared to respond to an ongoing threat. If the cortisol response gets triggered, a person can stay in the fight-flight-freeze response for hours, even days.

Therefore, it's important that you and the other person construct your timeout in a way that will not cause additional, ongoing distress. It would be ideal if both people could benefit from going into separate rooms and doing their own self-soothing during the timeout.

However, many people become additionally distressed if their partner leaves during a timeout. If this is the case, you may need to agree to stay in the same room during the timeout. Another creative response is reminding your partner that you are only leaving temporarily and offering to turn on GPS tracking on your phone so they can see where you are. Or you could leave and go to a place where your partner can see you, such as the backyard.

If you are going to stay in the same room, the next question to ask is, will you speak to each other during the timeout? Ideally, I suggest no talking at all during the timeout because the temptation to return to the argument is strong. However, some people become additionally upset by not talking. It feels like the silent treatment. If this is the case, you may decide to speak, but don't speak about the topic of the argument. Speak only of pleasant or neutral things.

Touch does not apply if you are in separate rooms, but if you stay in the same room, you may choose to touch in a soothing way. Some people don't like to be touched when they're upset. If you're staying in the same room, you'll need to discuss whether or not to touch and if so, in what way.

Timeouts should be a minimum of 20 minutes. As I said previously, it takes a minimum of 20 minutes for the adrenaline to leave your body. You will likely feel calmer and believe you're ready to talk in five or 10 minutes. Don't end the timeout early! The adrenaline is still in your bloodstream and you are very likely to return to the 3F response if you re-engage in the discussion with this hormone still activated in your body. Furthermore, a reactivation of the 3F response is likely to trigger the release of cortisol, which not only is damaging for your health, but will keep you revved up in the 3F response even longer.

At the end of 20 minutes, the person who called for the timeout should either check in with their partner and ask if they feel ready to re-engage, or check in with their partner and say, "I'm not yet calm. I need another 10 minutes, or 20 minutes."

If more than 60 minutes is needed for a time-out, then the person who is not able to calm themselves may be triggering their own cortisol response by thinking upsetting thoughts that keep them revved up in the 3F response during the timeout. I call this a spiral or emotional storm. It can be a shame spiral, anger spiral, guilt spiral, or fear spiral. These patterns can be difficult to change and professional help may be needed.

If this sounds like your experience, or that of someone you know, dialectical behavioral therapy (DBT) is the best method for changing these patterns and learning how to stop revving yourself up into an emotional storm. If you look up DBT on the internet, you'll see that it was originally developed to treat people with borderline personality disorder (BPD). And it's a very effective treatment for BPD. But it's not just for people with borderline personality disorder anymore.

The clinical term for the pattern of not being able to calm and soothe yourself, triggering the cortisol response, and being swept up in an emotional storm for 60 minutes or longer is "emotion dysregulation." Emotion dysregulation is one symptom of BPD, but it's also a symptom for post-traumatic stress disorder (PTSD), obsessive-compulsive disorder (OCD), attention deficit disorder (ADD and ADHD), bipolar disorder, and autism spectrum disorder (ASD), just to name a few of the most common.

You don't need to have a diagnosis or know your diagnosis to benefit from dialectical behavioral therapy techniques.

Action item: At a time when you are all calm and not engaged in a conflict, discuss with your partner or partners (or metamour, parent, friend, sibling, and so on) how you can each call for a timeout in a way that is kind, considerate, and effective. Also discuss if you will take timeouts in separate spaces or in the same place and what that will look like. If you can't agree on how to do this, you may need to ask someone to mediate this negotiation or seek professional help.

How to soothe the 3F response during timeout

I describe a lot of different self-soothing techniques in this section. I am not expecting anyone to use them all. But I do suggest you try many of them until you can create a list of favorites, or different ones to use in different circumstances.

First, try to assess how upset you are. Imagine that you could rate how upset you are on a scale from zero to 10. Zero means you're not at all upset and 10 represents a panic or rage level of distress.

Unless stated otherwise, the information in this section and the next section comes from the second edition of the *DBT Skills Training Manual* by Marsha M. Linehan.[30]

If your distress measures a 7 through 10, you are in a full-blown 3F response. At this level people tend to react to their emotions and often don't feel like they have much or any control in their choice of actions or words. Left in this state, we often do or say things that make the situation worse or damage our important relationships.

The skills you want to use for this level of distress are designed to soothe the physiological symptoms: slow the heart rate, slow the breathing, burn off the adrenaline, and prevent the cortisol response. This gets us out of the 3F response sooner and gives us back our executive brain functions.

Induce the dive response

The dive response is a bodily response to cold water. When a person falls through the ice and you fish them out 20 minutes later and they are not dead, or rescuers are able to revive them, that's because of the dive response. During this response, the body slows the heart and reduces the need for oxygen. You can employ this during emotional distress by putting something cold on your face, leaning forward and taking slow breaths. Sometimes putting something cold in your armpits works equally well.

Some people throw water and ice in a bowl or sink and stick their face in it. I think it's easier and less messy to use frozen gel packs, bags of frozen peas or corn, or homemade slushy packs. To make slushy packs, put 50% water and 50% rubbing alcohol in a plastic zipper bag. Then double-bag it to prevent leaks. Keep these in your freezer for use during high emotional distress.

Other variations on this skill are:

- Get in a cold shower or bath.
- Lie down flat, put an ice pack over your heart, and breathe slowly and deeply.
- Drink a big glass of very cold water.

---

30 Marsha M. Linehan, 2015. *DBT Skills Training Manual.* Gilford Press.

Caution! Using cold to induce the dive response can reduce your heart rate very rapidly. If you have a heart disorder, a heart rate below normal baseline due to medications or other health problems, anorexia nervosa, or bulimia nervosa, consult with your doctor before using this technique.

Paced breathing

If you don't have access to something cold, or you don't like putting cold things on your face, you can also get a calming effect with paced breathing. You can lean forward if that helps, or not. Notice the current pace of your breathing and focus on extending the exhale. Count the length of your exhale in your mind and work to extend the exhale a little bit with each count.

Your goal is to slow your breathing down to five or six breaths per minute (10 to 12 seconds per breathing cycle). I have had clients call me in the midst of a panic attack and I've been able to talk them through this method to end their panic attack in 30 to 60 seconds. Doing this on your own might take a minute or two longer, but that's still a pretty quick ending for a panic attack.

When our exhale is longer than our inhale, the vagus nerve sends a signal to the brain that calms, soothes, and slows down our nervous system. This is great for slowing down our system and helping us calm down from the fight or flight response. It doesn't work well for the freeze response.

Introduce movement

When someone is in the freeze response, the first step is to remove the threat. You may find it painful to hear, but if you are the person who triggered the freeze response in your partner, then you are the threat.

If you can, remove the threat. If you are afraid to leave your partner alone, see if there is another person (a non-threatening person) who can step in and coach your partner through moving out of the freeze response.

If there is no one else available and it's not safe to leave your partner alone (maybe you fear they will hurt themselves), physically back away. Talk in a soothing tone or use a higher-pitched voice rather than a lower-pitched voice. Talk about neutral or light topics.

Next, encourage your partner to introduce slow, intentional movement. Sway from side to side, walk slowly around the room, wave their arms in a slow and controlled way. Then, encourage your partner to increase that movement. They can shake the arms and legs more assertively and walk more intensely.

According to David Puder on the Psychiatry & Psychotherapy Podcast, once your partner is out of the freeze response, they are likely to experience fight or flight before they can calm themselves back to the safe and social mode.[31] They can use one of the other techniques: the dive response, intense exercise, or paired muscle relaxation if needed.

Intense exercise

The 3F response pumps adrenaline into the bloodstream so that we have the ability to fight or run away from an attacker. Exercise burns off the adrenaline. It also burns off any cortisol that might be dumped into your system, and is the best way to prevent chronic stress from damaging your physical health.

Do some sort of intense physical exercise for 20 to 30 minutes. Notice that "intense" is relative. Intense exercise for one person might mean a 20-minute walk around the neighborhood. But for a more athletic person it might mean a 20-minute run, jumping rope, or punching a heavy bag.

Ideally, your goal is to get your heart rate up to 70% of the maximum for your age, for 20 minutes or more. Look up on the internet "how to calculate heart rate training zones by age." But if you don't have time to do a 20- to 30-minute cardio workout, you can also try running in place, bringing your knees as high as possible for one minute, or doing jumping jacks, push-ups, or burpees.

Caution! Again, check with your medical provider before engaging in exercise. If you have problems with your back, joints, heart, lungs, or balance, exercise may be risky or harmful to your health.

---

31 David Puder, 2018. Psychiatry & Psychotherapy Podcast. Episode 023: Emotional Shutdown—Understanding Polyvagal Theory. July 9. https://www.psychiatrypodcast.com/psychiatry-psychotherapy-podcast/polyvagal-theory-understanding-emotional-shutdown

Paired muscle relaxation

The easiest way to learn paired muscle relaxation is to find a recording online and listen to it. The idea is to tense a muscle group while inhaling, and release it while exhaling. Sometimes people like to say "relax" to themselves as they exhale and release the muscles.

Start with one part of your body, such as your feet or hands, and progress through all the muscle groups. The final step is to tense and relax the entire body all at once, several times.

Rhythmic repetitive motion

Several trauma therapies use the soothing effects of repetitive movement. Eye movement desensitization and reprocessing, known as EMDR, uses rhythmic bilateral stimulation (left-right-left-right movement). Going for a walk or run is a form of rhythmic bilateral stimulation and can be soothing, burn off adrenaline and cortisol, and clarify and focus the mind.

EMDR and polyvagal theory use therapeutic forms of self-tapping for soothing and healing. Drumming, dancing, strumming a musical instrument, knitting, or rocking in a rocking chair or a hammock can all be soothing and calming.

Some repetitive movements, called stimming, are common to people on the autism spectrum, especially when they feel distressed: rocking the body while sitting or standing, flicking their fingers, flapping their hands, and twirling or spinning. If you are a person on the autism spectrum, I encourage you to allow yourself to do these soothing behaviors when you need them. Many people on the autism spectrum have been discouraged from doing stimming behaviors due to social or familial pressure.

Whether you are a person on the autism spectrum or not, if you find any of these rhythmic or repetitive behaviors to be soothing, use them to calm and soothe yourself out of fight, flight, or freeze during your timeout.

Self-soothing skills from DBT for moderate to low levels of distress

Go back to the concept of measuring your distress on a scale from zero to 10. If your distress is at six or below, or if you have lowered it to six or below using the skills listed just now, the following skills from DBT will help you to calm and soothe yourself even more.

Soothe the five senses

Think of each of your five physical senses and put together a list or physical collection of items that are soothing to each of them. Through this process, you'll identify some favorites. You'll also be able to identify things that are portable so you can access them anywhere, as well as things you can only access at home.

- Sight: Soothing visuals can be experienced in person or in photos or videos: art you enjoy, sunsets, sunrises, dim lighting, a view of the ocean, looking at a fire in the fireplace or a candle flame, hummingbirds, fireflies winking on and off, dragonflies, bees collecting pollen, watching maple seeds or dandelion seeds float through the air, horses or dogs running, baby goats jumping, kittens playing, and so on.
- Sound: Any kind of music that soothes you; nature sounds such as wind, rain, crickets, cicadas, hummingbird wings, bird calls, or a cat purring; and others, such as a white noise machine, ocean waves, binaural beats, ASMR recordings,[32] a meditation recording, wind chimes…
- Smell: Comfort food, scented candles, aromatherapy, salty ocean air, the earthy smell of a forest floor, your favorite cleaning supplies….
- Taste: Comfort foods, dark chocolate, hot tea. Be careful of engaging with disordered eating if this is an issue for you.
- Touch: Physical sensations of heat, cold, textures, and pressures, such as a weighted blanket, microfiber cloth, animal fur, a warm bath, a cool swimming pool, lying in the sun, feeling the wind on your skin or in your hair.

---

32 According to MaryKate Wust, the term "autonomous sensory meridian response" (ASMR) was coined to describe a tingly neurological phenomenon that some people experience as soothing in response to certain kinds of sounds. YouTube features millions of ASMR videos designed to produce this response. MaryKate Wust, 2018. "Sounds too good to be true? Delving into the strange and soothing world of ASMR." Penn Medicine News (blog), October 18. https://www.pennmedicine.org/news/news-blog/2018/october/sounds-too-good-to-be-true-delving-into-the-strange-and-soothing-world-of-asmr

Distraction

Distracting yourself temporarily is a healthy and soothing coping skill. Think about what activities you enjoy. What activities put you in a different state of mind or a happier emotional place? What are some skills or hobbies that you're good at and that feel fulfilling for you? The list is potentially endless. Here are a few examples:

- Play a video game
- Play a musical instrument
- Practice a sport or athletic activity
- Cook or bake something
- Clean a room
- Do volunteer work or help a neighbor or friend
- Watch a movie, TV show, or online video, especially uplifting or funny ones
- Play with or pet your pets
- Paint, sculpt, draw, sing, dance, drum, write

Half-smile and willing hands

Research shows that we can alter how we feel by changing our physical posture or facial expression. Our moods will shift (at least a little) to match the posture or facial expression we are acting out.

Marsha Linehan teaches the "half-smile and willing hands" technique. In this technique you start by relaxing your face, neck and shoulders, then turn up one corner of your lips into a half smile. Try to adopt a serene facial expression (no smirking.) Also hold your hands open and outward with the palm facing up as if you are accepting a bundle being handed to you by another person.

This is a way of physically acting out acceptance with your body. You might also try smiling and putting your hands over your heart to induce feelings of affection, or using power poses to induce feelings of confidence.

Mindfulness, meditation, and yoga

Meditation and yoga both include learning to focus on your breath and learning to not be caught up in your thoughts. Learning to notice your thoughts and let them go without engaging them is a beneficial skill if you have a tendency to get caught up in distressing thoughts that keep you revved up in an extended experience of the 3F response.

Mindfulness can be practiced during meditation, or separately from meditation. Mindfulness is the practice of being very intentionally present. To do something mindfully is the opposite of doing something mindlessly. If you are washing dishes mindfully, you are paying close attention to every motion, every smell, every sight, and every texture or sensation. If you are meditating mindfully, you are very present and aware in this moment, aware of your breath and your bodily sensations, and resisting the allure of thoughts or emotions that invite you to leave the present moment and contemplate the future or the past or to speculate on things that might not exist at all.

There are many ways to do mindfulness, meditation, and yoga. Explore these. Find a form you enjoy and try to work it into your daily or weekly routine. That way you will be more likely to think to use it when you're distressed.

> **Action item:** Reflect on the many skills listed here. Identify which ones might be helpful for you. Practice each of them when you are not distressed. This will make them feel familiar and more accessible when you're upset and not able to think clearly. Assemble the physical items you need to enact the skills you like. Compile playlists, bookmark webpages, pin photos on Pinterest and so on, so that your soothing music, photos, and videos are easy to find and use when you need them.

Avoid arguing if possible

There's a tsunami of online resources and relationship self-help books meant to teach people how to "fight fair" or "fight well." These books discuss at length how to choose language that is not attacking or blaming, and how to avoid behaviors that are manipulative or hurtful.

But if one or more people are in the 3F response, their ability to choose their behavior or words is impaired—sometimes greatly impaired. In other words, depending on how upset the people are, this kind of advice might be asking for the impossible!

You may have noticed that my approach seems to be "don't fight at all." What I mean by that is, if either person is upset, they're somewhere on the dimmer dial of the 3F response, which means they don't have full access to their executive brain functions. And remember, it's those executive brain functions, such as memory, empathy, and problem-solving, that we need most when trying to resolve a disagreement with a loved one.

Anything we do or say when in the 3F response is likely to be damaging to either the relationship or to the individuals in the relationship. Communicating with our partners when we're impaired within the 3F response is like driving while intoxicated. You might get lucky and not do any lasting damage, but it's dangerous and risky. It might even help to think of arguing when either person is impaired by the 3F response as being similarly irresponsible as driving while intoxicated.

Learn to identify the symptoms. Agree that taking a timeout is the responsible, kind, loving thing to do. Call a timeout, calm and soothe yourselves, and return to the discussion when you're not impaired. This is not going to happen overnight. Change and growth are incremental.

I'm also not suggesting that people become robotic and stop expressing their emotions when they're upset. An argument doesn't begin the moment one person expresses they are upset. An argument begins when they express their upset emotions in a hurtful way, and the other person responds in kind.

So, express yourself! As long as you don't lash out at, name-call, or insult your partner, or talk to your partner in a way that is disrespectful or degrading. I cover how to do this, as well as how to listen with compassion, later in the book.

Each relationship is unique. I've seen people comfortable with allowing some emotional back and forth and then one person interjects humor, and any real hurtful argument is derailed before it begins. I've also seen people do an incredible amount of damage while they appear to be having a calm, coolheaded conversation.

Some people think it's just semantics, but I think there's a difference between a disagreement and an argument. And in my opinion, arguments are not helpful. Sometimes they feel helpful to the person who wins, but by winning they have most likely done harm to the trust and safety their partner experiences in the relationship.

By definition, arguments typically result in enough harm that apologies and repair work are needed afterward. I think it's best to learn how to communicate in ways that bypass arguments in the first place if possible.

Conclusion

Here's a quick summary of what we covered in this chapter.

Arguments are upsetting, sometimes so upsetting they activate the fight-flight-freeze response in one or more of the people involved. The 3F response causes a number of physiological responses, including a shutdown of executive brain functions—memory, empathy, thinking, and decision-making—that are vital to resolving a conflict while also preserving and protecting the bonds of a relationship.

Continuing to talk or argue when one or more people are in the 3F response is unhelpful and possibly damaging. Don't do it!

Negotiate with the other person or people about how to call for a time-out. Take a 20- to 60-minute break and do self-soothing exercises during that time. If you can't soothe yourself to a calm state in 60 minutes, you may need to seek professional assistance. If you can't access professional assistance, seek out self-help groups, support groups, and other supports that could help.

In the next chapter I teach you what damaging communication to watch out for and how to be effective and kind when you speak. This will help you resolve conflicts in a constructive and collaborative way.

CHAPTER 3

How to Communicate Effectively and Collaboratively

In this chapter, we take a closer look at the communication and behavioral missteps that can create a rupture or rift in a relationship. This rift is the primary "problem" we will seek to address and repair anytime we're talking about relationship communication or interactions.

In the language of attachment theory, no one is perfect, and ruptures are bound to happen in any relationship. In order to experience our relationships as safe havens and secure bases, we need to have confidence in the ability of the people in the relationship to repair ruptures small and large so that we know the relationship is strong and flexible rather than fragile and easily destroyed.

I want to be clear on another point. Emotions or feelings are not, of themselves, problems in a relationship. Unpleasant feelings can be a task for an individual. If I feel angry and I don't want to feel angry because it's unpleasant for me, I have the task of trying to resolve and transform my feelings of anger into feelings of peace. (I'll begin addressing how to transform our emotions in chapter 6.)

In the context of my relationship, my anger is not a problem. My feelings are valid and they provide useful information. My behaviors might be a problem in my relationship, and the way I express my anger might be a behavior that could damage the bond in my relationship, creating a rift that's in need of repair. The rift itself is the problem that I encourage the relationship partners to come together and solve in a collaborative manner so the solution they find works for everyone involved.

Examine how you each communicate with the other people involved in your relationships. The way we communicate is often what causes a person to be activated into the 3F response. This chapter covers some very important skills to master and some very important things to avoid in order to create an environment where everyone feels safe to truly listen to others and express themselves.

Address the underlying emotional conflict

Now that we know how to recognize the 3F response and what to do when it happens, we're ready to move on to the next step. In the last chapter I explained that in any argument, there are really two different arguments: the surface-level argument and the underlying emotional argument.

Sometimes a conflict is more than just an argument. Sometimes the very security of the bond is damaged or threatened. When a partner fears their place in our heart or in our life is at risk—when they fear they will lose the relationship, that they will be replaced by someone else, that their relationship with us is being "downgraded," or that they will lose some important aspect of the relationship—this can induce intense pain, anger, or fear.

The first step to resolving any issue is to address the emotional argument or rupture to the bond that is hidden under the surface issue. The more intense the pain we feel, the more important it is to repair the relationship bond before trying to resolve the surface-level issue. There are several reasons for this.

First, as long as we fear the other person is disregarding our feelings, or hurting or attacking us, we will be emotionally activated. When we're activated, our executive functions are impaired. And the executive brain functions are precisely the tools we need in order to resolve issues well.

Second, the end result we want is for the people involved to feel close and bonded again. We want to feel safe and secure in our relationship and truly believe the other person is on our team. In arguments, our team member is transformed into an enemy. We need a process for turning them back into a teammate. The way to achieve this is to get each person to understand and empathize with the other person and communicate in a way that confirms that we each care about the other's feelings. This is what I mean by resolving the rift or rupture in the relationship.

Finally, we need a solution to the surface-level issue. That solution belongs to both people or all the people involved, and in an egalitarian relationship, it should be a collaborative creation and agreed upon unanimously. In a consensual power dynamic, depending on the terms of the relationship, the solution may still be co-created, or the dominant may have the responsibility of taking the submissive's feelings and needs into account and using that information to help formulate a solution that works for both of them.

Let's return to our example of Brian and Samantha arguing about the dishes. As I stated previously, the surface-level argument is about who will do the dishes and when. Under the surface, they both have feelings about this issue and they are arguing about whether those feelings are being well cared for in this relationship.

Let's imagine we could hear what they are each thinking:

Brian: Samantha knows my phobia of bugs. Seeing one literally gives me a panic attack. She doesn't seem to care about my feelings anymore. Not doing the dishes is more important to her than whether I have a panic attack. Also, if she doesn't do the dishes tonight, then I have to do them, and that's just not fair since I washed the daytime dishes and made dinner.

Samantha: He knows how exhausting my 12-hour work shifts are and I'm so tired all the time. I feel like I'm getting burnt out, but I know we need the money and I'm barely hanging on. But he doesn't seem to care how I feel or how much I sacrifice for us. Me doing the dishes is more important to him than my feelings.

They each want the other to understand and care about how they feel. They are each seeking to be understood. Unfortunately, each person is under the mistaken belief that the way to accomplish this is to argue their own perspective, like lawyers in a courtroom drama arguing opposite sides of a case.

The problem is that both people are thinking the same thing. Both are trying to get understanding. Both are trying to be heard. And neither is listening and trying to give understanding.

In order to successfully address the emotional issue, we need to take it from an unspoken subtext of an argument over dishes and bring it up to the forefront. We need to bring it out into the open and speak it as clearly and as kindly as possible. We need to move the argument away from the surface level of dishes and toward the deeper level of feelings.

Why? Because we need to repair the potential rift in the relationship and get these two people on the same team, addressing common obstacles together so they can solve the dishes problem as a team, together.

How do these two heal the rift between them? They need help communicating that they *do* care about each other's feelings. That help can come in the form of using two powerful tools: nonviolent communication (NVC), also sometimes called compassionate communication, and the Imago exercise. This chapter is primarily about how we communicate, so it involves a detailed discussion of nonviolent communication. The next chapter introduces the Imago exercise.

Think of these as building blocks stacked one on top of the next. At the top of the stack is the Imago exercise. But before we can do a communication exercise such as the Imago exercise, we need to learn how to communicate in a non-damaging way. That's NVC, the middle block. And before we can use NVC, we need to be physiologically able to think and access compassion. Therefore, we need an awareness of the 3F response, timeouts, and self-soothing skills. That's the block on the bottom.

So, to reverse that description, first we need to be in a physiological state where we can access compassion, our thinking brain, and other executive functions. We need to be in what polyvagal theory calls "safe and social mode," where we can approach problems with curiosity and where we want to connect with another person. Once we have that, we can use nonviolent, compassionate communication skills. These are new skills for most people, so you'll need your thinking brain. Using these skills requires the ability to feel compassion, tolerate being vulnerable, and express what you honestly feel. Once we are able to communicate in this way, we can then use the Imago exercise and achieve its best, most effective results.

Nonviolent communication

Nonviolent communication was developed by Marshall B. Rosenberg.[33] When he was eight years old, he and his family moved to inner-city Detroit just a week before the race riots of 1943, where 34 people were killed and 433 were injured. He also experienced extensive violence and bullying

---

33 Marshall B. Rosenberg, 2003. *Nonviolent Communication: A Language of Life.* PuddleDancer Press.

throughout his youth due to anti-Semitism. He became fascinated with what caused violence and how to interrupt that process.

Rosenberg earned his PhD in clinical psychology in 1961. He worked in a number of settings helping people communicate and resolve conflicts and eventually developed a system he called nonviolent communication. He helped desegregate schools, helped negotiate peace in several countries, and founded an institute to continue teaching these techniques around the world. In 2006 he was awarded the Bridge of Peace Nonviolence Award for his extensive international contributions to peace.[34]

Rosenberg begins from his belief that it is human nature to enjoy giving and receiving out of compassion for ourselves and others. If polyvagal theory had existed 70 years ago, I believe he would have said that it is human nature to want to stay in safe and social mode.

Rosenberg believed that cultural conditioning teaches us to disconnect from compassion and we use language in a way that alienates us from ourselves, our emotions, and each other. So he created a language system to help us reconnect.

The four components of NVC are:

1. Observe what is happening without judgment or evaluation.
2. State how we feel when we observe this.
3. State what needs, values, and desires are connected to the feelings.
4. Make requests for concrete actions that enrich our lives.

I'm going to explain in depth the first two steps of NVC in this chapter as well has how these concepts intersect with other therapeutic theories. The third step of NVC intersects well with the Imago exercise and I'll discuss them in the next chapter. The fourth step of making requests overlaps well with making relationship agreements; this is discussed in chapter 8.

How do our words impact others?

Communication is an interactive process. Though we are not completely responsible for how someone responds to us, we do have some influence.

---

34 The Center for Nonviolent Communication, 2020. "Marshall B. Rosenberg, Ph.D. (1934–2015): Our founder." https://www.cnvc.org/about/marshall

We can invite a cooperative, empathetic response, or we can invite a defensive, conflictual response by how we present what we have to say.

Another way of saying this is that we can de-escalate the combativeness of a conflict, or we can escalate that conflict through our choice of words, tone, and nonverbal signals such as facial expressions and body language.

If a person says something attacking, insulting, or accusatory, it's natural to expect the other person to respond defensively. Here's an example from my practice:

Harold: "When we argue and Jim gets upset, he starts using big words I don't understand and interrupts me just to shut me up. He doesn't want me to have a say. He bullies me!"

Jim: "Oh my God, that is not what happens! You get distraught and irrational and I'm just trying to calm you down. And I have gone out of my way to make sure you have a say in decisions! How could you accuse me of wanting to silence you?!"

Notice in this example how Harold accuses Jim of purposely hurtful motives. Furthermore, the use of the word "bully" evokes an image of a person who intimidates someone else or even uses violence, because they think it's fun or they feel entitled to control the other person.

Jim feels immediately defensive. He believes that he speaks the way he does for other reasons, so he defends himself and presents his alternate perspective.

Sports Analogy!

Communication is a bit like tennis. If you serve the ball all the way to the back right corner of the other side of the court, the other player will need to run to the back right corner if they are to engage that ball. If you barely lob it over the net, they will have to charge the net if they are going to engage that ball.

If we want a cooperative response—if we want to hear the other person and be heard by them—it's important that we learn how to invite that cooperative response. It's important that we learn to serve up tennis balls that are kind, considerate, and therefore easy for the other person to engage. Because relationship communication, unlike tennis, is not a combative, competitive sport. It's a vehicle through which we communicate and connect with our partners.

There's an important principle from NVC that we can use to increase the likelihood of cooperation and compassion, and decrease the likelihood of defensiveness and stonewalling.

The principle is to separate observations from judgments. This isn't a natural way of speaking for most people and will probably take practice. Let's look again at what Harold said.

Harold: "When we argue and Jim gets upset, he starts using big words I don't understand and interrupts me just to shut me up. He doesn't want me to have a say. He bullies me!"

What are the judgment words or phrases in this example?

- Just to shut me up
- He doesn't want me to have a say
- He bullies me

Harold is trying to communicate how he feels and what he believes needs to be addressed in the relationship, but he's doing it ineffectively. He's doing it in a way that increases the likelihood that Jim will *not* listen. He's communicating in a way that is likely to trigger defensiveness. Jim's attention will be drawn to the task of defending himself from accusations and judgments rather than the task of understanding Harold's feelings or what Harold is trying to say he needs.

When Harold uses these phrases, he's expressing assumptions about Jim's motives that reflect unspoken judgments of Jim's character. What kind of person would intentionally seek to silence his partner and prevent him from having a say in relationship issues?

Learning to express how we feel without adding judgment words and phrases will reduce needless conflict, reduce defensive impulses in the listener, and increase the listener's ability to actually hear what we want them to hear.

In nonviolent communication, Rosenberg says that we are culturally conditioned to continually evaluate the rightness and wrongness of everything and everyone. Especially in any verbal disagreement, rather than getting in touch with how we feel or seeking to understand how the other person feels, we tend to judge their thoughts, beliefs, values, or feelings as wrong, and we then express our judgment of their wrongness.

This expression of judgment is exactly what diverts the other person to defend themselves, their character, their action, their beliefs, or their ideas. Since the goal is for others to hear how something affected us, or to hear how we feel, we want to avoid diverting them to defensiveness. This is why Rosenberg instructs us, in step one, to separate what we observe from any judgments or evaluations.

Step two is to state what we feel. I recommend practicing a pattern of stating an observation without judgment, followed by an emotion word, which combines step one with step two. I call this the **observation-emotion format**.

> When _____ happens, I feel _____.

Or...

> I feel ____ when ____ happens.

In this example, Harold could instead say, "When you use big words and interrupt me, I feel angry." He could leave out his assumptions and judgments of Jim's motives or character.

Learn to recognize judgments

Learning how to separate observations from judgments may not be a simple task. It may be more helpful to learn what not to do. Learn to notice anything that could be considered a judgment, positive or negative. It may be fine to use them in everyday language, but as soon as a disagreement, conflict, or negotiation begins, judgments are like landmines waiting to be stepped on.

Cognitive behavioral therapy (CBT) and dialectical behavioral therapy (DBT) also invite us to challenge and forgo our judgmental thoughts and beliefs. The following are some examples of the kinds of judgments we might express when in an argument or disagreement with someone.[35]

Name-calling (and implied name-calling) is an attack on a person's whole character, rather than on a single observable behavior. Examples: jerk, bully, asshole, bitch, cheapskate, lazy, idiot, dingbat, dumbass, and so on.

- "You're such a jerk!"
- "You just lay around the house all day." (You're lazy.)
- "If you would just let us have something nice!" (You're cheap.)
- "You squander all our money on fast food, and we don't have enough to pay the bills." (You're irresponsible or selfish.)
- You're such an asshole!

Positive judgments: These are an issue when used to describe yourself, or some other third person, in comparison to the person you may be arguing with. Examples: accomplished, brilliant, handsome, beautiful, great, wonderful, and so forth.

- "Why can't you be accomplished, like your sister?"
- "Everyone looks so elegant tonight. You could have at least brushed your hair."
- "My other partner made a delicious meal tonight. You should really ask them for some tips."

Negative judgments: These kinds of judgments are more obviously problematic. Examples: failure, stupid, idiotic, ugly, terrible, and similar.

- "Give it up. That project is a failure."
- "How could you be so stupid?"

---

35 Some of these are taken from a 1996 handout entitled "Responsible Thinking" by Dr. Stephen Mathis.

- "How could you be so thoughtless?"
- "That looks like a terrible idea."

Also, learn to recognize **moralistic language**. These are judgments about what should be considered good and what should be considered bad. These can include: should, shouldn't, fair, unfair, just, unjust, right, wrong, good, bad, shameful, abnormal, normal, fault, blame, guilt, and lots more.

- "That's just not normal."
- "You shouldn't even want to do that."
- "You should be ashamed."
- "It's all your fault!"
- "That's sick."

As well, it's good to learn to recognize **catastrophizing language and other exaggerations**. These are exaggerated judgments of just how awful, or how unacceptable, something is. These are also used to dramatically emphasize how strongly a person feels. This can feel manipulative to the other person. Examples: awful, horrible, and terrible.

- "I can't stand it!"
- "It's the last straw!"
- "It's the worst thing ever!"
- "I can't deal with this!"
- "My heart is being ripped out of me!"
- "This kitchen is a disaster area!"

And finally, learn to recognize **totalizing** language. These are disguised judgments and exaggerations of the frequency, predictability, or repetitiveness of a behavior, thus drawing an unspoken conclusion about what the behavior means. In other words, these judgments assume that a given behavior means more than what is happening right now and is indicative of a pattern of behavior (and possibly a character flaw) with a greater, and hidden, meaning. Some examples are: all, none, always, never, any, ever, everyone, no one, nobody, anything, everything, nothing, and everybody.

- "Everybody knows that."
- "No one will ever want that."
- "You always do that!"
- "I can never count on you."
- "Everything you touch turns to shit."
- "You never finish anything."

Action item: Since it will take practice to separate judgments from observations, I recommend reviewing conversations, especially arguments and disagreements, but also discussions that appear to have been cooperative negotiations, to discern where you used judging language. You can do this on your own in a journaling practice, or with a partner by reviewing conversations you have had together and kindly and gently pointing out judging language. Then brainstorm together how you each could have expressed your observations without including judgments.

Name feelings, don't describe them

Now that we have addressed Rosenberg's step 1 of NVC, step 2 is to speak what we feel as clearly and kindly as possible. We are often unclear when we express our feelings. We frequently express thoughts, judgments, and beliefs instead. Very frequently, we try to communicate our emotions with graphic descriptions and metaphors, but never actually say what we feel.

- "I feel like my guts are being ripped out."
- "I feel invisible."
- "I feel like I'm being judged." (Or a shortened version of that: "I feel judged.")
- "I'm feeling very attacked!"
- "I feel like an old, unwanted toy, tossed aside and forgotten."

None of these actually name an emotion. The first one is a description of what sounds like intense pain. But in fact, it's saying that the person is on the receiving end of a violent act, which implies an accusation of the other person.

"I feel like I'm being judged," again, is more about assuming the motives and character of the other person than about communicating what we actually feel.

A good indicator to remember is the word "like." If you're saying the word "like," then you're most likely describing an emotion rather than naming the emotion.

Another indicator is the word "that." When we try to express how we feel and we hear the word "that," we are most likely speaking a thought or a judgment rather than an emotion.

- "I feel that you aren't listening."
- "I feel that it's wrong to do what you did."
- "I feel that you bully me."

Earlier, I suggested using the **observation-emotion format.** To use it, we all need to become practiced at using a vocabulary of emotion words.

Let's think about emotions for a minute. We feel emotions in the body. We learn to associate the physical sensations with certain emotion labeling words. These physical sensations are created by the interplay of hormones and many other factors. The commonly known neurotransmitters that impact emotions (serotonin, dopamine, and oxytocin) are also hormones.[36] Hormones are chemical messengers that are meant to encourage or drive us to take action.

A couple of non-emotion examples of hormones driving action are hunger and sexual arousal. Both of these physical sensations are created by hormonal chemical messengers. The physical sensations we feel encourage us to take action to resolve the sensation and thus obtain something of benefit: nutrition, calories, sexual pleasure, relaxation, connection.

Each of the human emotions serves a positive purpose, even the ones that feel unpleasant. Sadness encourages us to slow down. Grief encourages us to reflect on the memories of something lost. Reflecting on a memory of an event strengthens that memory. Anger motivates us to protect a boundary for ourselves or a loved one. This is why I don't refer to any of our

---

36 Endocrine Society, 2022. "Brain hormones." January 24. https://www.endocrine. org/patient-engagement/endocrine-library/hormones-and-endocrine-function/brain-hormones

emotions as "bad" or "good." I refer to emotions and pleasant or unpleasant, but not good or bad.

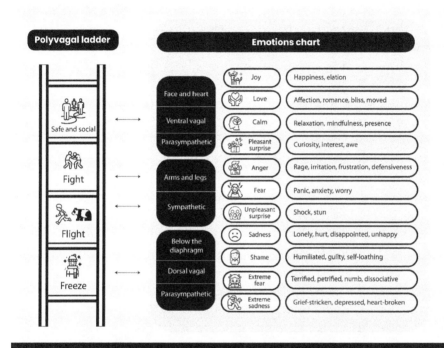

It's very helpful to expand our vocabulary of emotions and feelings. The emotions chart here combines a vocabulary of feeling words with a polyvagal map of the body. This chart is of course an oversimplification of human feelings and emotions because it leaves out many of the factors that give rise to our feelings, but it provides some handy examples of the body-mind connection and how emotions relate to polyvagal states.

The current scientific understanding of emotions and feelings involves an interplay between conscious and unconscious brain functions, multiple brain regions, hormones and neurotransmitters, the limbic system, an interceptive network (including the vagus nerve) that monitors bodily sensations, conscious recall of memory and thus a person's individual history of experiences, conscious and unconscious interpretation of our external environment, and conscious and unconscious biases and cultural beliefs.[37]

Lisa Barrett, author of *How Emotions are Made: The Secret Life of the Brain*, defines emotions in this way: "An emotion is your brain's creation of what your bodily sensations mean, in relation to what is going on around you in the world."[38]

We can feel a wide array of emotions without being in a full blown 3F response. But in reality, the 3F response is not an all-or-nothing experience. We don't usually go from calm to 3F instantaneously. As I explained previously, it's much more like a dimmer dial. We can be a little bit activated where we might feel anxious, nervous, or irritated. Or we might be moderately activated and feel anger or fear. Or we might be completely activated and feel enraged or terrified.

In order to use the observation-emotion format, we need a useful, descriptive vocabulary of emotion words. In the previous example, if Harold and Jim were going to apply NVC, Harold could have said, "When Jim uses big words and interrupts me, I feel angry." Or he could be more specific and select a more detailed word in the anger category: "When Jim uses big words and interrupts me, I feel exasperated."

There is considerable research showing that naming painful or unpleasant emotions helps to decrease the intensity of that pain. It helps calm and soothe the person (a little) and move them in the direction of being able to once again engage in constructive negotiations.

Conversely, naming a pleasant or enjoyable emotion helps to intensify the enjoyable experience of that emotion and also helps the person solidify the memory of that experience for later retrieval.

37 Antonio R. Damasio, 2022. Keynote address: The Science of Emotion. https://www.loc.gov/loc/brain/emotion/Damasio.html

Patrick Zimmerman, 2019. "How emotions are made." Behavioral Research Blog by Noldus Information Technology, June 11. https://www.noldus.com/blog/how-emotions-are-made#:~:text=And%20yes%2C%20emotions%20are%20created,%2C%20surprise%2C%20sadness%20and%20anger.

38 Lisa Feldman Barrett, 2018. *How Emotions are Made: The Secret Life of the Brain.* First Mariner Books.

> **Action item:** On your own or with a partner, review how you have communicated your feelings in the past. Do you tend to describe rather than label? Practice identifying your emotions by describing the physical sensations you experience with each emotion label. Be aware that these may vary from person to person.

Avoid intellectualizing

Some people have learned to avoid talking about their feelings at all. This can also be associated with male gender socialization or very regimented social environments. Sometimes people have a history of being shamed for talking about their feelings, or for displaying outward evidence of emotions.

Please understand, I am not singling out men. Anyone can internalize these messages if they either have a low tolerance for vulnerability or believe they should be in control of themselves or others. This way of relating to emotions just happens to also be part of an old-school gendered paradigm. Adhering to this way of restricting emotions reduces observable vulnerability and projects power and self-mastery. Unfortunately, by blocking vulnerability, it also blocks the vulnerable experiences of love and intimacy; it can keep relationships shallow, and it interferes with creating egalitarian relationships.

In traditional male gender socialization, people are taught that only a narrow band of emotions are appropriate for them. These tend to be emotions that lead to dominating others since, according to this worldview, masculine people are supposed to be in control of themselves and others. Therefore, they are allowed to feel anger, pride, confidence, sexual arousal, and controlled happiness. Uncontained happiness, fear, sadness, grief, pain, despair, shame, hurt, insecurity, anxiety, and doubt are off-limits.

Given these rules, people may struggle to allow themselves to name any variant of these emotions. They may feel shame at the thought of admitting to feeling one of the "off-limits" emotions. They tend to speak of their thoughts and judgments instead. Here's an example I encountered in my therapy practice:

Client: (Referring to kink/BDSM play) I think my boyfriend feels threatened when I want to play with another male dom.

Me: What does he say when you ask him?

Client: He has no objection when I get together with someone and I'm topping them. When I try to make a date with a woman to top me, he's okay with that. But when I try to make a date with a male to top me, he says, "I don't know. I think you should think about that some more." These are people we know well. One guy is someone I played with before my boyfriend and I got together. So it's not about safety. But I can't get him to talk about his feelings. He just keeps questioning my judgment instead.

Why is it important for a person to name their feelings (and name them accurately) rather than resist talking about their emotions? Because otherwise, the conversation centers on the merits of an idea rather than on the feelings motivating a disagreement. For example, a person might avoid saying to their partner, "I feel nervous when we talk about taking money out of our retirement account," and will instead say, "I don't think it's a good idea."

Why is this distinction important? Because "I don't think it's a good idea" sets up a win/lose debate over the merits of the idea. It also sets up your partner to feel insulted and try to defend their idea rather than listen for what you're feeling.

Let's say your partner can make a very good case for why it's a good idea to take money out of your retirement account, but you still feel uncomfortable. If you still don't talk about your feelings, you might seek to shut down this conversation. Your partner might feel unduly silenced or insulted.

On the other hand, if you are willing to talk about your feelings, you can say, "I see the merits of the idea, and yet I feel uncomfortable. Let's find ways to help me feel safer, or we could choose to explore other options for getting the money, simply out of compassion for my feelings."

Remember that anger is often a smokescreen

Anger often hides more vulnerable emotions. Sometimes the gendered emotion rules lead a person to translate all their vulnerable emotions into anger. Anger is safe and allowed, whereas fear, hurt, sadness, and doubt are not.

Here's another example from my practice:

Client: When I came into the room, I heard her on the phone mak-
            ing plans with her boyfriend. We had just agreed that she
            would talk with me about plans before talking with him, and
            here she was breaking that agreement!

Me: How did you feel when this happened?

Client: Angry!

Me: Why do you suppose you felt angry? Was there another
            emotion that happened with or before the anger?

Client: I guess so. (Then, after a long pause…) I felt hurt and
            betrayed. Maybe I felt a little scared that I couldn't trust her.
            Then I felt angry that something made me feel scared or
            hurt.

Avoid shutdown language

Before I explain shutdown language, I want to make one premise clear: I
believe all relationship decisions need to be unanimous. I go into more detail
in chapter 8, but for now the important concept is that whether there are two
people involved, or three, or five, they would ideally all have to agree to something for the group to take action. If they don't agree, then nothing changes
until they do agree. It's important that if they don't agree, they need to all stay
open to the discussion until they all agree to say yes or they all agree to say no.

The two exceptions to this are when you have a right to make a unilateral
decision or when you are willing to accept that making a unilateral decision
is going to change (or damage, or end) the relationship. I explain rights in
much more detail in chapter 5.

Shutdown language is language that operates like a veto—even though
the speaker may not mean for it to operate like a veto.

For example, Carol and Bill had an open relationship for several years,
and they also had two young children. They agreed when they opened their

relationship that they would not tell the children about polyamory or introduce them to their other relationships.

Bill developed a serious relationship with Janet and wanted to renegotiate. He wanted to introduce the children to Janet. Carol felt panicked by the thought and said, "That's a hard no for me."

A hard no means "I am not open to negotiation on this." I'm sure you can see how this would sound like a veto and would shut down communication.

Vetoes and shutdown language leave other people feeling frustrated and unheard. It would be more helpful, and keep the spirit of the relationship collaborative and welcoming, to at least hear why something is important to that person.

Let's revisit the conversation, but this time Carol will avoid shutdown language.

Bill: I'd like to introduce the kids to Janet.

Carol: I'm feeling a bit panicky. I'd like to take a break and calm down so I can really hear what you have to say.
            (They take a 20-minute break, then return to the conversation.)

Carol: Until now, we've always agreed to not tell the kids about our other relationships. Tell me why you feel differently now.

Bill: I've been seeing Janet for two years. I love her a lot. I see that relationship continuing for a long time. The kids are older now and I believe they can handle this information. And it just hurts to not be able to share this part of my life with Janet.

Carol: I hear you. And I can imagine it would be hurtful to not be able to share the kids with her... I'm still concerned that the kids aren't old enough to understand Daddy having a girlfriend in addition to me. I wonder how open you want to be with them about the nature of that relationship. I worry that they won't be discreet enough and might tell their grandparents or our neighbors. I worry that asking young kids to keep secrets causes them undue stress. And I worry a little bit about feeling replaced. It might feel like they have a step-mother even though you and I are still together.

Bill: I hear you. And you have some good points. I hadn't thought about secrets putting stress on kids. Can we talk about how we might create what I want without creating problems?

Carol: Sure. How about we get together with Janet and include her in this conversation, too?

Bill: Okay.

Notice that for Carol to stay open to the conversation, she didn't have to give in. She held her ground. But now they can brainstorm ideas that could possibly work for all three of them. Also, if she ends up still not wanting the children to meet Janet, she can express compassion for both of them and their hurt feelings while expressing why she is not willing to agree. She may also be able to outline under what circumstances she would be willing to reconsider, such as when the children are two years older, or if they went to an after-school program rather than seeing their grandparents every week-day afternoon.

Action item: On your own or with a partner, review how you have communicated in the past. Do you tend to avoid talking about feelings? Do you intellectualize or talk about your thoughts rather than label your emotions?

Action item: Review discussions where you have felt shut down by a partner. Review where you may have shut down conversations prematurely. If you can, ask your partner or other people to help you identify some of these moments. Identify your fear. Why did you shut down the conversation? Practice how you might continue the conversation without necessarily giving in or giving up the thing you want.

Conclusion

When we speak, it's important to speak in a way that is more likely to result in the other person being willing to hear us, and less likely to activate the other person into the 3F response. Using nonviolent communication, naming our feelings, using the observation-emotion format, and avoiding shutdown language are useful tools and techniques I encourage you to practice when trying to resolve a conflict in a collaborative and cooperative way.

In the next chapter I explain the Imago exercise and illustrate several ways to use it to improve the communication and problem-solving in your relationships. I also explain how it links with NVC steps 3 and 4, and share some recommendations I have for using both NVC and the Imago exercise in non-monogamous relationships.

CHAPTER 4

Listening Well and Resolving Disagreements

Now that we know how to speak in a way that will reduce the likelihood of activating the 3F response in others and increase the possibility of an empathetic and cooperative response, I will explain the complete Imago exercise.

Purpose of the Imago exercise

Let's return to our example of two people fighting over who washes the dishes. When we left, Brian and Samantha were arguing with each other. They had become opponents and had taken up opposite sides of the issue (who will wash the dishes, you or me, and when will they be washed?). The chasm between them was quickly growing as they each stated their case and struggled to be heard and understood. But they both forgot to try to hear the other person.

The Imago exercise, developed by Dr. Harville Hendrix and Dr. Helen LaKelly Hunt in 1980, is an excellent tool to bring Brian and Samantha back together so that they can address the problem of the dishes as a team.[39]

The purpose of the Imago exercise is to give each person an opportunity to explain what they feel about an issue and why, and to give the listener the opportunity to understand a perspective different from their own. The goal

---

[39] Harville Hendrix, 1990. *Getting the Love You Want: A Guide for Couples*. Perennial Library.

is to validate each other's feelings and resolve to work together as a team to find solutions to the issue that take both people's feelings and needs into account.

I'd like to explain what validation is. Therapists are well known for saying, "Everyone's feelings are valid." And people hearing this are well known for rolling their eyes and scoffing. I believe this is due to a misunderstanding of what therapists mean when we say "valid."

If you have a phobia of cats and seeing a kitten causes you panic, trembling, fear, and nausea, I can say, honestly, that your feelings are valid. What that means is that I can understand, given your history, given your phobia, why you feel the way you do. I can even say, "If I were you, and I had your history, and I had your phobia, I can imagine I would feel the same way you do." And, I'm saying that your feelings of terror and nausea matter to me. I care, and we should act in ways that show I care about your feelings.

I am not saying that I feel the same way. I don't. I adore kittens and love cats and seeing one makes me feel giddy and gooey and I want to pet it with every fiber of my being! I am also not saying that your feelings are justified by the facts. Cats and kittens are fairly harmless and, unless you are deathly allergic, they are very unlikely to do significant harm to an adult human, especially if that human respects the autonomy of the cat.

Everyone's feelings are always valid. They are not always justified by the facts. I cover this in chapter 5 on boundaries.

How to do the Imago exercise

First, I'll explain the Imago exercise step by step. At the end of this description is a flow chart for visual representation of the Imago exercise. After the chart, I'll follow with some very important tips for doing the exercise well, and then I'll illustrate how to use the exercise with the concrete example of Brian, Samantha, and their conflict over doing the dishes.

When using the Imago exercise with two people, one person is designated the speaker and the other person is the listener. The speaker states (non-judgmentally) what they observed or experienced and how they felt about it. They express what is important to them, what they value and how these are related to what they felt. And they inform the listener when they are done speaking.

The listener listens, all the way through, without interrupting or adding any comments. They may need to take written notes of what the speaker says. When the speaker is done speaking, the listener still does not comment or respond to anything they heard. The listener's role at this time is simply to repeat back what they heard, focusing primarily on what the speaker felt and why. When finished, the listener asks the speaker if they got it right.

If the speaker feels the listener got it right and the speaker has nothing further to say, then the speaker answers yes and goes on to the next step. If not, and the speaker needs to clarify something the listener didn't understand correctly, or if the speaker simply feels they need to clarify something better, the speaker says no and they enter Loop 1 in the flow chart.

Loop 1 is where the speaker clarifies what they are trying to express, and the listener listens, then repeats back what they heard and asks if they got it right. They continue to repeat this process until the speaker says "yes, you got it right" and they don't feel they need to clarify any further. Here, they leave Loop 1.

Next, they determine whether they need to enter Loop 2. To determine that, the listener must ask themselves, "Do I feel I truly understand the speaker, what they were feeling and why, or do I need to ask some questions so I can fully understand?"

If the listener does not feel they truly understand the speaker, they enter Loop 2 on the diagram. In Loop 2, the listener asks open-ended, non-judgmental, probing questions designed to help them understand the speaker. The speaker answers the questions. The listener repeats back what they heard and asks if they got it right. They continue repeating this loop until the listener feels they completely understand the speaker, and the speaker has said yes to all of the "have I gotten it right" questions.

At the end of Loop 2, the listener should feel they truly understand the speaker, what they feel, and why they feel as they do. And the speaker should feel heard.

The next step is the validation step. After the validation step, the speaker should feel understood and feel that their feelings are accepted and respected. In this step, the listener says, "I get it. I understand. And, if I were you, and had the same history, perspective, and values, I can imagine I would feel the same."

The final step is for the listener to express care and the desire to work together as a team. "I care about your feelings and I want to work together with you to find a solution that works for both of us."

After going through the whole exercise, the two switch roles and repeat the entire process with the former speaker now being the listener, and the former listener being the speaker. It is very important to always switch roles so that both people get a chance to speak, be heard and understood, and to have their feelings and perspective validated.

After both people have had a chance to be the speaker and to be validated, and both have been the listener and have a new understanding and compassion for the feelings of the other, the final process is for the two people to brainstorm solutions to the surface-level issue as a team, looking for solutions that take both people's feelings and needs into account.

Here is a visual flow chart of the Imago exercise.

Imago exercise flow chart

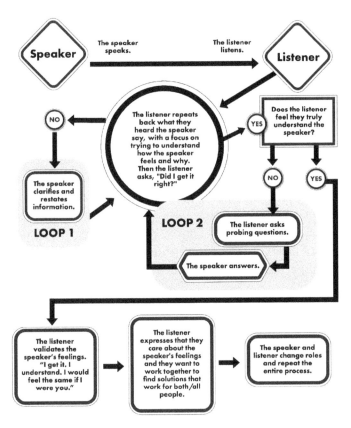

> **Action item:** When you and a partner, or you and any other person in your life, use the Imago exercise for the first time, practice it with something easy first. Especially if arguments tend to get heated with this person, practice several times with topics where you already agree or where you disagree but the emotions are neutral to mild. It's difficult to use the exercise with a heated argument when you are still unsure of how to use the format.

Important tips for doing the Imago exercise well

1. <u>When you're the listener, drop your agenda.</u> When you are the listener, it's important to listen with your sole focus on trying to really understand what the speaker is feeling, what's important to them, and why. What's it like to be them? Completely set aside your own agenda and your own feelings for now.

   Abandon the tendency we all have to listen like lawyers. What I mean is, we tend to listen for the thing we disagree with so we can say "I object!" We tend to listen for the points where our perspective disagrees with the perspective of the speaker. When we hear it, we tend to stop listening and hold on to that point so that when it's our turn to speak, we can present our counter-argument. If you are the listener, part of your job is to resist this tendency.

   Instead, you want to listen to understand. Learn to assume that the other person is a rational person. Despite the fact that their position may not make sense to you right now, accept that their position makes sense to them. Your job as the listener is to understand how that is so, from their perspective. Your goal in the end is to be able to truly empathize with and validate their feelings.

2. <u>When you're the listener, take notes.</u> As the speaker speaks, take notes if necessary, because at the next step in the exercise, the listener's job is to repeat back what they heard, especially the emotional part—what the speaker feels and why—and then ask if they got it right.

3. <u>When you're the speaker, be gentle.</u> The speaker's job is to express how they feel and why. Avoid using blaming or judgmental language while doing this. Do your best to use nonviolent communication techniques.

This will decrease the listener's tendency toward defensiveness, objections, and counter-arguments.

4. <u>When you're the speaker, be concise, if you can.</u> Sometimes people have difficulty finding their own point and talk around something for some time before getting there. This makes it difficult for the listener to follow or maintain attentive focus. If you trust the process, the back-and-forth of Loop 1 and Loop 2 can help you find your point more easily and is less challenging for the listener. (I'll give you concrete examples of these loops in action in a moment.)

    Other times, a person can be verbose because they feel they have to get out the *complete* thought. And the complete thought might be several pages of material. If being more concise is difficult or impossible for you, try to remember that it's difficult for others to focus for that long, and have compassion for your listener. You may need to exercise patience and understanding as they try to repeat back what you said and miss several important points, and you have to repeat those points for them.

5. <u>When brainstorming solutions, focus on what you *do* want, rather than on what you *don't* want.</u> Each person as individuals, or the relationship members as a group, will do best if you focus on what you want to feel or experience rather than on what you think you don't want. Once the issue is resolved, how do we want to feel about each other? How do we want to feel about ourselves? What do we want our relationship to feel like? What experiences do we want to have? I'll explain this more toward the end of this chapter.

The Imago exercise in action

Let's look at these first steps using the dishes example with Brian and Samantha. Brian will take the speaker position first and Samantha will take the listener position first.

Brian: I asked you to do the dishes before you went to bed because leaving dishes overnight invites roaches and ants! I'm feeling unappreciated because I did the daytime dishes and prepared dinner before you got home. And I'm angry that it's a struggle to get you to do this one thing. But mostly it's about the bugs. Just seeing dishes in the sink in the morning makes me fear I'll see a bug and it can mess up my whole day.

Samantha: Ok. I heard that you are feeling unappreciated because you are doing a lot around the house and it's a struggle to get me to do this one thing. And that just seeing a bug in the morning is so frightening that it can mess up your whole day. Did I get that right?

From here, the speaker asks himself, "Do I think Samantha really understands how I feel and why?" If the answer is yes, they go on to the next step. If the answer is no, they enter Loop 1 on the flow chart.

If the speaker feels the listener missed something important and they enter Loop 1, the speaker speaks again. They may add information or clarify something said previously, and it's very important to stay on the one topic. If tempted to add in a second topic (no matter how related it seems), the speaker should resist that urge and save it for a complete, second application of the Imago exercise.

Next, the listener again repeats back what they heard and asks if they got it right. They continue with this cycle, over and over, until the speaker can say, "Yes, I believe the listener really understands me now."

Brian: Almost, but it's not just seeing a bug. Seeing dishes in the sink causes me to fear that I *might* see a bug, and my heart starts to pound and I literally fear approaching the sink in the morning. I begin to fear I will have a panic attack. If I see a bug, I *will* have a panic attack. And starting my day this way … I feel angry and resentful for hours because it can all be avoided by washing the dishes before bed. But then I feel resentful that I have to do that too, because I did all the other stuff.

Samantha: Ok, I heard that it's not just seeing a bug, it's the fear that you might see a bug, and seeing dishes in the sink in the morning triggers that. This fear can trigger panic attacks and can mess up your whole day. So, it is really important to you to have the kitchen cleaned up at night but then you feel resentful if you have to do that on top of all the other things you did that day. Did I get that right?

Brian: Yes. (Now he feels heard.)

Notice Brian's use of nonviolent communication. He used a bit of blaming language the first time he spoke (and Samantha did a good job of letting it pass without getting defensive), but the second time Brian spoke, he did great! Notice he said, "When I see… I feel."

Next, the listener decides whether they enter Loop 2. The listener asks herself, "Do I feel I truly understand Brian?" If the answer is yes, they go on to the validation step. If the answer is no, they enter Loop 2.

In this case, she answers yes, and they go on to the validation step. The validation step is very important. Don't skip it! Here, the listener expresses that they understand why the speaker feels as they do. The listener's goal is to validate that the speaker's feelings make sense. It is the opposite of "you shouldn't feel that way" or "you're being too sensitive" or "that's just not logical." All of those are invalidating statements and do damage to your relationships.

Validation essentially goes like this: "I get it. I understand. And I would feel the same if I were you."

Samantha: I get it. I understand. And, if I had panic attacks related to bugs, I would feel the same way you do about the dishes being left out overnight.

It is important that the listener avoids saying, "but I don't feel the same way." Remember, your turn is coming in just a minute. This is the wrong time. Let this moment be only about validating the speaker.

To strengthen the relationship, now the listener expresses that they care about the speaker's feelings and want to work with them to find a solution.

Samantha: I care about how you feel, and I don't want you to feel fear or resentment. I want to work with you to find a solution that works for both of us.

Notice that Samantha did not give up and let Brian have his way. The listener didn't say "You are right and I am wrong." None of that has happened. Just "I get it, I understand, and I would feel the same if I were you."

Timeouts during the Imago exercise

The listener role is an emotionally demanding role. It's common for the listener to struggle with getting activated into the 3F response. If this happens, gently call a timeout and self-soothe for 20 minutes. **When you return to the discussion, always start where you left off.** Don't go back to the beginning. It's very important that both people get a full turn at being the speaker, being heard, and getting validated!

Your ability to self-soothe and develop the skills to listen without becoming activated will increase with practice. If the listener is activated into the 3F response or frequently needs to self-soothe during the Imago exercise, reflect on whether the speaker is consistently using nonviolent communication techniques. If the use of NVC could be improved, gently point out the link between you being activated and any judgmental, blaming or attacking language, and ask the speaker to try to use NVC consistently.

Switch over!

Next, the two people switch roles. Some people struggle to remember to switch roles. In those cases, the speaker may struggle to give up the speaking role until the disagreement is resolved. Or, one person may struggle with the requirements of the listening role and the necessity of putting their own agenda and perspective on hold long enough to really listen to the other person.

Remember, you can't resolve an issue ethically unless both people have been heard and understood, and both people's feelings and needs are taken into account as you craft possible solutions. Keep working on it until you can both listen and validate the other person well.

The second time through the exercise, Samantha speaks and Brian listens.

Samantha: On the days that I work, I work 12-hour shifts, and when we add commuting, I am gone for 15 hours on those days. I come home so exhausted that I literally only have energy to eat something, unwind in front of the TV for an hour or two, and go to bed. Then I sleep, get up, and do it all again. The thought of doing even one work-oriented task makes me want to cry. I feel unappreciated because I feel this is a sacrifice I make for us, and when you talk about me doing dishes, it seems clear you don't know how badly I already feel.

Brian: Okay, I heard that you are exhausted after working long hours and the thought of doing a chore makes you want to cry. You feel hurt and unappreciated that I don't seem to understand how you feel. Did I get that right?

Samantha: Yes.

Here, the listener got it right, and Samantha doesn't feel a need to clarify anything, so they bypass Loop 1, but Brian doesn't feel he truly understands all he needs to understand about Samantha's experience. He decides to ask some open-ended, non-judgmental, probing questions, causing them to enter Loop 2 before doing the validation step.

A probing question is one that seeks information. It's very important to avoid embedding any judgment in your questions or any implication that the speaker is wrong for wanting what they want or feeling what they feel.

Some examples of hidden judgment questions are: "When you did that, did you think about if it was fair to me?" "Can you see where that creates a problem?" "Did you just feel entitled to let me do all the work?"

It's also important to avoid framing these questions in the form of criticism, such as "How can you think that?" or "How could you feel that way?" or "Why would anybody want that?"

Also, avoid asking closed-ended questions that limit the speaker to options you predetermine by the way you ask the question, usually meaning they only leave room for a yes or no answer, or for a choice of options determined by the listener. Some examples of closed-ended questions are: "In that moment, did you think about washing the dishes?" "When you were going up the stairs, were you thinking you would do the dishes in the morning?" "Did you feel angry or sad?"

One of the best ways to avoid adding judgment or criticism to your follow-up questions, and also to avoid imposing limits on the answers the speaker might offer, is to use an open-ended question format. This format invites more information and details without limiting or restricting the speaker to any preconceived limits on the answers, and typically avoids adding judgments.

Some examples of open-ended questions are: "Help me understand what you felt in that moment?" or "Can you tell me more about how you felt and why?"

In the next section of dialogue, Brian askes some open-ended, non-judgmental, probing questions.

Brian: You said the thought of a chore makes you want to cry, and your job feels like a sacrifice you make for us. Can you tell me more about that?

Samantha: What do you mean?

Brian: It sounds like you hate your job. (Brian offers a possible answer to his question only because Samantha didn't seem to understand what he was getting at.)

Samantha: I don't really hate the work I do. But I enjoy it a lot less than I used to. I think these 12-hour shifts are killing me. But we need the money, and jobs with eight-hour shifts pay less per hour. So I stay at this job and it makes me really unhappy, but I do it for us.

Brian: Okay, I think I understand now, the way your job is structured makes you really unhappy and exhausted, but you stay with it for us because we need the money. And when I talk to you about the dishes, you feel this sacrifice is unappreciated and that I don't know or care how tired you are. Is that right?

Samantha: Yes.

Now Brian does the validation step.

Brian: I get it. I didn't realize how tired or unhappy you are because
                of your job, and if I felt I was sacrificing for us like that, I
                would feel the same way you do about my requests that you
                do dishes on your work nights.
                     I care about your feelings and I want to work together to
                find a solution that works for both of us.

Samantha: Thank you.

Notice that Brian and Samantha still have not solved their dishes problem.
But they have solved the threat to the relationship. They should be feeling
closer and less angry or upset, and feeling more compassion for each other's
experience.

Before moving on to the brainstorming step, ask, "Do we both feel
heard and understood enough to brainstorm solutions to the dishes issue?"
If not, go back to the beginning and keep working through the Imago exercise until you can both (or all) say yes to this question.

At this stage, it's important to resist the tendency to feel stuck or discouraged. Sometimes when we can see both sides of an issue, we can feel
immobilized and unable to imagine resolving it. This is because we tend to
get attached to the first solution that seems right when we are only seeing
things from our own perspective. I'll discuss this tendency more toward the
end of this chapter in the example of Bob, Adam, and Charlie. For now, try
to stay open-minded and trust the process.

As Brian and Samantha move forward to solve the dishes problem, they
can approach this problem as a team. As a team, they are on the same side,
and they want to find solutions that work for everyone on the team. The next
step is to brainstorm solutions to the problem that take both of their feelings
and needs into account.

Any proposed solution to the dishes issue needs to also be sensitive to
the emotional issues that have been voiced: one person's bug phobia, the
other person's exhaustion and burnout, and both people struggling with
feeling unappreciated.

Brainstorming

One of the fun things about brainstorming is agreeing in advance to allow yourselves to make suggestions that may seem ridiculous, unrealistic, and unreasonable, without judgment. This is important to help each person open up to creative ideas and bypass the tendency to self-censor or reject ideas before they are shared.

However, there is one rule about what's not admissible in the brainstorm. These solutions should not require either person to change who they are, how they feel, or what they value, or to change contributing factors such as their job. At this stage, we need to do our best to ensure any solutions we offer up are consistent with the validation step we just completed.

It would be counterproductive and possibly hurtful if, right after validating our partner, we offered a solution to the problem that effectively invalidates them. For example, offering up that Brian could get therapy for his bug phobia is essentially saying that he is wrong to feel the way he does. He is the problem, and the solution is to change who he is.

It's not always the case, but it may be helpful to think of this stage as brainstorming that focuses on seeking immediate, short-term solutions. Longer-term solutions can be offered if they don't require a person to change. But be aware that if they require a change that would need to be negotiated, like saving to buy a dishwasher, or moving to a new home, there may need to be a whole, separate negotiation around that suggestion.

Here's what Brian and Samantha came up with for their short-term, immediate solutions:

1. Hire someone to wash the dishes.
2. Buy all new dishes every day and throw away used dishes.
3. Eat out or get take-out food and thus avoid creating dishes.
4. Use paper plates and plastic utensils.
5. Buy a dishwasher.
6. Increase pest control measures.
7. Get a big plastic container with a tight lid that the dishes can go in overnight.
8. Make a new agreement that he will do all the dishes and cooking on her work days and she will do all the dishes and cooking on her off days.
9. Do the evening dishes together.

After the brainstorming, they can discuss and eliminate the solutions that would not work for them. Samantha wanted to eliminate #9 because it would still require her to do a chore on a work night, even though the chore is shared. They both eliminated options 1, 2, 3, and 5 because these are outside their budget. They also eliminated #4 as not being consistent with their values to reduce waste and care for the environment.

In the end, they decided to do a combination of options 6, 7 and 8. They decided to increase their efforts regarding pest control, and to institute a split-shift agreement regarding meal prep and dishes where Brian does all the cooking and dishes on Samantha's work days and Samantha does all the cooking and dishes on her non-work days, and they got a large plastic tub with a tight-fitting lid for the times when they are both exhausted and they want the luxury of letting the dishes wait until the next day.

> **Action item:** After you've used the Imago exercise successfully a few times on easier topics, then try using it with a more difficult topic. Remember to call for and allow timeouts as needed. If you take a timeout, remember to start where you left off when you return to the exercise.

Suggesting someone change

It's clear in this example that certain contributing factors are setting the stage for the dishes conflict. Each person has individual issues they could address that might remove the entire basis of the argument. Brian has a bug phobia and panic attacks. Samantha has a painfully structured job and burnout. The couple has financial issues that add pressure to the situation.

Asking someone to do the individual work to change something can be delicate, especially if they have a reason for not wanting to change it, or a reason for not doing the work involved to change it. Chapters 5 through 9 cover individual change as it relates to relationships. For now, I will say that Brian has a right to choose to not address his bug phobia and Samantha has a right to not change her job, so any suggestion from the other person should be presented as a completely optional request. (I cover individual rights and boundaries in chapter 5.)

Some of the suggestions that could help Brian and Samantha but would require individual work and change are:

- Brian could get therapy for his bug phobia.
- Brian could explore anti-anxiety medication with a psychiatrist.
- Samantha could change jobs.
- Samantha could explore a career change.
- Samantha could increase her self-care on non-work days to combat burnout.

There are still other suggestions that would require the two to negotiate new relationship agreements that go well beyond who will wash the dishes and when. (Relationship agreements are covered in detail in chapter 8.) Some of those suggestions could be:

- The two could look at their spending habits and see if they can free up some funds for Samantha to work eight-hour shifts and take a reduction in pay.
- They could adjust their spending habits to enable them to save for a dishwasher.
- They could change spending habits to pay for education for either person to make a career change that would bring in more money.
- If therapy or a psychiatrist for Brian to address his bug phobia would require funds, they could change their spending habits to fund one or both of these.

At this time, I recommend reading through chapter 9 before attempting to negotiate individual change or more extensive relationship agreements.

Avoiding arguments before they begin

The principles and steps of the Imago exercise can be used to avoid arguments before they start. Here are three ways to do that.

1. Lead with feelings.

Let's go back to the beginning of the dishes example and look at what was happening inside the thoughts and feelings of each person.

What was Brian's moment-to-moment experience? First, he saw Samantha begin heading off to bed. Then he looked at the sink and saw the dishes still there. He felt irritated. Then he thought, "I did the cooking and cleaning earlier, she should do these dishes." He decided that if she goes to bed, this would be unfair. He thought Samantha wasn't appreciating his efforts in cooking and cleaning that day. His irritation grew to anger. Then he said to Samantha, "You didn't do the dishes!"

Samantha's experience was different. She began heading to bed. Then she heard, "You didn't do the dishes." She felt surprised. She thought Brian understood how tired she was. She interpreted his demand that she do the dishes as a sign that her sacrifices were not appreciated by him. She felt hurt and angry. She retorted, "Why can't they wait until morning?"

It may not be obvious, so I will point out that both of them began speaking *after* they created interpretations of what the other person was thinking and feeling, and assumed what it meant for the relationship.

To reduce or avoid arguments, it's helpful to begin speaking *before* each person's unique (and biased) interpretations take hold. Begin speaking by naming the emotion. This is a great opportunity to use the observation-emotion format.

At the moment Brian saw Samantha heading for bed and he felt irritation, he could have said, "I'm feeling upset because I see the dishes in the sink."

If Brian begins with NVC and the observation-emotion format, Samantha is less likely to respond defensively. She is more likely to be able to stay in safe and social mode and respond with curiosity regarding Brian's feelings.

Another example would be if Brian still responded as he did in the original story and said, "You didn't do the dishes." Samantha felt surprised. Before her interpretation of Brian took hold, she could have said, "I'm feeling surprised. I didn't think I was expected to do the dishes after a long work day."

Let's look at another example of how NVC and Imago can be used to stop an argument before it starts. Adam and Bob are a couple who live together and they are arguing about whether Adam will go out on a date with Charlie. First, we will look at how the argument might play out without the NVC and Imago principles.

Adam: I'm planning to go out with Charlie again this weekend.

Bob: Again?! I don't want that.

Adam: But this is only my second date with Charlie in the last month. I hardly see Charlie at all.

Bob: You and I don't spend enough time together.

Adam: You and I live together. I spend every day with you.

Bob: But most of our time is not spent really connecting. It's spent at work, or doing chores, or sitting in front of the TV for an hour before sleep. I feel like I get all the work stuff and Charlie gets all the fun stuff.

Adam: That's what living together is. I'm sorry you don't find living with me to be fun anymore. If you think living with me is so boring, how is one more "boring" evening at home going to help?

Bob: You don't care how I feel! It's like you don't even love me anymore!

Adam: Ugh! Why do you have to be so dramatic?

Let's again go back to the beginning and see what each person in the couple was thinking and feeling during this exchange.

From Adam's perspective, he's feeling good. He's planning a date with Charlie and he feels happy about it. He goes to inform Bob out of courtesy (and based on their relationship agreement regarding communication about dates) and he's not thinking there is going to be an issue. When Bob says "Again?! I don't want that," Adam sees his happy plans threatened. He thinks, "Surely my partner wants me to have this happy experience," and he attempts to explain that he hardly ever gets to see Charlie. But Bob doesn't back off. In fact, he presses on. Adam thinks, "Maybe he doesn't want me to have this happy thing." This thought hurts. Now he's beginning to feel truly upset. As he goes into the fight-flight-freeze response and his executive functions begin shutting down, empathy also shuts down, and he becomes sarcastic, mocking, even a bit contemptuous.

From Bob's perspective, Adam announced that he is planning another date with Charlie. Bob felt a pang of unpleasant emotion: hurt, sadness, jealousy, even a bit of panic. He'd been wanting a special date with Adam and hadn't consciously realized it yet. His next thought was an image of Charlie on the date with Adam that Bob wanted to have with Adam. Bob then said, "Again?! I don't want that."

And that is where they got stuck. They got stuck on whether Adam was going to have another date with Charlie: yes or no. They took up opposing sides of the argument around this and they each dug in and fought for their own side.

This pattern is so common! Something happened that triggered hurt or upset feelings in Bob (Adam announced a date with Charlie). Bob didn't want the unpleasant feelings. A solution flashed through Bob's brain (the opposite of the triggering event—no date with Charlie). Bob grabbed onto it as the solution to his upset feelings, and he fought for it.

But if Adam and Bob had started with the feelings rather than what they each *think* is the solution, they might avoid an argument altogether. In other words, they would start with the underlying emotional discussion before getting sidetracked into the surface-level argument.

They need to start at the beginning! Bob's problem began with the pang of unpleasant emotion. *That* is where the conversation needs to begin.

If Bob had begun by naming what he felt, the beginning of the conversation might have looked like this.

Adam: I'm planning a date with Charlie.

Bob: Hmm. I just felt something. Maybe a pang of jealousy or disappointment?

Adam: Really? What's going on?

Here, they begin with a shared problem. Because they bypass Adam's defensive response, or Adam getting activated into the 3F response, Bob invites Adam's curiosity and empathy about his hurt feelings. Curiosity and empathy are possible because Adam is still in safe and social mode. Adam expresses concern for Bob's feelings and they begin exploring them together. This way, they are not limited to one possible solution (the one that Bob invented all on his own). There are many possible solutions to a painful emotion.

2. State what you *do* want rather than what you *don't* want.

This may seem like a repeat of the brainstorming suggestion earlier in the chapter. But it's different because this is outside of the Imago exercise. Here, we are using some of the NVC and Imago principles to defuse an argument before it begins. And we are applying the questions for a single person to use introspectively.

Bob got stuck on what he thought he didn't want. When he heard Adam say he was planning another date with Charlie, Bob felt pain. He didn't want that pain, so he thought, "The date is causing the pain, so to not feel the pain, I need the date to not happen." He got stuck there and it created a conflict with Adam.

But what happens if Bob asks himself, "What do I want? How do I want to feel? What experiences do I want to have?"

If he asks himself these questions, Bob will probably find that he wants dates with Adam. And he wants to feel connected. He wants to feel his relationship with Adam is still special and meaningful.

Bob noticed his distress when Adam told him he is planning a second date with Charlie in a month. But demanding Adam *not* go on a date with Charlie will not make Bob feel loved and connected.

When having a disagreement with someone, go deeper. Ask yourself, what do you want to feel when the negotiation or conversation is over? What experiences do you want to have?

Bob wants to feel loved and connected. He wants to spend time with his partner doing fun things. He wants the two of them to make happy memories. He wants a date night (or two! or three!).

Typically, when a person feels their needs are being met in their relationship, they can more easily give an enthusiastic yes to something their partner wants. In this case, if Bob felt the connection he wanted to feel, and he had the positive, romantic dates he wanted to experience with Adam, he would be more likely to feel happy that Adam was going out with Charlie again.

I'll discuss the use of these questions for introspection in much more detail in chapters 6 and 7.

> **Action item:** Review past disagreements. Ask yourself, "What did I want to feel? What experiences did I want to have? Did I know this at the time? Did I communicate what I actually wanted?" In new discussions and disagreements, try to incorporate these questions in the dialogue. Ask yourself or the other person, "What do you or I want to feel? What do we want to experience?" If one person is asking the other for an accommodation ask, "What do I need (or what do you need) to get to an authentic, enthusiastic yes?"

3. Create a second chance to avoid an argument.

But what if Bob misses the opportunity to avoid the argument and instead reacts to his painful emotions? Can Adam still help them avoid an argument before it begins? Yes, possibly!

Remember the analogy from chapter 3, where I said that communication is like tennis? I said that if I hit the ball to the back of the court, you have to run over there *if you are going to engage that ball.* This next suggestion involves choosing to let that ball pass by. Don't engage a ball that invites you to engage in an argument.

Let's imagine Adam has announced that he is planning a date with Charlie. Bob reacts to his hurt feelings and says "Again? I don't want that!"

If Adam can resist responding defensively, he can sidestep the surface-level issue (will he have another date with Charlie, yes or no) and go right to the emotion-level issue. He could say, "You sound upset. Let's talk about how you feel. I want to hear it."

They can also use the entire Imago exercise. Once Adam has asked Bob what he's feeling, this can lead into step 1 of the Imago exercise, with Bob speaking first and Adam listening. In the end, they can brainstorm solutions that work for both of them.

It's very important for all the people involved in the conflict to remember that each individual person is responsible for regulating their emotions and responding to those emotions with ethical behaviors, regardless of whether their feelings are justified by the facts of the situation or not. Therefore, Adam taking steps to calm Bob's emotions is a beautiful gift, not a responsibility.

The example with Adam and Bob is fairly mild. If we alter this story to include Bob becoming very dysregulated and lashing out at Adam in a harsh or even abusive manner, Adam can still choose to help soothe Bob's distress, but it's very important that at some point (preferably in the same discussion) Bob acknowledge his harmful behavior and his responsibility to learn to regulate his emotions and behaviors, express that he knows he is not entitled to Adam's help in that moment, and express gratitude for the gift of Adam's help with emotional soothing.

It's also important to remember that the greater the harmfulness of Bob's response, the more likely it is that when Adam helps to soothe Bob it will cause harm to Adam's mental health. I will discuss the role of power imbalances and their potentially damaging impact on a person's mental health in the next chapter.

Using Imago with more than two people

The mechanics of using Imago with more than two people are almost the same. Each person takes a turn at being the speaker. When any one person is the speaker, everyone else is the listener.

Each listener repeats back what they heard and asks if they got it right. If the speaker needs to clarify something with any individual listener, the speaker initiates Loop 1 with each individual listener. Before going on to the next step, it's important that each listener repeat back all Loop 1 clarifications, even if they took place with a different listener.

If a listener needs to ask follow-up questions, each listener will have a chance to initiate going into Loop 2. When the speaker clarifies something based on a Loop 2 question, each listener needs to repeat back what they heard and ask if they got it right, just as they did in Loop 1.

It's very important to avoid triangulation, or any appearance of coalition-building. It may be helpful to remind everyone present that any solution the group comes to must take everyone's feelings and needs into account, and any agreement, decision or course of action the group takes must be based on a unanimous vote. The group will not be taking a majority vote to resolve the issue. (See chapter 1 regarding unanimous votes rather than majority votes.)

It also helps to avoid using language (whether as speaker or listener) that implies or states agreement with another person in the group. It's common to try to strengthen the influence or acceptance of our ideas or experiences by attaching them to another person with the same idea or experience. Let your statements stand independently rather than linking them to someone else's statements.

For example, if I were a person in a triad relationship with Brian and Samantha, and it was my turn to speak, if I said, "I also don't like bugs," the word "also" suggests I share that experience with Brian. It seems to bring some of the intensity of Brian's phobia to my experience, which might be inaccurate. If instead I say, "I don't like bugs," it feels independent and unique.

When all the listeners feel they understand and are able to validate the speaker's feelings, and the speaker feels heard and believes all the listeners understand, the group moves on to the validation step. Each listener individually expresses validation for the speaker's feelings and experience, and expresses that they care about the speaker's feelings and that they want to work together as a team to find a solution that takes everyone's feelings and needs into account.

Then they move on to the next round, in which the next person becomes the speaker. It's important that every person involved get to be speaker and get to be understood and validated. It's also important to remember that the solutions offered during the brainstorming step must take everyone's feelings and needs into account.

Though this process certainly becomes more cumbersome and time-consuming with each additional person added to it, it also becomes quicker and easier with practice—more conversational and less rigid. Also, some parts may drop off if they feel unnecessary, especially when everyone involved stays curious and open because they are able to stay in safe and social mode.

If the group you're working with is large enough that the Imago exercise feels too difficult, there is a version called Communologue, designed for larger groups.[40] I haven't studied it, but you may wish to give it a try!

Including relationships of different levels of commitment

Hierarchy can be a touchy subject among non-monogamous communities and individuals. Some people prefer to reject hierarchy all together, and others feel it is just natural to prioritize relationships involving greater commitments such as relationships where children are being raised, where people live together or own property together, or where the partners are planning a long-term future together.

When considering using Imago to resolve an issue, when should a third or fourth person be included? The focus of this book is skills and tools for sexual, romantic, and committed relationships in ethical non-monogamy, but I'd like to remind readers that the principles and techniques in this book can be applied to all kinds of relationships between adults. (I'm excluding relationships between adults and children because adults have responsibilities to children and children have needs from adults that make these relationships very different from the relationships between adults.) Imago and NVC can benefit relationships between co-workers, parents and their adult children, friends, and relationship partners of any level of commitment.

Let's imagine that Bob and Adam have gone through the Imago exercise. They discover through the process that Bob wants more dates with Adam. As they brainstorm solutions, they realize that their conflicting schedules is a reason they have not spent much special time together. They realize they could resolve this by reworking their schedules and they could make Sunday their special day together.

But Bob has been spending some Sundays with his adult daughter Stephanie for the last few years. If Bob and Adam make a new agreement without consulting Stephanie, it could leave her feeling unimportant to Bob

40 The Imago Center of Washington, DC, n.d. Communologue: dialogue used in community groups. https://imagocenterdc.com/communologue-dialogue-used-in-community-groups/

and damage their relationship. Before Bob and Adam can make a new agreement about how they spend their Sundays, it's best to include Stephanie in some way.

I like a slogan used by disability rights advocates to help me determine when a person should be included in a discussion: "Nothing about us without us." That's from South African disability activists Michael Masutha and William Rowland.

If the new agreement or the solution to a problem would impact another person, or would require their cooperation or consent, then they should be included. How to include the other person and how much input they get will vary a great deal based on the nature and depth of involvement of each relationship.

Much of the time, we keep a protective boundary around our partner relationships where we don't expose arguments, hurt feelings, and strife to friends, relatives, our adult children, or our parents. Stephanie, in the example, would probably prefer to not be included in the entire Imago exchange between Adam and Bob regarding date nights. But she might deeply appreciate Bob coming to her and saying, "Stephanie, the time we spend together is very important to me. At the same time, Adam and I are looking at our schedules to try and create more time for us to spend together as a couple. Can you and I look at our schedules and see if there is some flexibility and maybe you and I could identify other days of the week we could spend together? Or maybe spend part of a Sunday, then Adam and I could have the other part of that Sunday?"

But what about Charlie in the original example? As Bob and Adam are brainstorming ideas that will help Bob with his painful emotions, if they settle on ideas that will impact Charlie, then it's very likely that it would be ethical to offer to include Charlie in some way before they commit to that solution.

Charlie, of course, is free to choose to not engage in processing that is primarily between Adam and Bob. The more casual the relationship between Adam and Charlie, the less likely she will want to be included. The deeper and more involved the relationship, the more likely she will want to be involved and have input into solutions that impact her.

If the impact on Charlie is minor, such as simply changing the date of the next meeting, and the relationship with Adam is fairly new or superficial, then Adam could possibly make that change without including Charlie in any in-depth discussion. "Hey Charlie, something has come up and I'm no longer available on that date. Can we schedule a new date?"

If Charlie's relationship with Adam is more serious or more committed, and if a greater accommodation is needed from Charlie, such as less frequent dates overall, or refraining from texting or calling when Adam and Bob are having a date, then Charlie should be included and will most likely want to be included. This doesn't necessarily mean the three of them need to have a sit-down. Before Adam and Bob commit to a solution that would require consent or cooperation from Charlie, Adam can probably just have a separate conversation with Charlie.

It's important that Adam approach this conversation collaboratively and seek input from Charlie, not simply tell her of a change and pressure her to accept it. He can tell her the situation and some of the ideas he and Bob are floating, point out how they might impact her (unless that is obvious) and ask her how she feels about these ideas. From there, they can easily go into the Imago exercise, with Charlie taking the first pass at being the speaker. Brainstorming in the end will involve Adam and Charlie brainstorming ideas that will meet the needs of all three people.

Before Adam and Charlie commit to a solution, Adam must bring these ideas back to Bob. If Bob agrees to one of the ideas Charlie and Adam came up with, then they all communicate their agreement, and they are done.

If there are hard feelings between Bob and Charlie, if either of them feels the other is trying to hurt them, or they are misunderstanding the other's motives, it might be beneficial for Charlie and Bob to communicate directly about their feelings toward each other (with or without Adam present) and avoid the tendency to put Adam in the middle.

Additionally, if Adam isn't good at relaying information accurately, or the relay communication method isn't working for any number of reasons, then the three of them could consider getting together for a three-person Imago exercise.

Keep in mind that each person has the right to consent or not consent to any conversation or interaction. If Charlie doesn't want contact with Bob, that's okay. If Bob doesn't want contact with Charlie, that's also okay. Polyamory doesn't have to be done in "kitchen table" style to be healthy.[41]

---

41 Kitchen table polyamory (KTP) is where all the people in a polycule have a baseline of friendship and mutual respect where they could all sit down (presumably at a kitchen table) and share a meal together. KTP implies that all the people involved are comfortable enough with each other to interact amicably and communicate cooperatively. https://feeld.co/blog/feeld-guides/what-is-kitchen-table-polyamory

Learn to bring up topics before they become arguments

It's great to avoid arguments before they start in the moment by naming your emotions instead of simply reacting. And if one person starts a conversation that could turn into an argument, it's handy when the other person can deflect it by letting the ball pass by and addressing emotions instead. But it's even better to see problems coming from far away and manage them before they bring up tough emotions in the first place.

This is where being attuned to our partners and aware of our own emotions is very helpful. As I said before, our emotions serve a positive purpose, even unpleasant emotions. They give us information. If I'm sitting at home watching TV and my partner is out doing something, and I feel irritated (or anxious, or any other unpleasant emotion), I might be tempted to quash the emotion. I might think, "This is an unpleasant emotion. I don't want to feel this. I shouldn't feel this. I'm being too needy." And then I set about suppressing the emotion and trying to drive it away or put it in a box and ignore it.

This is the first place many people get stuck, and it can lead to relationship arguments later. The problem with this approach is that suppressed emotions don't go away. They just go underground. They stay there, hidden from our awareness and they grow, like mycelium.

Mycelium is the underground part of mushrooms. It spreads in the soil, unseen, sometimes over long distances, then pops up unpredictably as a mushroom, when conditions encourage it to become visible.

Suppressed emotions are like that. In the example where my partner is out of the house, if I suppress my irritation, the emotion and beliefs it's based on remain. They just go below the surface of my conscious awareness, and they grow.

My irritation is based on thoughts and beliefs, such as, "I would sure like to know where she is, what she's doing, and when she'll be home, so I can plan my evening." If I suppress the emotion and the thoughts and push them out of my awareness, they aren't resolved. They don't go away. They just go below my conscious awareness. The suppressed emotion and the belief that she is inconsiderate in her lack of communication is spreading, finding and creating other things to attach to.

Next, I may feel irritated when she doesn't do the dishes and I expect her to. Or, I feel irritated when she doesn't communicate about a purchase from our shared account. They all become examples of her lack of consideration instead of individual small incidents. And like a mushroom cap, one day, unexpectedly, my emotions will rise up over some small thing that seems inconsiderate to me, and we'll have a big, complex web of resentment to untangle.

Instead, I can treat my unpleasant emotions as needed messengers. They are bringing me useful information. As I sit there in front of the TV feeling irritated, I can recognize and name what I'm feeling, and why I'm feeling it. "I'm feeling irritated because I don't know when to expect my partner home, and I would like to plan my evening." Then I can ask myself, "Based on this, what do I need or want?"

Chances are, I want something from my partner. This is the second place people tend to get stuck. It's important to remember to use this question only to help you clarify what you're feeling and why, and be sure to avoid getting too attached to any solutions you come up with on your own. Remember that solutions need to be negotiated by all the people involved and take everyone's feelings and needs into account.

Going back to my example of being irritated, when I ask myself what I want from my partner, I might identify that I want more information or better communication. I want her to think of me and of how her actions may impact me. Then I ask myself, "What do I want to feel?" I might find that I want to feel considered and I want to feel free to plan my time.

But since she's not a mind reader and she's not going to automatically give me what I want, I'm going to have to ask for it if I'm to have any hope of getting it.

For many people, the thought of bringing up something or asking for something is hard. Our history with this partner, with other partners, and with our family of origin can all play a role in making it difficult to ask for what we want or need.

Maybe our partner tends to respond defensively or tends to become painfully emotional. When we think of the resistance this partner tends to give us, or the cost of bringing up an issue, it just doesn't feel worth it.

We may be under the mistaken belief that if there are no obvious arguments or fights happening, then we have peace in the relationship and to bring something up is to start a fight. It just feels wrong to rock the boat and disrupt the current peace.

Sometimes a history with other partners or our family of origin can make us reticent to start a discussion even though this partner tends to respond well. And sometimes, our relationship or family history can leave us feeling unworthy of asking for anything.

Learning to overcome our own fears of starting these conversations is a very important element of growth for our relationship skills. And learning techniques that increase the likelihood of a peaceful and cooperative outcome will make starting these conversations feel more rewarding and less costly, especially as we get better at doing this.

First, it's important to pick a favorable time and place. Pick a time when you and your partner are most likely to be in safe and social mode, have low stress, are not pressed for time, can give adequate focus, have adequate privacy, and it's not a special time meant for something else. In other words, if you're sharing a date night, or some other time set aside to truly enjoy each other, that's not a good time to bring up something about them that's annoying you.

Likewise, it's unwise to start a potentially charged conversation during the car ride to spend time with friends or family, or when your partner is exhausted, sleepy, hungry, on a deadline with a work project, or during the big game showing on TV. These are not good times to broach the topic.

If you have trouble identifying a good time to start the conversation, ask your partner to schedule a time with you. Avoid the temptation to say, "We need to talk." I think that sentence sends everyone's blood pressure through the roof. Try, "I want to talk about something that's been bothering me. I'm hoping it will be relatively minor and a quick thing we can fix. But I also want us to give it adequate time and attention. When is a good time we can both sit down and talk?"

Once you've got your partner in front of you, a good way to start these conversations is with a variation of the compliment sandwich. The compliment sandwich is a business management technique for giving a subordinate constructive criticism without leaving them feeling broken and disheartened. You start with a compliment, follow with constructive criticism, and then close with another compliment.

In business, it might sound like this: "Bill, I want you to know that I really appreciate your enthusiasm for this job. You're here every day and you're often early. I'd like to see you apply some of that wonderful enthusiasm to the research aspect of your reports. The research was thin on your last report and I need you to go into more depth. I know you can do it. I was very impressed by the thoroughness of the summary you wrote last month."

There are two variations of the compliment sandwich that can be useful for initiating relationship conversations. The first one is to start by saying what you fear, then what you hope for, then expressing the issue.

It might sound like this: "I have something I want to talk with you about. I'm really nervous because in my last relationship, anytime I asked for something, my partner would get upset and berate me and tell me I was being needy. I don't think you'll do that, but I have the fear anyway. My hope is that you'll be willing to give me a small accommodation and I'll feel loved and cared for. So, here's the thing. I noticed when you were out the other day, I felt irritable...."

Remember to use the principles of NVC and the observation-emotion format, and you may need to go into the Imago exercise if it's not an easily solved issue.

The second variation is good when the thing you fear is your partner's response pattern. If your partner has a tendency to respond defensively, or jump in and cut you off before you finish speaking, or get upset when you try to talk about things, you can attempt to interrupt that pattern by saying something in the beginning about how you would like your partner to respond, not respond, or listen.

An example of this would be: "I have something I want to bring up. I'd like you to listen all the way through before responding and in fact, I'd like you to consider not responding right away. Just listen all the way through and then take a few minutes to think about it before you respond. And if you start to feel upset, let me know and we'll take a 20-minute break."

Action item: If you are a person who tends to avoid confrontation, this could be challenging for you. Talk about this with your partner or other significant people in your life. Agree to create opportunities for you to practice bringing things up. Consider establishing regular relationship check-ins where you are expected to bring things up. You might also negotiate the use of text or email to bring things up. Practice bringing up neutral topics and then expand that to potentially difficult topics.

What if it doesn't work?

What happens if you use all of these tools and you still find yourself at an impasse in a disagreement? Your partner wants something and you are upset about it. Your feelings matter. Your partner's feelings matter just as much, and they are upset if they don't get the thing they want. How do you resolve a situation like this?

This is where the difference between our feelings being valid versus justified becomes an important distinction. Sometimes we're justified in feeling upset with someone, and sometimes we're not. When we are not, we need to look at ourselves and resolve whatever inner issue is causing us to feel upset. The next chapters address this process.

Part 2

Fostering Autonomy

CHAPTER 5

Rights and Boundaries

Sometimes even after doing the Imago exercise and the brainstorming, the people involved are unable to agree on a solution that meets everyone's needs and is compassionate to their feelings. Sometimes we're trying to resolve disagreements with people who are unwilling to engage in the Imago exercise with us. And sometimes people get stuck on having the solution they want (or think they want) even if it doesn't work for the other people involved.

Imagine if Bob from the last chapter was so attached to believing that the one thing that would make him feel better was for Adam to cancel his date with Charlie. If Adam refused, they would have continuous, unrelenting conflict in their relationship. Bob would feel hurt and believe his feelings and needs were disregarded. If Adam gave in, he would feel resentful, his relationship with Bob would be damaged, and his relationship with Charlie might also be damaged.

In addition to a collaborative process for resolving conflicts, we also need a set of ethical guidelines for relationships, based in human psychology and healthy relationship practices, that help us to identify when we're successfully taking responsibility for ourselves and when we're stepping into areas that are not ours to dictate or control.

If we voluntarily seek to be responsible for ourselves and respect our partners' rights and autonomy, we increase the safety, affection, and bonding in the relationship and also support the growth and development of healthy, happy individuals within those relationships.

The individual vs. the relationship?

When I look at popular literature on the elements that promote healthy self-esteem and self-respect for an individual, I immediately find discussions of individual boundaries. However, the literature often presents this as though the individual must have boundaries to protect themselves against the demands of their relationships. In other words, a person's personal boundaries protect them from the demands of their partner, their employer, their parents, their adult children, or any other adult person with whom they may have a relationship.

And yet, if healthy, happy relationships are an important and vital aspect of an individual having a happy, healthy life experience (and they are!), then these two things—the individual and the relationship—should work together, in concert, *symbiotically*, not in opposition or in conflict.

I believe the literature reflects on individual boundaries as though they are in opposition to the demands of relationships because this is where the pain is. If two people are at an impasse in a disagreement, this is where they feel trapped between choosing to protect themselves and damage the relationship, or protect the relationship and damage themselves.

The solution, I believe, is to manage *how* we negotiate through these painful disagreements, not to choose one over the other. If we're in a relationship with someone who is unable or unwilling to adopt cooperative communication methods such as the ones outlined in this book, then we find ourselves forced to choose to either maintain our self-respect and self-esteem or protect the stability of the relationship.

The final step in learning how to resolve conflict cooperatively is knowing when to take a hard look at ourselves and to take responsibility for ourselves and our behaviors. We need to know when to back off of the demands we make of our partners and others, and when to push forward; when to hold people accountable and when to require changes in their behaviors.

A boundary is a limit

Much like a fence or a wall is a limit on a person's ability to move forward physically, a personal boundary is a limit on a person's behavior. There are two types of boundaries:

- boundaries on your own behavior
- boundaries or limits you put on other people's behavior toward you.

Boundaries on your own behavior

A boundary on my own behavior is a limit *based on my values* that helps determine both my behavior in the face of pressure from other people, and the behaviors I will allow myself when struggling alone with a difficult situation.

It's important to know what you want, and to decide what you value and what you don't. Creating boundaries on our own behaviors helps us act more consistently with our values.

For example, if I'm a person who loves pets and thinks of them as members of the family, it would be damaging to my self-respect and self-esteem if I let a difficult financial or housing situation pressure me into dumping a pet at a shelter or at the side of the road. Likewise, it would also be damaging to my self-esteem and self-respect if I allowed another person to pressure me into dumping a pet because they didn't like animals.

The more thought put into difficult decisions such as these, and the more you have identified your values and the limits that are important to you, the stronger and clearer your personal identity will be. A great exercise for identifying your personal values can be found in chapter 2 of the book *Ecstasy is Necessary* by Barbara Carrellas.[42]

Keep in mind that what's healthy for a person is found in an appropriate balance. In this case, that means the balance between limits on our own behavior and self-compassion.

If we erect harsh, strict boundaries on what behavior we allow ourselves, then we are refusing to recognize that, as humans, we have limited power and influence. Sometimes the world, circumstances, other people, or our own human nature and physical, material, or mental health limitations will make acting in accordance with our values nearly impossible. When this happens, we need to temper those expectations of our own behavior with self-compassion, understanding, and when needed, self-forgiveness.

On the other hand, too much self-compassion leads to not holding ourselves to standards we could achieve. Knowing we have not lived up to our values when we could have leads to shame, guilt, and regret. Ultimately, this damages our self-esteem and self-respect.

---

42 Barbara Carrellas, 2012. *Ecstasy is Necessary: A Practical Guide to Sex, Relationships, and Oh So Much More.* Hay House, Inc.

Finding that ideal balance between living up to our values and self-compassion is important to feeling at peace with ourselves and feeling that we are content with how well we live up to our values.

Action item: Reflect on what is important to you. What are some of your values in life? What are some behaviors that you would regret or feel ashamed if you did them? What are some responsibilities for which you would feel regretful or ashamed if you didn't fulfill? Clarify whether you want to set these as personal boundaries on your own behavior. Also, consider the need for self-compassion. What are circumstances in which it would be unreasonable or harmful to require yourself to live up to each expectation?

Ethical boundaries on other people's behavior

A boundary is also a limit we enforce on the behavior we will allow other people to direct toward us or inflict upon us.

In the example we just saw, I stated it would be damaging to my self-esteem and self-respect if I allowed someone else to pressure me to violate my own values and relinquish a pet. In that moment, the other person is likely accessing a source of power they have over me and using it to pressure me to do something I normally wouldn't choose to do. Their power over me could be based on financial, emotional, social, or physical resources. They might be inducing fear in me of financial or physical harm if I don't do what they want. They might be threatening to socially shame or embarrass me. Or they might be threatening to emotionally harm or abandon me. Using power to coerce someone into violating their own values is an abuse of power.[43]

Not many people put active thought into what their limits are and how they'll respond if someone oversteps those limits, but we're responsible for doing that thinking and deciding how we will and will not allow other people to treat us.

Keep in mind that none of this absolves the person who may be engaging in insulting, derogatory, controlling, or manipulative behavior from blame or responsibility for their abusive or damaging actions. Interpersonal power

---

43 I plan to address power and manipulation in greater depth in my next book.

is a real thing. When someone uses their title, position, influence, or physical advantage to violate our limits, and when we lack the personal power to enforce the limits we need to maintain our self-esteem and self-respect, this damages our sense of safety and self-efficacy in the world, and can result in debilitating internalized shame, humiliation, and even trauma.

Action item: Reflect on memories of when you have been harmed by someone else's behavior. If you could say anything you wanted to that person, without any negative consequences, what would you say? Can you use this as a template for a rule or boundary you'd like to have that limits how other people can treat you? Some examples are:

- "No one can touch me without my permission."
- "It's not okay to laugh at me."
- "I won't tolerate a person who lies to me about something important."

Think about what actions you can ethically take to enforce these boundaries. Some examples are:

- I will respond to uninvited touch by saying loud and clear that it's not okay and they must stop.
- If someone laughs at me, I will hold my head up, verbally protest, and walk away.
- If a person lies to me about something important, I will confront that person with the truth and strongly consider ending whatever involvement I have with that person.

If you feel embarrassment or shame when reviewing memories where you were hurt by someone else, practice engaging self-compassion. Interpersonal power is real, and if awareness of the other person's power influenced your decision to not defend yourself (or not defend yourself as strongly as you would have liked), work to embrace self-compassion for the past you who did the best they could in a very difficult moment. If the fight, flight, or freeze response happened to you in this memory, remember it's an involuntary response. It happened *to* you. You didn't choose it and you likely had no ability to change that response in the moment.

How to enforce boundaries

There is more detailed discussion on how to enforce boundaries in my next book. For now, what I mean by enforcing boundaries begins by telling the other person to stop.

If I have a boundary that it's not okay to speak to me disrespectfully, and another person calls me stupid, I need to respond in order to preserve my self-esteem and self-respect. I need to tell that person that it's not okay to call me stupid.

Clearly, I can't force my will on this person. I lack the magical powers to force them to only use respectful words when addressing me. So, what I am seeking is their agreement to change their behavior back to respectful words.

Typically, my feelings on the matter should be enough of a motivator. "I feel offended and disrespected when you call me stupid. It's not okay to use that language toward me."

If my feelings matter to this person, they will most likely apologize and correct themselves. "I'm sorry. I didn't mean to offend you. I just felt frustrated in the moment. I won't do it again."

But sometimes people don't respond this way. Sometimes they try to defend their disrespectful behavior. It's now up to me whether I let them get away with not apologizing and correcting their behavior, or if I allow them to justify their disrespectful behavior. If they succeed at getting me to back down, they have set a precedent for future interactions where they now believe they can get away with disrespectful behavior.

Here's an example of someone justifying their disrespectful name-calling toward me. "Well, you just stepped in wet cement! I don't know what else to call that. If it's not stupid, then what is it?"

What happens next has a lot to do with interpersonal power. If I'm a friend helping a friend pour a cement walkway in their front yard, and I'm doing this free of charge, out of the goodness of my heart, I am in a much better position to defend my boundary than if I am an employee of the verbally abusive person and I desperately need this job and this paycheck.

If I'm helping a friend, I can take a gentle tone: "I know you may have been feeling frustrated, or maybe you're used to people talking to each other this way, but I need you to agree that I have a right to require that people speak to me respectfully. I need you to agree to only speak respectfully to me going forward." If the person either refuses or continues to defend their language, I can choose to leave and withdraw my help on their project. I can even distance myself from the friendship or end it.

Or, I can take a harder tone and say, "It's not about what I did. It's about what you said. You are welcome to judge my behavior in your mind all you want. But nothing makes it okay to speak those thoughts to me out loud. It's not okay to call me stupid. I need you to acknowledge that, or I will leave."

If I am the employee, the fact that I need the job and the paycheck puts me at a power disadvantage. If I say, "It's not okay to call me stupid," and my employer defends his actions, the situation forces me to choose between two things I value: my self-respect and my job. This can become damaging to my self-esteem and self-respect. I could quit and accept the loss of the job and income. I could threaten to quit if my boss doesn't apologize. Either way, I risk losing things I value.

I could continue to verbally defend my boundary. I could state my disapproval of the abusive language and stop there. "I don't think it's right for my employer to call me stupid, no matter what I've done." However, I still risk a reprisal from my boss.

Or, I could say nothing and swallow it, at the risk of damaging my self-esteem and self-respect. But I can take steps to repair my self-esteem and self-respect by deciding to leave that job at the first opportunity. I can begin job hunting, and once I've accepted another job I can go back to my employer and say that I left because of the day he called me stupid and then refused to acknowledge that his behavior was wrong.

To be a healthy individual

I've just thrown a bunch of new concepts at you, so let me summarize:

- To be a mentally and emotionally healthy individual, we need to reflect on and determine our **values**. This is a very important aspect of clarifying and strengthening our identities as individual people.
- Based on our values, we need to determine our **boundaries**. These are limits we place on ourselves and our behaviors that will keep our behaviors consistent with our values. Acting consistently with our values is important to maintaining positive self-esteem and self-respect while avoiding behaviors that induce regret and shame.

- There is another set of **boundaries** that are limits we place on other people's behavior toward us. These are limits by which we do not allow other people to treat us poorly. It's important to our self-esteem and self-respect to defend our boundaries when they are violated by other people. It is important that we know we have the courage to confront other people when they treat us poorly, and if possible, assert our interpersonal power and require that the other person correct their behavior.

- **Interpersonal power** is real, and when it's used to violate someone's rights, boundaries, or relationship agreements, it's an abuse of power that can cause debilitating psychological and emotional harm as well as damage the bonding and feelings of safety in the relationship.

The balance between interpersonal ethics and individual boundaries can be difficult to find. The use or abuse of interpersonal power and the harm that can result makes the stakes of getting this correct pretty high.

Treating someone unethically—violating their rights, boundaries, or the relationship agreements we have with them—damages our relationship with them. The anxiety we can experience as we worry and second-guess ourselves because we're unsure of whether we're defending a rightful boundary or treating someone else unethically can also be debilitating.

And finally, no one wants to be taken advantage of by unscrupulous and manipulative people who play on this anxiety with those of us who are simply trying hard to be ethical toward others while also protecting ourselves from harm.

Here is where it can get confusing

This is where the topic of personal boundaries starts to get sticky. Other people have personal boundaries too. Is it possible that I may have a boundary that's in direct conflict with someone else's personal boundary? What if my boundary of "people must speak to me respectfully" conflicts with my boss' boundary to never let anyone challenge his authority, or my friend's boundary to always speak the truth of what's on their mind?

This is why I think it's very important to be able to explain clearly why some boundaries are appropriate and some are not. Boundaries need to reflect our values, but they also need to be ethical toward other people.

I believe we have a right to make certain boundaries. Which by default means that we don't have a right to make certain other boundaries. Knowing which is which is key to ensuring that the boundaries we create are actually ethical.

Ethical boundaries are based on individual rights

Being in a relationship does not mean losing yourself or giving up your right to have individual boundaries in service to the "us" of the relationship. To be two healthy individuals, you need to maintain your individual identities along with fostering a healthy "us."

Part of how this is done is by knowing what's yours to control, what's yours to decide, and what's yours to make boundaries around. And part of this is knowing what your partner (or other person) has a right to control, decide, and make boundaries around, and respecting their right to do so. And finally, there are relationship agreements that belong to both of you, and you must agree to them freely and unanimously.

I believe healthy, ethical boundaries begin with the individual person's rights. The list that follows is based on what's important for navigating a healthy individual identity and negotiating healthy, ethical relationships.

I like this list because it is not based on what kind of relationship you are in. This is not a list of rights for a primary partner or a list of rights for a secondary partner. In fact, I believe this list works for *every* adult relationship: parents and adult children, employers and employees, friends, hook-ups, casual dating partners, long-term dating partners, and life partners.

Individual bill of rights

Each person has the right to:

1. Full bodily and sexual autonomy.
2. Be safe from physical, mental, and emotional violence or the threat of violence.
3. Have access to adequate food, water, medication, medical care, disability accommodations, and sleep.
4. The privacy of their thoughts and personal space.

5. Determine their own identity and values—including the right to explore who they are and to identify their natural orientations, and the freedom to build their public social identities around these things, or to keep these things private if they wish—and the right to determine limits on their own behavior based on their values.

6. Decide their own interests and how they want to spend their time and energy.

7. Decide with whom they wish to be friends and whom they love, and to invest time and energy into maintaining those relationships.

8. Be spoken to respectfully and treated with dignity.

9. Express themselves as long as, while doing so, they speak to others respectfully and treat others with dignity.

10. Control and protect their possessions, livelihood, money, and assets.

11. Consent (or not consent) to be in a physical space, to interact, to have sex, to engage in relationships, to determine the depth of a relationship, and to consent or not consent to relationship agreements.

12. Withdraw those consents at any time, as long as while doing so they consider the ethics around *how* they withdraw their consent.

13. Be given the information they need in order to engage in informed consent, provided in a timely, clear, and honest manner.

Action item: Reflect on these rights and whether your rights have been violated in current or previous relationships. Has this caused you pain or trauma? Reflect on whether you have violated the rights of others in current or previous relationships. Consider how you might mend any harm you have done. Can you apologize? Can you make amends? Do you need to do this in order to foster healthy self-esteem and self-respect? If that's not possible, can you embrace self-compassion?

Ethical boundaries and a generous attitude

These individual rights become guideposts for understanding what's yours and what you can ethically make boundaries around, decide on, or control in situations where another person is involved. I call these rightful boundaries because they are based on your rights. The list of rights is also helpful in recognizing what belongs to someone else and thus what they have a right to control, decide, and make boundaries around.

In other words, it's *not* ethical for me to make a boundary around something that's *not* mine. If I tell my partner she cannot take a job that requires her to travel, whether I try to claim it is a boundary for me or not, I'm being unethical. I do not have a right to make a boundary around her job, her travel, or her choice. I do not have a right to that boundary, and if I try to declare my control over that choice (which rightfully belongs to my partner) I am being unethical toward her.

If I work late on Thursday evenings and I would like my partner to prepare dinner for me before I get home, I can ask for it, but do I have a right to it? No. Does it matter if I do a lot of other things for her and I feel it's only fair? No. It's her time, her energy; she gets to decide what to do with it.

Treating my partner respectfully means that I don't demand something I have no right to. And I don't passive-aggressively suggest that she should want to do it because I've done other things for her. It means I voluntarily acknowledge I have no right to expect her to make dinner for me, and then I ask her if she would be willing to do it anyway.

The difference between a demand and a request is that when it's a request, we're willing to gracefully accept no for an answer. And if we have fostered a healthy relationship, we both *want* to do things for each other, but we know we're free to say no if we want to, guilt-free.

This is useful because it helps us approach conversations with a different attitude. If we believe we have the right to demand altered behavior from our partners anytime we feel upset by something, we run the risk of being controlling, demanding, or possibly manipulative. However, if we approach a conversation with a gentler, more generous, more respectful attitude, our partners are more likely to feel respected. We increase the feelings of safety, security, and affection in the relationship. And we are more likely to get compassion and possibly generosity from them as a result.

Can boundaries collide?

Not really. They can appear to collide, but in reality, one of those boundaries is probably an unethical boundary and should instead be presented as a request.

This example is based on a situation I have seen several times among a number of different people in my private practice. This story is an amalgamation of several stories, plus some fictional elements.

Jim sits on the edge of my office sofa with his head in his hands. He has recently separated from his wife. They opened their relationship three years earlier, but she eventually decided polyamory was not for her, and she also no longer wanted to be married to Jim. It was a fairly amicable split.

Jim has a serious relationship with Betty as well, and she was pushing hard for her and Jim to set up house together as soon as he moved out of the house he shared with his wife.

He says he tried to tell Betty that he wanted to live by himself for a while. When he was a young adult, he had moved directly from his parents' home to a college dorm, and then in with his wife when he graduated. He had never been an independent adult, on his own, with some freedom.

He says, "She said I could only want to live alone if I was going to pick up lots of people and start new relationships. She said I'm wrong for wanting to do that when she's waited for me for years and she's ready to move to the next level. I think she's afraid that if I have this freedom, I might meet someone I like better and eventually set up house with someone else. She accused me of using her all this time and that if I can't get serious about our relationship now, then she's done with me."

He continues, "I'm so confused. She sounds so calm and reasonable when we talk. Her reasons make sense. And she's right, I do want to pick up people and start new relationships, and I want to have the freedom to do that. But I love her. I love her so much! I don't want to lose her! I don't want to go through two serious breakups at once! I just also don't want to jump right back into a marriage-like relationship again. Maybe I am being selfish, but when I think about giving in, I feel so trapped and depressed."

Jim's relationship with Betty is very important to him and it's teetering on the edge of a cliff. Must he give up the freedom he wants in order to keep his relationship alive? How he handles this will shape his relationship with Betty by either setting precedents for future conflicts or possibly ending the relationship altogether. What's he going to do and how should he decide?

Examining this conflict using the list of individual rights, based on right #11, Jim has the right to determine what depth of relationship he wishes to engage in and when. He has the right to live alone if he wishes. Based on right #1, he has the right to engage in new sexual relationships.

You may be wondering, if Jim has the right to determine the depth of the relationship he wants to be in, why doesn't Betty? She does. But determining this is just deciding what they each want. What depth of relationship the two people actually engage in must be a relationship agreement to take action and move this from what they want to what they are doing.

In this example, Betty wants a deeper commitment than Jim wants or has agreed to. All relationship decisions need to be unanimous. If they both want to move in together, great! They can move in together. But (much like sex) they can only do together what they *both* want to do. If only one person wants something, that's not unanimous, and continuing to push for something the other person doesn't want, and to which they don't have a right, is unethical.

You can probably also see that based on right #12, Betty has the right to withdraw her consent to be in a relationship with Jim, if she chooses.

Most of the problem here is in *how* Betty is talking to Jim about this conflict. She's telling him he's wrong for wanting what he wants and that he deserves to be broken up with if he doesn't comply with what she wants.

Remember from the Imago exercise that people's feelings are always valid. Jim's desire to live alone is valid. Betty's desire to escalate the relationship is also valid. But pressuring him to comply with something he doesn't want is unethical. She has no right to demand that he move in with her and escalate their relationship to living-together partners. She can ethically request this. She can even ethically say that she is ready to withdraw from the relationship if he says no. But she can't ethically demand it or tell him he's wrong for wanting what he wants. Doing this is a way of weaponizing her boundaries.

Weaponizing boundaries is when we use a rightful boundary to pressure someone to submit to our will.

I first heard the term "weaponizing boundaries" on the Multiamory podcast.[44] To weaponize a boundary is to voice a boundary and then use it as a threat to coerce something from someone else.

Any boundary can be weaponized, but I have most often seen it in the form of threatening to end or downgrade a relationship. We all have the right to withdraw our consent from any relationship agreement at any time, including our consent to be in the relationship at all. So how can we tell if we are simply asserting our rights, or if we are weaponizing that right or boundary?

The key is in why we are using it. A clue is to ask ourselves what response we're expecting from the other person. If I were to say, "I can't be in a relationship with you if you are going to smoke," am I saying that to protect my boundary to not be in a relationship with a smoker? Or am I saying it to pressure someone I want to be involved with to quit smoking?

If they were to accept my boundary and say, "Okay, you have that right. I guess this is goodbye," how would I feel? If I would feel respected, but sad, then I voiced a boundary with no weaponizing motive. But if I would feel shocked, surprised, caught off guard, angry, insulted, devastated, or abandoned, then I was weaponizing that boundary.

Let me explain. If I actually have a boundary that I will not be in a relationship with a person who smokes, and I get involved with someone who either takes up smoking or returns to smoking after the relationship began, I have a dilemma. I would most likely sit down with this person and tell them about my boundary. I would also tell them how much I care for them and don't want to end the involvement. And then I would ask them if they were willing to consider quitting smoking.

If their answer is no, I can reflect on this boundary and ask myself if I can be flexible about it without doing damage to my self-esteem or self-respect (or maybe my agreements with someone else). But if I determine that I need to adhere to this boundary, I would express regret for the pain I'm about to cause. I would express the pain the decision causes me. And then I would express my need to end the relationship.

If the person accepts my decision and my boundary, then I feel respected, and also sad.

---

44 Multiamory podcast, 2018. Episode 178: The basics of boundaries. July 3. https://www.multiamory.com/podcast/178-basics-boundaries

On the other hand, if I express that I can't be in a relationship with someone who smokes, the other person accepts that, and then I feel angry, shocked, betrayed, or otherwise deeply hurt, it's clear that I wanted a different response. The only other response they can give is to offer to quit smoking. Therefore, my actual intent was to use the boundary to pressure them to quit smoking.

Basically, weaponizing a boundary is a bluff. If I'm weaponizing a boundary, I don't really want them to accept and respect my boundary. I want them to change their behavior so I don't have to enforce the boundary. I can tell I'm bluffing if I feel angry or upset when they call my bluff.

Returning to the story of Jim and Betty, does it seem like Betty would feel respected, but sad, if Jim said, "I understand. I guess this is goodbye"? Or does it seem like she would feel angry, shocked, or deeply hurt? My guess is the latter.

Rather than take the position of respecting his rights and acknowledge that he has every right to get his own place, pick up new people, and enjoy being a solo adult for the first time in his life, she took the position that if he didn't move in with her, then he had been using her all along. She tried to tell him he was wrong to want to be solo for a while. These are the clues that tell me that her intention was to use the ultimatum to pressure him into doing what she wanted. And that is weaponizing a boundary.

Warning! Don't stop reading here!

If you stop reading here, you run the risk of going into your next relationship conversation with the attitude, "I have a right to _____ and you are a controlling person if you try to have anything to say about it!"

In which case, you will have succeeded at defending your rights and protecting your autonomy, but you are teetering dangerously close to doing damage to your relationship and the connection you have with that person.

When trying to resolve a disagreement, it's important to always start with the NVC and Imago techniques. Ask what the other person is feeling and why. Express what you are feeling and why. The more intimate and more sensitive the feelings involved, the gentler your approach needs to be.

Most of the time, in a close relationship, if the person is stepping on your rights in an emotionally charged situation (like Bob telling Adam to cancel his date with Charlie) it's because they need something in order to feel safe and loved in the relationship. Unfortunately, at this early stage in the disagreement, they're unclear about what it is they need or how to get it without stepping on your rights. What they need to hear in that moment is that you understand what they feel and that their feelings matter to you. If instead you launch into, "But I have a right to do what I want with my time!" All they will hear is, "Your feelings don't matter to me." They will feel hurt, and your relationship will be damaged.

This information on individual rights is best used to examine ourselves and ask ourselves: Am I respecting my partner's rights? And if I need something I don't actually have a right to, am I remembering to ask rather than demand, and to show appreciation if it's given?

If we need to point out to a partner that they're insisting on something we don't want to give and to which they don't have a right, only do this after the Imago exercise. Approach the topic gently at first and only increase your firmness if they continue to insist or resist. Remind them that you care about their feelings and there are many ways to meet their needs without insisting on the thing you don't want to give. If they continue to resist, you may need to become increasingly firm in clarifying and defending your rights. The degree to which a partner resists acknowledging your rights can become a clue in helping you to identify whether your partner has a pattern of manipulative, coercive, or abusive behavior toward you.

Most of the time, people can successfully use a combination of the Imago exercise and a shared awareness of each person's rights to identify solutions that work for both people. These solutions become relationship agreements.

You will learn in chapter 8 that relationships are literally defined by their agreements, and in those agreements the people involved agree to *not exercise* all of their rights. To be ethical and healthy, these agreements must be freely negotiated. This book is dedicated to explaining *how* to ethically negotiate those agreements and how to communicate through disagreements to create an amicable conclusion that respects the individual rights, feelings, and wants of each person.

By living this process, you'll foster safety, mutual respect, mutual appreciation, and a spirit of generosity in your relationships. You'll create an environment within those relationships that supports the elements the individuals need in order to live up to their values and maintain their self-respect and self-esteem. And you'll be building a relationship in which each person has the opportunity to nurture a strong individual identity; in which the bonding, security, and safety is strong; and, if it is an attachment-bonded relationship, can be a safe haven and a secure base for the people involved.

Obstacles to implementing ethical boundaries

As I'm sure you can imagine, it's not a simple task to know the right thing to do and then just do it. It's not helpful to label ourselves weak or inadequate for not automatically being able to do this. (That would be a lack of self-compassion.)

There are real obstacles to implementing healthy, ethical boundaries. In order to succeed at implementing these boundaries, we must first identify the obstacles and then figure out how to get around them or remove them altogether.

For example, Jim didn't know what to think of Betty's behavior. On one hand, he perceived her as being "so reasonable" when she spoke about what she wanted, and on the other hand, he felt controlled when he thought about agreeing to what she wanted.

I call these external obstacles: the pressure and opposition we receive from others as they express what they want or object to what we want. We'll explore these external obstacles in the next chapter.

CHAPTER 6

External Obstacles to Implementing Rightful Boundaries

External obstacles are the obstacles other people create that interfere with our ability to act on our rights or defend our rightful boundaries. These obstacles can be verbal or nonverbal.

For example, I have the right to leave a physical space if I wish, but if someone takes my car keys, physically blocks my access to the door, or hides the medical equipment I need in order to leave, they are violating my rights and creating obstacles to my ability to enact my rights. These are examples of nonverbal obstacles.

Obstacles can also be verbal. They might verbally deny that one of my rights is actually something I have a right to. But most often the verbal obstacles people create are related to their upsetting emotions. Here's a conversation I had with a client, Renee, in which she realized in session that due to her upset feelings, she may have created obstacles interfering with her husband's ability to maintain his relationship with his girlfriend.

> "They broke up two weeks ago and he still talks to her every day!" Renee was frustrated. Her husband, Martin, had been dating a woman named Janine for the last three years or so. Over time, Janine seemed to need more and more emotional processing with Martin, and it was taking a toll.
>
> Martin and Renee were not people who enjoyed deep emotional processing. "It seemed to me that Janine was draining the joy and

energy out of Martin. He'd be so frustrated after their phone calls. So I started telling him he should break up with her."

"How long did you encourage Martin to break up with Janine before he finally did?" I asked.

"Probably six months." Renee said, "I don't know why it took him so long. He was miserable."

"I'm curious," I said, gently searching for more details. "Was his misery your only motivation, or were Janine's emotional needs affecting you directly?"

"Well, you know I depend on Martin a lot to help manage my ADHD. If I forget something or lose something I can usually count on him to help me out. One time he had to come to the grocery store and bring my wallet or I would have had to leave the store and come back. Another time, I would have been stranded at work because I lost my car keys, and he brought me the spare set from home. But Janine and her constant need for processing seemed to drain him. Sometimes he'd be on the phone with her for hours. I was afraid he wouldn't be able to be there for me if I needed him."

"Renee, I'm going to say this as gently as I can, but if I fail, I hope you'll forgive me. Do you know whether Martin actually wanted to break up with Janine, or if he only did it because he felt pressured by you to do so?"

Her eyes got a bit larger. "Oh, God, I hope not."

I explained to Renee that though it was a wonderful gift that her husband was willing to help her when she forgot or lost things, it was still her responsibility to manage her ADHD. If she truly did pressure him into ending a relationship against his will so that she could continue to rely on him, this was unethical, could lead to him resenting her, and could create a rift in their relationship.

External obstacles to defending an ethical boundary

Let's say you want something, and you've looked through the list of rights in the previous chapter and determined you are within your rights to have the thing you want. External obstacles are the ways other people might oppose you when you try to exercise one of your rights.

Or, like Renee in the story, you might oppose someone else having something that is within their rights. In that case, your actions would be an external obstacle to them defending their rightful boundary.

Opposition usually comes in the form of emotional expressions (anger, anxiety, fear, hurt, and so on), and you may experience it as a pressure to take an action you don't want to take, as an expression of judgment, or as a threat of punishment if you take the action you want (and have the right) to take.

In Renee's story, she may have verbally pressured her husband to break up with his girlfriend because she feared he would not be available to help her manage her ADHD. Her husband had the right to stay in the relationship with Janine if that was what he truly wanted. And he had the right to step back from helping manage Renee's ADHD if that is what he truly wanted.

In the story of Jim and Betty in chapter 5, Betty threatened to break up with Jim if he didn't move in with her, even though he wasn't ready and had the right to decide for himself where he wanted to live and with whom.

When people are hurt, afraid, anxious, frustrated, or angry, these feelings are unpleasant. People want relief from these feelings. So, they treat these feelings as problems that need to be solved.

As I stated previously, I don't think of painful emotions as problems. All emotions have a useful purpose as long as they are happening within their constructive parameters. Even when they are outside those parameters, they provide useful information that can help us resolve the underlying issue and transform our feelings to more pleasant ones. Painful emotions are often an indicator that work needs to be done, and they can also provide us with useful information about the underlying issue.

The important question I am presenting here is: Whose responsibility is it to resolve the underlying issues related to painful emotions? Who should sacrifice what they want in order to help transform painful feelings? Often, we're responsible for resolving our own painful emotions. When we create an external obstacle for someone else, we are not taking responsibility for our own feelings.

As discussed in chapter 2, both (or all) the people involved in a relationship should work together to resolve painful emotions. But sometimes, when people are at an impasse in those negotiations, it helps to identify who is responsible for what, and who is giving the gift of helping with something that is actually another person's responsibility.

Taking responsibility for our own emotions and actions

Mark Manson, author of *The Subtle Art of Not Giving a F*ck*, wrote a blog post entitled "The Guide to Strong Relationship Boundaries."[45] In it he says that good boundaries mean "taking responsibility for your actions and emotions while NOT taking responsibility for the actions and emotions of others."

This can be confusing. You might be asking, "Shouldn't other people be held responsible if they are being purposefully hurtful, neglectful, manipulative, or abusive?"

Yes. Yes, they should. Sometimes, we're dealing with situations of abuse and manipulation. However, most of the time that's not what's happening. So I'm going to make it very clear when we are responsible for our feelings, and when our upset feelings are justified and others need to be held accountable for their hurtful behaviors.

When none of our rights (see the previous chapter) are being violated and no relationship agreement is being violated (see chapter 8), yet we are upset about something, we are responsible for our own painful or unpleasant feelings, and for any actions we take in response to those feelings.

When none of our rights have been violated, but a relationship agreement has been violated by the other person, we are justified in being upset with them and the solution will involve both people. I explain this more in chapter 8.

When one or more of our rights is being violated, the other person is responsible for our painful or unpleasant feelings. The actions we take are still our responsibility, but they may be justified and necessary in order to defend our rightful boundaries, preserve our self-esteem and self-respect, and prevent the damage we would suffer if we did not take action.

When are we responsible for our own emotions and actions?

First, when none of our rights or relationship agreements have been violated, what we feel is ultimately our responsibility. I know this can be a mind-blowing concept, so let me break it down.

---

45 Mark Manson, n. d. "The guide to strong relationship boundaries." Blog post. https://markmanson.net/boundaries

Earlier in my career, when I was working with (presumably monogamous, mostly heterosexual, mostly binary, cisgender) teenagers, I would explain it this way:

Me:	Let's say you are walking to school and you see your boy-friend, girlfriend, or significant other (SO) on the steps of the school. What do you feel?
Teen:	Happy! Excited to see them.
Me:	And how would you act?
Teen:	I might smile, or wave, or walk faster.
Me:	So, you're walking faster and let's say they haven't seen you yet. Then another person comes up behind your SO, they smile at each other, and the other person puts their arms around your SO and kisses them on the cheek. Now how do you feel?
Teen:	I'd be upset!
Me:	And what are you thinking?
Teen:	They're cheating on me.
Me:	So, what do you do now?
Teen:	I'd walk up there and tell somebody off!
Me:	For the sake of this exercise, I want you to imagine that you continue walking up to your SO with the intention of getting an explanation. But as you walk up, your SO smiles at you. Then they say, "It's great to see you! I want to introduce you to my cousin," and gestures toward the person who kissed them. Now how do you feel?
Teen:	Relieved and kind of embarrassed because I was wrong.

Me:	You see, what you felt at different times in the story (first happy, then upset, then relieved) was actually based on your thoughts and beliefs about what was happening, not on what was actually happening. Your feelings were created by your thoughts, not by the actions of your SO.

Let me repeat this, because it is very important: What we feel is determined by our thoughts, beliefs, and values and on how *we combine them* with a real-life situation to create our interpretation of what's happening.

Those feelings are *our* creation, based on *our* interpretation, and are thus *our* responsibility.

Our feelings are not created by the actual event or the other person's actions. Additionally, the actions we choose, *based on* our feelings and our interpretations, are also our responsibility.

This is why *we* are responsible for our own feelings—because *we create them* out of our thoughts, beliefs, values, and interpretations. And *we have the power to choose* what we think, what we believe and what we value. *We can choose to interpret events differently.* We can choose to challenge those thoughts, beliefs, and values, *and thus change how we feel.*

Of course, this is a lightning-fast process, and we don't experience it in a way that feels like we are making conscious choices.

When an upsetting event happens and we have fast, powerful feelings in response, it feels like it is *happening to us.* When someone says or does something we interpret as hurtful, it feels like *they are hurting us* with their words.

Here's an example.

Simone had been having a once-a-week sleepover with Khyree for the last 18 months. She had fallen madly in love and was struggling with feeling insecure. She wanted more in her relationship but wasn't able to get it because Khyree also had a spouse, a family, and a busy career.

When Simone was talking with Khyree on the phone one afternoon, he expressed that he was happy his wife was taking the kids somewhere overnight, and he was going to enjoy a night in his house all alone. He called it a bachelor night and said he hadn't had one in a long time.

Simone was immediately upset. She asked him to spend that time with her. He listened and gently declined. He said he really needed and wanted the time alone.

When Simone came to see me, she had not been able to get to a place of acceptance and peace. She was hurt and crying and considering ending her relationship.

She said, "It clearly means he just doesn't love me the way I love him. I'm just a third wheel. I'm going to get dumped at some point. I just know it!"

"How do you know he doesn't love you the way you love him?" I asked.

"Because I wouldn't do this! If I had any opportunity to spend more time with him, I would. If he has the opportunity to spend time with me and chooses not to… then he's not in love with me. Not the way I love him!"

She was in tears and hurting, so I was patient and gentle. "I completely understand that. You miss him a lot during the six days apart each week. And loving him this much with the current limits on his time must be difficult, especially since you don't have a life partner meeting your other relationship needs."

"Yes. It is hard. I wonder all the time if I'm being foolish."

"And I'm sure you get more than enough alone time."

"I have a social life. But you're right, I never notice a need for alone time."

"So… He's not you. He has a different life experience. I wonder if he really needs alone time and really struggles to get it?"

She thought about that for a moment and said, "Maybe… but it still hurts."

"Since he's not here and we can't ask him, how about we try to look at the evidence? What evidence can you point to that tells you he really, really loves you?"

"He never misses a date. He is very sweet to me. He compliments me all the time. He tells me he loves me… a lot. He drives all the way across the city to see me every week. When he's with me, I can just tell that he loves me."

"And also," I said, "he seems to enjoy alone time, but every week, without fail, he spends a full 24 hours with you that he could be spending alone."

Her face relaxed. She seemed to understand.

"Okay, I'll ask him about it and maybe he can help me understand how spending this time alone is good for him."

"If you're saying that now you don't have to believe that him choosing a bachelor night over spending time with you means that he doesn't love you, what can you choose to believe instead?"

"That he just rarely gets alone time and he really needs it. But I want to ask him about it before I just start believing it."

"And how do you feel now?"

"Better. Calmer. And more secure that I'm safe and loved in this relationship."

She did ask. And that was what he said. He was a person who needed alone time, and he almost never got an adequate amount of it. He also wanted to sleep alone and spread out in the bed. This was another experience he rarely got. He also reassured her that he loved her very much and his desire for alone time was not a reflection of how much he loved her.

You see, Simone first interpreted the interaction through what it would mean if *she* did what her boyfriend was doing, and *based on that interpretation*, she felt very hurt.

But later she interpreted the events differently, and thus felt differently.

This therapeutic method is based in cognitive behavioral therapy, or CBT. In cognitive behavioral therapy, we guide clients through examining the thoughts, beliefs, and values that give rise to their emotions. If the client wants to feel differently in a given situation, they may be able to achieve that by challenging and changing what they think, believe, or value.

I tell you this so that if you want to research it further, you know what it's called. There are cognitive behavioral therapy workbooks to help a person work through jealousy, anger, anxiety, and even trauma.

You see, we are not helpless victims of our emotions, and we are not completely powerless in the face of them. We may be stuck feeling what we feel in the moment, but we can revisit our feelings, do some internal work, and quite possibly change those feelings in the direction of peace, love, and generosity.

In the next section, I explain this process in more detail.

Action item: Reflect on some events where you felt unpleasant or painful emotions. Review the list of rights to determine if your rights were violated in these memories. Only in the events where your rights were not violated, and a relationship agreement was not violated, reflect on what thoughts, beliefs, or values you had that caused the painful emotions. You may or may not choose to challenge those thoughts, beliefs, or values. If you do wish to challenge them, examine the evidence that supports your current interpretation of the event, and look at the evidence that does not support your current interpretation. Then ask, what could you choose to think, believe, or value that would help you to feel better?

How to respond ethically to painful emotions

Typically, people become aware of events happening in their environment and then they have feelings about those events.

What we are aware of:

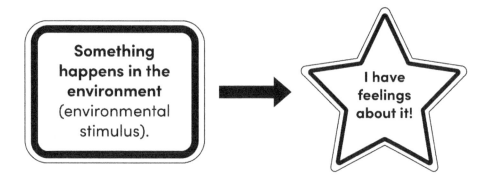

For instance, an event could be that my partner says, "I'm going rock climbing." I then feel fear.

But the event (my partner saying they are going rock climbing) doesn't directly *cause* my feelings. The event gets filtered through my thoughts, beliefs, and values first, and based on those *I create an interpretation of the meaning of the event.* I may think about how the event will impact me, and *then* my feelings and emotions arise from this.

What's really happening:

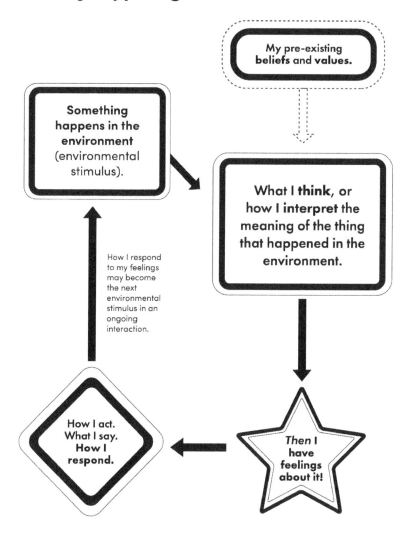

For example, I may have thoughts or beliefs such as, "Rock climbing is dangerous. My partner could get killed." Based on that interpretation, I feel fear.

But if I have the thought, "I've been rock climbing. I know it's fun. I trust my partner to keep themselves safe." Based on that interpretation, I would feel happy for them.

Notice how my feelings of either fear or happiness are coming from *me* and *my interpretations* of the meaning of my partner telling me they are going rock climbing.

So, let's get clear on what we mean by "making other people responsible for our feelings."

What would it look like if I were trying to make my partner responsible for my feelings? I might say something like this: "How can you do this to me? You know how scared I get! When you go rock climbing, all I do is worry and worry until you call me afterward and tell me you're okay. How can you put me through that again?! I insist you don't go. I can't stand this anxiety!"

You may notice that this choice of words suggests that my partner is responsible for my fear, rather than my thoughts and beliefs are responsible for my fear.

"How can *you do this to me?*" (You are doing this to me.)

"How can *you put me through this* again?" (You are putting me through this again.)

What would it look like if I were expressing my feelings while also taking responsibility for them? I might say something like this: "The thought of you going rock climbing fills me with fear. I know you have every right to go rock climbing, and I respect that. I know I am responsible for dealing with my fear. But I've been in therapy for a year now trying to get over this fear and I have not been able to. Please don't go."

Now let's start over and imagine that I am having this interaction, but I'm using the information learned so far in this book.

Let's imagine that I am still the person who thinks rock climbing is dangerous and I feel fear at the thought of my partner going rock climbing.

First, I look at the list of personal rights and I realize that my partner is within their rights to go rock climbing if they want to. They have the right to determine what they do with their body as well as their time. And they have the right to determine their own interests, hobbies, and activities.

I don't have the right to tell them they can't go rock climbing. The intensity of my fear doesn't change this. Even if my fear and anxiety is nearly debilitating, I do not have the right to tell them they can't go rock climbing.

It's perfectly okay for me to express my feelings about them going rock climbing, as long as I express myself respectfully: "I feel afraid when I think of you going rock climbing. I fear this is a dangerous activity. And I fear you will get killed."

It's even okay to ask my partner to not go: "Please don't go."

The difference between *asking* and *demanding* is that with asking, I am prepared to gracefully accept no for an answer. In fact, I would probably say it this way, just to make sure my partner knows I am not attempting to pressure or control them: "I know you have every right to go rock climbing, and dealing with my fear is my responsibility, but I would still be grateful if you chose not to go rock climbing."

An example related to polyamory

Let's look at an example directly related to polyamory.

Imagine that JaNae and Jadyn have agreed to open up their marriage. All seems to be going well until JaNae meets a non-binary person, Wren, and there is a shared attraction.

JaNae comes home and, in the manner they agreed to communicate about such things, tells Jadyn that she intends to move forward with Wren. Suddenly Jadyn feels anxious.

Jadyn expresses his feelings, respectfully, to JaNae. He expects her to respond by breaking things off with Wren. But JaNae doesn't want to.

Jadyn feels even more anxious, and now feels angry and betrayed, too. He expresses his feelings more loudly and aggressively, and he threatens to withdraw his consent to polyamory if she doesn't break things off with Wren.

What's happening here? If we look at the list of personal rights (see chapter 5), JaNae is completely within her rights. She is only looking to make decisions and exercise freedoms regarding her own body, emotions, relationships, and expenditure of time. She has also acted ethically, because she and Jadyn had agreed they both wanted to open up the marriage to ethical non-monogamy. And she followed the agreement about how to communicate regarding a potential new partner.

Jadyn, on the other hand, is not within his rights. He appears to be trying to push JaNae to break things off with Wren as a solution to his anxiety, and JaNae doesn't want to.

Is Jadyn acting ethically? He began ethically by expressing himself in a respectful way, but when he didn't get the result he wanted, he left ethical behavior behind and expressed himself in an intimidating and aggressive manner, and he made a threat.

Now, Jadyn *does* have the right to withdraw his consent to polyamory, but in this case, he's using the threat of it to try and force JaNae to give up something she wants and to which she has a right. So though he may have the right to withdraw his consent, he's weaponizing a boundary.

Looking at each person's rights is a good place to start when we want to determine which of the people involved needs to examine their thoughts and feelings, and which person needs to try to change how they feel or act. In this case, it's Jadyn.

Let's say Jadyn and JaNae have reviewed the list of personal rights. Jadyn and JaNae agree that JaNae is within her rights to see Wren and to continue that relationship if she wants. Jadyn asks if she's willing to stop seeing Wren, and JaNae says no. Jadyn admits that he's responsible for his feelings of anxiety and he's willing to examine his feelings and see what he can do to change them.

Jadyn goes back to the beginning and asks himself, "Why did I feel anxious when I learned that JaNae and Wren have a mutual attraction and want to advance their relationship?"

He realizes that his next thought was, "What if she has great sex with Wren, falls in love with them, and leaves me?" He has a belief that the power of sexual passion and the quality of sexual experiences (or a person's sexual performance) can cause someone to fall in or out of love and influence major, life-altering actions, such as JaNae leaving him.

This belief didn't spring from Jadyn's head—it's a common cultural myth here in the United States and in other cultures as well. But is it true? And is it true of JaNae? Rather than assuming it's true, Jadyn might want to ask JaNae about this and ask for the reassurance he needs. For most people, choosing to leave a marriage has to do with a lot more factors than just the quality of sexual experiences.

When Jadyn expressed his feelings, he expected JaNae to accommodate him and break things off with Wren. When she didn't, Jadyn felt betrayed. If he asks himself why, he might realize that he has a belief about how a committed relationship is supposed to work.

Like many other people, Jadyn believes that if you have strong feelings of pain, especially if triggered by your partner's actions, your partner should change what they are doing in order to relieve your pain for you. This belief leads directly to *making someone else responsible for your feelings.*

In Jadyn's mind, JaNae was responsible for solving the problem of his painful emotions, and her choosing not to was the equivalent of choosing her new love interest over him. To Jadyn, this looked like JaNae was showing a lack of commitment to their relationship, and so he felt betrayed.

If Jadyn is going to find relief for his jealousy and fear, he will need to become convinced that JaNae would not leave him even if she has great sex with someone else. And he would need to believe that it's not JaNae's responsibility to back down just because Jadyn's emotions are strong.

This can be accomplished through inner work, examining his thoughts and beliefs, examining the evidence that contradicts his beliefs, engaging in healthy communication with JaNae, asking for reassurance from her, or negotiating some other consensual relationship agreement that might reduce his anxiety.

> **Action item:** Reflect on how you speak when expressing painful emotions when your rights have not been violated. Do you have a pattern of speaking as though the other person is responsible for your feelings? How might you rephrase the things you say so that you clearly acknowledge that you are responsible for solving the problem of your painful emotions?

> **Action item:** If you are unaware of how you speak when expressing painful emotions, begin keeping a journal. Write down as much as you can remember when you have conversations or arguments related to your painful emotions. Determine whether any of your rights were violated or a relationship agreement was violated. If not, how did you express your feelings? Did you make the other person responsible for them? Or did you own them as your responsibility? Practice rephrasing so that you are clearly taking responsibility for your own emotions.

When can we hold other people responsible for their hurtful behavior?

Imagine I'm on the public bus, it's crowded, and someone tries to steal my wallet. I feel angry about this. Is it my responsibility to examine my thoughts, beliefs, and values, and try to become at peace with someone taking my wallet? Of course not!

Look at the list of personal rights. I have the right to control and protect my possessions, livelihood, money, and assets. This stranger on the bus has violated one of my rights. Thus, I have every right to make a boundary around my wallet, my money, and my possessions, and to *demand* that this person respect that boundary.

When someone violates one of our rights, our upset feelings (hurt, anger, fear, and so on) are *justified*. These painful emotions are meant to motivate us to take action to defend our rightful boundaries or to protect ourselves.

Furthermore, to have someone violate one of our rights and to not defend that right, or to not be able to defend that right due to an imbalance of power, is damaging to our self-esteem, self-respect, and feelings of safety in the world. It can be so damaging that in such situations, people sometimes develop post-traumatic stress disorder, depression, or some other mental health disorder.

For example, if, as an adult, I visit my parents and they have a pattern of talking to me in a disrespectful or derogatory manner, this is a violation of one of my rights (to be spoken to respectfully and treated with dignity).

I could call them out on the way they speak to me. But because they are my parents, I might find that difficult. The parent-child relationship, even as adults, can be very power-imbalanced in favor of the parents. But if I do call them out, or find the courage to talk with them about how their words are hurtful, or if I simply take steps to distance myself and insulate myself from being exposed to them and their words, this exercise of my personal power to create and defend my boundaries builds my self-esteem, self-respect, and feelings of safety in the world.

Action item: Think about times when your rights were violated. Did you realize it at the time? Were you able to hold the other person responsible? Did a power imbalance, fear of that person, or a trauma history interfere with your ability to stand up for yourself? Allow yourself to feel compassion for the historical you in these memories. Rehearse how you might respond to similar situations that might happen in the future.

Physiological causes of unpleasant emotions

Just to ensure that human emotions continue to be the perplexing enigma they often are, I want to point out that unpleasant emotions such as anxiety, anger, and sadness or depression can also have physiological causes. When the primary cause of an emotion state is physiological, cognitive behavioral therapy will not help much.

We feel our emotions in our bodies. We learn, over time, to associate a certain combination of physical sensations with an emotion label. I have found that different people sometimes feel different sensations for the same label. For example, when I feel anxiety, it's like an all-over, uncomfortable jitteriness combined with worry thoughts. Fear is like amplified anxiety plus a feeling like ice water in my intestines. Anger feels like a hot energy in my chest and arms, sometimes also my legs, like I want to hit and stomp things. Other people have described their anxiety to me as including a brain fog plus a desire to run, or anger as a heat in their neck and seeing red in their mind.

However you might experience your emotions, they are a physical experience. Hormones are powerful chemical messengers involved in the experience of emotions, and they can be impacted by a number of medical issues, medications, and non-prescription drugs.

Anxiety can be a symptom of, and can precede, the following diagnoses:[46]

- Heart disease
- Diabetes
- Hyperthyroidism
- Respiratory disorders, such as COPD and asthma
- Chronic pain or irritable bowel syndrome
- Rare tumors that produce certain fight-or-flight hormones.

Medications that can cause anxiety include:[47]

- Medications with caffeine, such as migraine or PMS medications
- Corticosteroids used for treating inflammation, allergies, and auto-immune disorders

46 Mayo Clinic, n.d. "Anxiety disorders." https://www.mayoclinic.org/diseases-conditions/anxiety/symptoms-causes/syc-20350961

47 Rachel Reiff Ellis, 2021. "What meds might cause anxiety?" WebMD. https://www.webmd.com/anxiety-panic/anxiety-causing-meds

- Stimulant medications for ADHD and narcolepsy
- Asthma medications such as bronchodilators
- Vasodilators such a topical minoxidil[48] and medications for erectile dysfunction[49]
- Thyroid medications
- Seizure medications
- Medications that treat Parkinson's disease, such as Sinemet and Rytary.

Depression can be a symptom of, and can precede, the following diagnoses:[50]

- Gastrointestinal or pancreatic cancers
- Chronic pain disorders, such as fibromyalgia
- Hypothyroidism (and sometimes hyperthyroidism)
- Heart disease
- Autoimmune diseases, such as lupus
- Multiple sclerosis
- Vitamin B12 deficiency.

Some medications that can cause depression are:[51]

- Beta blockers
- Glaucoma medications
- Corticosteroids
- Benzodiazepines, such as Xanax and Valium
- Estrogen hormones used for birth control and menopause symptom relief

---

48 John P. Cunha, 2021. "Minoxidil topical." RxList. https://www.rxlist.com/consumer_rogaine_minoxidil_topical/drugs-condition.htm

49 Mohammadreza Shalbafan, Maryam Orooji, and Leila Kamalzadeh, 2022. "Psychosis beas a rare side effect of sildenafil: A case report." *Journal of Medical Case Reports*, vol. 16, no. 120. https://rdcu.be/cUtiL

50 Amanda Gardner, 2022. "10 medical conditions linked to depression." *Health*, September 25. https://www.health.com/condition/depression/conditions-linked-to-depression?slide=08332dd0-9513-4455-99ad-1cf9d903f4cb#08332dd0-9513-4455-99ad-1cf9d903f4cb

51 Nancy Schimelpfening, 2022. "Depression with drugs: Are your medications making you depressed?" *Verywell Mind*, October 7. https://www.verywellmind.com/drugs-that-can-cause-depression-1067458#types-of-drugs-that-can-cause-depression

- Drugs used to treat Parkinson's disease
- Stimulant medications for ADHD and narcolepsy
- Anticonvulsant medications
- Proton pump inhibitors and H2 blockers
- Statins and other cholesterol-lowering drugs
- Anticholinergic drugs for treating irritable bowel syndrome
- Acne medications
- Pain relievers
- Allergy medications
- Thyroid medications
- Antibiotics

Anger can be a symptom of:[52]

- Personality changes due to dementia
- Diabetes
- Epilepsy
- Hepatic encephalopathy caused by liver failure
- PMS or menopause
- Personality changes after a stroke
- Hyperthyroidism
- Wilson's disease, a rare genetic disorder
- Depression.

Medications that can cause anger or irritability include:

- Benzodiazepines
- Statins for lowering cholesterol
- Anti-inflammatory steroids used for chronic pain[53]
- Anabolic steroids used in sports.[54]

52 WebMD editorial contributors, 2022. "Is my medical condition making me angry?" WebMD. https://www.webmd.com/balance/guide/why-am-i-so-angry#2-13
53 Ava Meena, 2022. "Steroid rage and pain management." Lupus.net. https://lupus.net/living/steroid-rage-pain-management
54 Etienne Benson, 2002. "More male than male." *Monitor on Psychology*, vol. 22, no. 9. https://www.apa.org/monitor/oct02/moremale

Alcohol and recreational drug use or withdrawal can also cause episodes of anxiety, depression, and anger.

If you seem to feel these unpleasant emotions frequently regardless of what's going on in your life, or if they have started out of the blue and don't appear to be related to events happening in your life, you may have a medical disorder, or may be having a drug reaction best addressed by a medical doctor. Another possibility is that you may have a psychiatric disorder best addressed with a combination of medication and therapy. An evaluation with a psychiatrist might be needed. (A psychiatrist is a medical doctor who specializes in the biochemistry of emotions and thought patterns.)

Conclusion

If we are going to have happy, healthy relationships with others, we need them to respect our rights and the rightful boundaries we create around our rights. As long as we have not violated their rights or a relationship agreement, if they are upset with us, they can show they respect our rights by expressing their upset feelings in a way that acknowledges that they are responsible for their own feelings.

If we have violated their rights or a relationship agreement, then we are responsible for their upset feelings, and we are responsible for helping to resolve those feelings. But when we are not responsible for their painful emotions, and the person speaks in a way that claims we are, this can become an external obstacle to defending our own rightful boundaries. I explain how to determine who is responsible for what in much more detail in chapter 9.

There are also internal obstacles to implementing our rightful boundaries. This is when our own feelings of guilt, fear, and shame cause us to block ourselves from taking rightful actions. I address internal obstacles in the next chapter.

CHAPTER 7

Internal Obstacles to Implementing Rightful Boundaries

"That just sounds so mean!" Connie said.

"What does?" I asked.

"Telling someone I don't want to be family with them. That just sounds so mean."

Connie came to see me because she was struggling to cope with the many needs of the people in her polycule (a group of people in interconnected polyamorous relationships). She had already made a lot of progress in how she expressed herself when frustrated and was no longer having screaming meltdowns with her husband, Ben. However, she was still frustrated that her metamour, Lisa (her husband's girlfriend) was at the house almost all the time.

Connie managed to negotiate with her husband that they should each have 50% control over the home environment, and she preferred the girl-friend not be at the house for her 50% of the time. Her husband agreed. But now Lisa was complaining that Connie's restrictions were interfering with the increased commitment and depth she wanted in her relationship with Ben.

Earlier in the session, Connie and I had the following conversation.

"Lisa and her husband Greg seem to want to move in and have all four of us living like a commune, and be one big family, and I just don't want that."

"You know," I said, "you have every right to determine for yourself what depth of relationship you want with Lisa or Greg, and if you don't want them to be family to you, you have the right to say so and have that respected."

That's when Connie said, "It just sounds mean."

I replied, "They may feel hurt by it. But just because they feel hurt doesn't mean you are being mean. I'm sure you realize that when Ben asked you to marry him, you had the right to decide whether you wanted him to be family to you. Saying no would have hurt, but if that was the truthful answer, it would be wrong to say yes just to avoid hurting his feelings."

"That's true," she said.

"I don't see where this is much different," I said. "Do you know what Ben wants?"

"I'm not sure, but if I had to guess, I'd say he probably doesn't want them that close either, but he has a difficult time telling Lisa no."

"It sounds like your first task might be to talk about this with Ben, find out what he truly wants, and then negotiate a solution that respects both your feelings and desires and Ben's feelings and desires on this issue. If it turns out that he doesn't want to escalate his relationship with Lisa, but he has a hard time telling her no, the two of you could support each other in setting limits with her and Greg. What do you think?"

"Yes. Let's discuss how I might approach him about this."

Internal obstacles to defending a rightful boundary

In the last chapter we covered external obstacles to implementing rightful boundaries. These are the obstacles we experience that arise from the resistance other people express toward us as we attempt to implement the boundaries we have a right to put in place.

In this chapter, we'll be looking at internal obstacles to implementing rightful boundaries. As you may have guessed, these arise from within ourselves. We may notice them as feelings of guilt, fear, anxiety, or some other painful or unpleasant emotion when we think about expressing what we want or need, telling someone no, or defending a boundary. Or we may notice them as judgmental thoughts about what we want, such as "that's selfish" or "I don't deserve that."

As I explained in the last chapter, these emotions are created by thoughts, beliefs, and values. In the example, Connie didn't want to escalate her relationship with Lisa to live-together-family, but she hadn't let herself say it clearly because she felt guilty, and thought it was "just mean."

She had a belief that if someone wants a deeper relationship with you, rejecting them is mean. She predicted Lisa would feel hurt or angry. She believed if an action by her "caused" someone else to feel painful emotions, then she was responsible for that pain. This belief resulted in her feeling guilty and therefore she stopped herself from expressing what she wanted.

According to Mark Manson in his blog post "The Guide to Strong Relationship Boundaries,"[55] another way of saying this is that Connie is "taking too much responsibility for the feelings of others."

Sometimes we take so much responsibility for the feelings of others that we don't even get clarification from the other people involved about what they actually feel or why. We simply anticipate what we think they will feel, and we take on fixing their painful feelings as our responsibility by compromising what we want or need.

In the last chapter we looked at an example where Jadyn was feeling anxious and angry about JaNae's relationship with Wren. We determined that JaNae was acting within her rights and Jadyn's first response—whether consciously or unconsciously—was to try to make JaNae responsible for his pain. Jadyn tried to pressure JaNae to take action to "fix" his pain by breaking up with Wren.

In our first telling of this story, JaNae gently confronted Jadyn, who admitted he was asking for something outside of his rights. JaNae stuck to her guns and said she didn't want to break off her relationship with Wren. Jadyn began examining his thoughts and feelings and took responsibility for finding his own emotional peace.

But if JaNae had been like a partner in many real-life couples, the same scenario could take a different turn. JaNae could have chosen to never confront Jadyn about his behavior, or with how hurt or controlled she might feel in response to his demands that she stop seeing Wren. JaNae could have been a person like Connie who feels guilt, fear, or shame at the thought of standing up for what she wants or needs. She could have been

---

55 Mark Manson, n. d.

a person who takes too much responsibility for the feelings and emotions of others.

Beliefs about yourself based on personal life experiences

Why do people have internal obstacles to implementing ethical boundaries? As I explained in chapter 6, our emotions are a product of our thoughts, beliefs, and values. We often come to these thoughts, beliefs, and values due to a lifetime of experiences that teach us to predict certain responses from others as a consequence to our actions. Here are a couple of examples I've encountered in my therapy practice.

Tracy grew up with a father who threw temper tantrums anytime other family members didn't readily give him what he wanted. Once, he threw a coffee pot and narrowly missed Tracy's head. He also had a pattern of ignoring Tracy or criticizing her accomplishments, and would praise girls Tracy perceived to be skinnier and prettier.

Tracy learned to fear standing up for herself and to expect angry outbursts if she didn't immediately bend to what her father wanted. As an adult, this impacted her relationships. She often felt guilty even thinking about expressing a need or want. She was typically comfortable with polyamory, but would sometimes become anxious when her partner showed an interest in other women. If she perceived them to be skinnier or prettier, she feared he would lose interest in her and abandon her for these other women.

Thanks to her father's behavior, Tracy learned growing up that she was of little value compared to supposedly skinnier and prettier girls.

In another example, a different client, Andreus, came to believe he was of little value compared to his mother's career, as she missed all his events and left him home alone for long hours. In his adult relationships, Andreus resented his partners' missing social events, dates, and vacations due to the demands of work or career, but he never spoke up and expressed his resentment. When I asked him why, he realized he predicted he would never "win" in such a conflict. He assumed his partners' careers would always come first.

Both of these examples show people who, deep down, question their value to their partners. They feel unworthy, sometimes they feel unlovable, and they assume that if they put their partners in a position to have to choose between them and some other thing of value (a "prettier, skinnier" new partner or a career-boosting event), they will not be chosen.

Based on this belief, they choose what appears to them to be the safer route; the route they believe is necessary to preserve their relationship; the route that allows them to not challenge their own fear; the route that builds their simmering resentment under the surface. This route is one in which they say nothing and immediately accommodate their partner without speaking up for themselves or their needs.

Another belief about the self that can interfere with standing up for your rights or voicing what you need is the belief that you're not a good person unless you put everyone else's needs before your own. Another way that I've heard this expressed by my clients is, "If I can do it, I should."

This is another way of devaluing oneself. This belief says that your needs and your wants don't compare to the needs and wants of others, and that their needs are more important than yours.

All people can be conditioned to take on responsibility for other people's emotions, especially if they have been raised by emotionally unstable adults, immature adults, or adults who have simply never questioned the coerciveness of the emotional norms with which they, themselves, were raised.

Imagine the child who expresses a normal childhood desire for a new game, a game that the parent can't currently afford to buy for them. A healthy parental response would be to validate the child's desire for the game: "That sounds like a great game, Todd, I totally understand why you would want that." And then, "I wish I could afford to get it for you, but I can't. Let's talk about ways you can earn the money and buy it for yourself."

The child may feel disappointed, but we all need opportunities to learn how to cope with disappointment.

An emotionally unstable, immature, or unaware parent might feel immediately ashamed or angry that they can't afford the game and lash out at the child, making the child responsible for the parent's feelings: "Todd, I can't believe you would ask me for that when you know how little money we have! Are you trying to kill me with your constant wants? It's like you don't care how hard I work just to feed you. You are so selfish!"

This response is likely to induce feelings of shame or guilt in the child, teaching them that they will be seen as bad and selfish if they want things. It even teaches them that expressing their wants actively hurts the parent.

In other words, as the parent expresses that the child is responsible for the parent's feelings of anger or shame, the child internalizes these beliefs and learns to believe that they are responsible any time someone is upset with them.

This is very important! If you have a tendency to feel guilty, anxious, afraid, or ashamed at the thought of expressing a need or want, of having any expectations on how someone else should treat you, or of inconveniencing anyone for any reason, you may have internalized the justifications of a person who was not taking responsibility for themselves and their own emotions.

The parent's response doesn't have to be this extreme to have a negative impact on the child. A non-verbal sigh or grimace will do. What does the harm is the absence of validation of the child's feelings or desire combined with an expression of displeasure, especially if this is the majority of parental responses throughout the child's life. A child in this environment will grow up feeling apologetic about expressing their wants or needs, and they are unlikely to have a clear concept of their personal rights or to have healthy emotional boundaries or healthy relationship communication skills.

People can also be conditioned in adulthood if they find themselves in a relationship with someone who tends to not take responsibility for their own emotions, or is mentally, emotionally, or physically abusive.

Let's imagine JaNae is one of these people. When Jadyn expresses his pain, JaNae might feel guilty. She might take responsibility for Jadyn's feelings so fast that Jadyn doesn't even have to suggest she break off her relationship with Wren. Even though it's not what she wants, JaNae might quickly volunteer to end her relationship with Wren.

Many people have such a strong negative emotional response (guilt, fear, or shame) when their partner feels pain or discomfort that they jump to accommodate their partner *in order to relieve their own pain!*

The examples we just saw describe this form of devaluing the self when it's based on individual experiences. But it can also be based in cultural beliefs.

Ingrained dominant culture beliefs about yourself, and expectations on you, regarding your place in the social fabric of the world

We typically think of power imbalances based on gender, race, age, ability, financial resources, looks, and so on as being structural power imbalances. This means they are baked into the structures of our society as part of systems, institutions, and traditions. As a result, these structural power imbalances are built into institutional policies and norms, as well as expressed between individuals within one-on-one and small group interactions. Within these interactions people often carry with them and act out assumptions based on power and social capital. They bring with them expectations of how others should behave due to their social status relative to them. Often people from a more powerful or influential group expect members of a less influential group to defer to them and to give up what they want. People in a dominant group may feel something is owed to them, or feel entitled to have the others bend to their wishes.

These group experiences are the aggregate of many individuals living out power imbalances in millions of interactions between individuals every day. These power imbalances come down to how others see your value, or how you see your value in comparison to others in relation to these elements and intersections of identity. They also have to do with how much social power or social capital you believe you have, or other people believe you have. And in relationships, they have to do with how your partner or partners see your status and interpersonal power, and how you see your own status and interpersonal power in comparison to others.

One example is the classic binary framework of gender and the expectations placed on people based on how others interpret their gender.

In the traditional binary gender model, there are only two sexes: male and female. The label of "male" or "female" is assigned to a child at birth based on what their physical body looks like. People assigned "male" are expected to be masculine and grow up to be men, and people assigned "female" are expected to be feminine and grow up to be women. This binary gender model organizes social life and interprets virtually every aspect of human experience through the lens of men and women as polar opposites. Opposite but supposedly complementary gender roles, gender stereotypes, compulsory heterosexuality, and monogamy are said to reinforce and continually reconstruct the binary gender model.[56]

Within this model, girls and women are told they must almost always put their desires, goals, and needs absolutely last relative to other people (especially family members) in order to be thought of as good people. This kind of self-sacrifice is seen as being nurturing or caregiving, and is praised

---

56 Marion Godman, 2018. "Gender as a historical kind: A tale of two genders?" *Biology and Philosophy* 33 (3), p. 21. https://www.ncbi.nlm.nih.gov/pmc/articles/PMC5943372/

in girls and women and is considered a central aspect of being adequately feminine.

Another belief is that women should submit to men, and particularly to a partner who is a man. In order for a partner who is a man to feel adequately masculine, she must help create this experience of power and dominance by deferring to him, submitting to his will, praising his accomplishments and abilities, and downplaying her own.

Additionally, there is the belief that for a girl or woman to be assertive, ambitious, or focused on herself or her needs is not feminine and is therefore grotesque. In this belief system, femininity is partly defined by a girl or woman's desire to give to others, to nurture others, to *want* to put others' needs and wants before her own.

The counterpart to this belief is a traditional component for boys and men. They are taught to prioritize, actively seek, and compete for what they want, and to continue to push for what they want even in the face of opposition from others. If they are to sacrifice what they really want, it's in order to live up to the responsibilities of being a breadwinner or the family disciplinarian.

Boys and men are also taught to believe that they must live up to the expectations of masculinity—such as dominance and not expressing weakness or insecurity—or they risk losing their own self-respect as well as the respect of their partners, their friends, and society as a whole.

This traditional gender binary also includes the belief that it's not masculine to express feelings or emotions other than anger, sexual desire, or confidence. Since boys and men are supposed to be dominant over girls and women, expressing vulnerable feelings such as hurt, fear, or insecurity is seen as weak and can expose boys and men to social and interpersonal ridicule.

We've already seen in earlier chapters that the ability to express these emotions is important to honest communication, such as when using nonviolent communication and the Imago exercise. And we'll see in later chapters that expressing vulnerable emotions is essential to honestly and fairly negotiating healthy relationship agreements, while also expressing respect for your partners' rights.

Anyone can pick up traditional binary gender components, regardless of their gender assigned at birth or sexual orientation. Those of us in the LGBTQIA+ community may have felt considerable pressure from others who expected us to conform to gendered expectations with which we did not or do not identify. Or we may have taken on gender roles and expectations that others did not expect of us, or even forbade. But even when we choose and fight for our right to inhabit these roles, to the extent that we internalize their unhealthy aspects, they may still be problematic within our relationships.

All of the social power relations listed earlier (gender, race, age, ability, financial resources, looks) can play out on the individual level in this way. In response to an ableist social context, a person with disabilities might avoid expressing a need to their partners because they don't want to appear weak or in need of "special" accommodations. A person of color might hesitate to express reasonable anger to a partner out of concern they will be seen as more emotionally or physically volatile than they are, in keeping with racist stereotypes. A person who perceives themselves too unattractive based on narrow social standards and media portrayals might be overly accommodating because they fear their partner "could do better."

Additionally, circumstantial inequalities can hinder us from feeling safe enough to stand up for our rights in a relationship. Maybe we agreed years ago to be the stay-at-home parent while our partner built a lucrative career, and we now feel financially dependent. Maybe we feel isolated and lack social or family support, while our partner seems to have friends and family willing to validate their perspective on the couple's disagreements. Maybe we're in a secondary relationship position and we fear we would be easily discarded if we express our needs and our partner then perceives us as being difficult.

Regardless, none of the motivations listed are psychologically or emotionally healthy, nor are they building blocks for a healthy relationship. When pushed on us by social power structures or by other individual people, these power imbalances are external obstacles to our rights and rightful boundaries. When we internalize beliefs about these power imbalances, meaning we believe them about ourselves, they are internal obstacles. The painful feelings that result from internalizing these beliefs—such as guilt, fear, or shame—block us from standing up for our needs, wants, and rightful boundaries.

If we engage in our relationships as though we are of lesser value than someone else, not only is this damaging to our self-esteem and self-respect, but we may also create a self-fulfilling prophecy where we train those involved with us to devalue us or to expect us to be extra accommodating even if they don't share those biases.

For example, if I enter a relationship with internalized sexism, and I haven't questioned these beliefs, then I am unlikely to be consciously aware of how those beliefs impact my emotions or the actions I take and choices I make based on those emotions. When I go to my new partner's apartment and see housework that needs to be done, I may feel a pull to do that housework. My unexamined beliefs behind that emotional pull might be, "I should do this for them," or "they will see me as a potentially good partner if I do this." Even if my new partner has no expectation that I will or should do their housework for them, I might volunteer this service without having truly examined whether I want to do it, whether I want to create this precedent in my relationship, or whether I am taking the first step toward creating a power imbalance.

Even if my new partner objects, if I haven't examined why I feel compelled to do their housework, I might defend my actions with a justification such as, "Acts of service is one of my love languages. Please don't reject this show of love." If my partner accepts this justification, then I have effectively trained my partner to allow me to do their housework, to expect that I will do their housework, and that I will be hurt if they do their own housework.

The key here is to deeply examine why we do these things. I offer some tools to help in this self-examination toward the end of this chapter. If our motivation comes from a positive place of wanting to be helpful or to share the load within a balanced relationship where we also accept help with chores or receive an equivalent contribution, then acts of service can be a healthy part of the relationship. But if our motivation comes from a place of feeling unworthy, or that we must do things for others to earn their love, or that because of some element of our identity it's expected of us even though we don't want to do it, then we owe it to ourselves to grow out of this behavior and become a person who is authentic to our true wants and who honors our own equal value in relation to others.

If we provide service as a love language or as part of a negotiated power dynamic, we need to do this with adequate self-esteem (or to be working on that), relationship security, fully informed consent and thorough negotiation.

A more subtle example might be if my partner is short-tempered with me one day. If I have internalized beliefs, such as sexism, where I tell myself it is my role to "bear this pain and don't correct him or make him feel small," then I will say nothing and passively wait for him to correct himself or apologize without me prompting him.

Let's say he doesn't apologize or correct himself. This could be motivated by his sexism or a more personal explanation, such as that his parents used to shame him by making him perform publicly humiliating apologies in front of the whole family. Regardless, if I go back to acting like nothing happened, then I have effectively taught him that he can treat me this way and I won't require him to apologize or otherwise repair the relationship.

I fully acknowledge that if someone treats us badly due to racism, sexism, ableism, and so forth, the responsibility for their actions and the harm caused is on them. They have violated our right to be treated with respect and dignity.

I am also saying that if someone treats me badly, whether it is motivated by racism, sexism, ableism, or some other more personal reason, how I respond or don't respond communicates to them whether I will tolerate their behavior, make excuses for their behavior, disapprove of their behavior, openly object to their behavior, or demand a change in their behavior.

These can be very emotionally challenging moments. It takes incredible courage, strength, and energy to actively choose conflict for the purpose of making things better in your relationship. If in that moment you don't have the energy, or you assess you don't have the interpersonal power and will be more damaged by standing up for yourself than you are willing to risk, be kind to yourself. You don't owe that work to anyone.

But if you choose to do this work, especially if it's part of maintaining and improving a relationship that's important to you, I encourage you to think of this as empowering. Because this work takes energy, it's personal growth to develop the strength and courage to do it. That growth is primarily around increasing your awareness of and ability to use your interpersonal power, and results in dismantling your internal obstacles to implementing your rightful boundaries.

A note regarding consensual power dynamics

In a consensually negotiated power dynamic, the power between the two people is not equal, but their value is equal. It's important to remember that you can only negotiate away your personal power if you have that power to begin with. And that negotiation can only be considered consensual if you began the negotiation with equal power.

I strongly urge people in the beginning stages of a power dynamic relationship to begin as equals and negotiate the power exchange at a slow enough pace that the needed trust can be demonstrated and earned.

I know that for some people it's exciting to think of being in a consensual power dynamic, and because of this, people often rush the process. But it's important to remember that turning over your personal power to another person is serious business and is a situation that, in the wrong hands, lends itself easily to abuse of that power or neglect of your needs. On the flip side, taking up personal power in someone else's life can be a heavy responsibility, and slowing the pace can help you discover your own needs and limits within that dynamic to help keep things healthy and sustainable for all concerned.

If you're considering entering a consensual power dynamic relationship, you may want to check out some of the very good books that teach communication skills and ethics particular to these types of relationships.[57]

Pushback from our partners

Sometimes people do well with expressing their initial wants, but the internal obstacle arises after their partner responds with pushback or opposition. The person tries to stand up for themselves, but finds themselves quickly confused as their partner justifies and rationalizes why they should be accommodated. And sometimes the partner has a frighteningly strong emotional response. For example, what if our partner responds like Tracy's dad, by throwing tantrums or throwing objects?

We explored in the last chapter that when other people try to make us responsible for their feelings and refuse to acknowledge our rights, this becomes an external obstacle to implementing our rights and defending our rightful boundaries, and it introduces coercion into the relationship. But our fear or guilt over this response, or our anticipation that this might be our partner's response, is an internal obstacle. Whether that fear or guilt is based on our partner's historical patterns, or whether our partner has never acted this way but other people in our past have conditioned us to expect

---

57 Sabrina Popp, M.D. and Raven Kaldera, 2014. *Unequal by Design: Counseling Power Dynamic Relationships*. Alfred Press.
Raven Kaldera and Joshua Tenpenny, 2013. *Building the Team: Cooperative Power Dynamic Relationships*. Alfred Press.
Raven Kaldera, 2010. *Power Circuits: Polyamory in a Power Dynamic*. Alfred Press.

this response, it is still our internal obstacle and our responsibility to address it and unlearn it.

Are you trying to manage the other person's strong emotions?

As we discussed in chapter 2, there are a number of mental health diagnoses that can contribute to a person feeling very strong emotions they don't readily have the ability to control. They may also currently lack the ability to reduce their painful emotions or to effectively self-soothe when they are painfully upset.

Keep in mind, however, that sometimes people consciously choose to display strong emotions as a way of coercing, pressuring, manipulating, or controlling others. You'll need to decide for yourself which situation you are facing. (I cover this in depth in my next book.)

If you're interacting with a person whom you believe cannot control their strong emotions, you may recall from chapter 4 that the solutions brainstormed at the end of the Imago exercise must be based on accommodating the feelings of both people as they currently are. And yet, it's important to not give in and give accommodations you don't actually want to give. While these ideas may appear to be in opposition to each other, it's important to strike a balance.

Here's an example:

Colin complained, "Every time Keshav and I make an agreement, he breaks it."

I asked for an example and Colin said, "When Keshav had a date with Jared last week, he agreed to be home by 8 p.m. But he didn't get home until almost 9."

When I asked Keshav for his perspective, he said that he never really wanted to agree to the 8 p.m. curfew. He said, "Colin gets so upset, I say 'yes' just to get some peace. And I start out with the intention of being home by 8, but when the time comes to cut my date short or interrupt an emotionally important conversation with Jared, the restriction feels so unfair that I don't comply."

It's perfectly okay to negotiate solutions with another person that respect their feelings and yours and that don't require either of you to change. I even prescribe that in chapter 4, where I said the solution must respect *both* of your feelings. Here, I want to emphasize that this means it must respect your feelings, too!

When we try to manage other people's strong emotions by giving up things we want and to which we have a right, what's happening is that our fear or dislike of the other person's emotional response is so strong that it's skewing our decision-making in an unhealthy direction.

You may even believe you *want* to give this compromise. Conflict may be so painful for you that you don't even let yourself realize what you want. You're more focused on watching for the first signs of conflict or strong emotions from the other person so that you can jump to quickly compromise, make nice, and defuse conflicts before they begin.

You want peace. You want to avoid the pain of experiencing their strong emotional response. That's not the same thing as wanting to freely give them the accommodation. Rather, you feel coerced or pressured by their emotional response, and any accommodation you give under coercion or duress is not consensual.

This is a very important distinction. It is very important to know whether you are agreeing to something freely and consensually, or if you are agreeing to something under duress. The first step in learning to tell the difference is learning how to identify *what you truly want*.

How to get better at identifying and defending boundaries

When a person tends to take on too much responsibility for the feelings or behaviors of others, what can that person do to begin identifying their boundaries and defending them?

Let's return to our second iteration of the story of JaNae and Jadyn where JaNae felt pressured to end her relationship with Wren due to her own feelings of guilt and her aversion to conflict. Just like Jadyn in the last chapter, in this chapter JaNae has her own work to do. She needs to take some time to think and explore her feelings, thoughts, and beliefs. She may ask herself, "When Jadyn expressed his anxiety and anger, I immediately felt guilty and ashamed. Why?" And she may realize that her next thought was, "It's selfish of me to want something that would make him unhappy."

Or, she might hear cultural messages in her mind saying, "A good wife puts her spouse's needs first."

Challenging these beliefs can be difficult, and the more deeply ingrained they are, the more difficult it is to change them. Also, the amount of resistance from the partner or other person increases the difficulty. Often, professional help is needed. But some tools can be helpful, even outside of therapy. Here are some suggestions:

1. **Identify *your* wants and needs independent of other people's wants and needs.** If this is difficult, try imagining that other people will happily accept your wants and needs and give no resistance. Or imagine there are no other people affected by you having the thing you want. Let yourself feel how it would feel to have that thing. Use this to determine whether you want it.

2. **Try imagining the same scenario but replace you and your partner with two other people in your imagination.** Reimagine the whole scene using these other people with all the same dialogue and actions. If you find yourself thinking, "They (the person playing out your part of the dialogue) shouldn't have to put up with that," ask yourself why you allow this person more respect and autonomy than you allow yourself.

3. **Try changing the genders (or ages, or races, or physical abilities, or life circumstances) of the imaginary actors.** By doing this, if you have a different emotional response such as in #2, ask yourself the same questions: "Why do I afford this other person more rights, more autonomy, and more humanity than I allow myself in the same situation?"

4. **If you identify cultural or identity-related components to your deeply ingrained thoughts, read extensively on equality for that social identity.** All people can benefit from reading material on equality in relationships, whether that is based on gender, race, age, ability, socio-economic status, or any other potential factor subject to a social power imbalance.

5. **Join support groups and discussion groups with other people who have similar struggles.** Social support and validation can be very helpful in learning to value ourselves equally.

6. **Journal daily about when you feel you are accommodating others and you don't really want to,** and what you might do differently if you felt stronger, braver, more supported, or more independent.

7. **Start standing up for yourself, maybe in smaller ways at first, and pay attention to what responses you get and how you feel when you take different approaches.** Notice if your partner puts up no resistance and happily accommodates what you want. Are you predicting or imagining resistance that isn't there? If you do get resistance, consider how you might counter resistance that violates your rights. Experiment, see what works, what doesn't, and how good it feels to succeed, even in small things.

8. **Consider whether you may have an anxiety disorder.** If your partner tends to be supportive of you when you exercise your rights, but you have strong fears or anxieties that get in your way, you may have an anxiety disorder. If this is the case, you may deny yourself things you want and have a right to in order to avoid experiencing your own anxiety or panic. Anxiety disorders are very treatable and respond well to behavioral therapies. There are also medications that can help.

9. **If you realize that you are not standing up for yourself because you are avoiding conflict with the other person, or the emotional meltdown that happens when you do stand your ground, then your programming and feelings of guilt or anxiety are only part of the problem.** The other part is the controlling effect those conflicts and meltdowns have on you (and would probably have on anyone).

    a. Some controlling behavior is not intended to be controlling, but rather is a reaction to fears and anxieties the other person has not questioned. Bringing it to their attention with compassion may start them down the path of taking responsibility for their own fears and anxieties.

    b. Sometimes the behavior is simply habitual. As a child, the person may have watched adults get their way by throwing tantrums, and somewhere along the way they learned to get what they wanted from others by throwing tantrums, too. If this is all they know, they may think this is normal behavior in relationships. They may not intend this behavior to be controlling or abusive, but it is.

c. Other times, the behavior is conscious. When controlling behavior is conscious and intentional, the other person will often escalate this behavior when you try to stand up for yourself, in order to regain control over you. You may want to ask yourself some serious questions about whether you wish to continue in that relationship or step back from it. You may also wish to reach out for community or professional support in making these decisions.

Conclusion

Internal obstacles are the painful emotions that arise within yourself that block you or interfere with you defending your rights and rightful boundaries. Like most feelings, they are a result of your thoughts, beliefs, and values. You can develop a stronger individual identity and promote your mental and emotional health by reflecting on these thoughts, beliefs, and values and by working to shape them in the direction that will promote your self-esteem and self-respect.

Your rights and your rightful boundaries should not be ignored, forcibly challenged, or coercively pressured away. Whether you feel that pressure coming from another person or from within yourself, it would be unhealthy for you and for the relationship to allow yourself to be pressured into something you don't really want.

Yet, some of the most beautiful, healthy, and loving interactions in relationships happen when we consciously, voluntarily, give something we don't have to give. When two people negotiate a solution to a problem in their relationship, often one or both people voluntarily choose to give up something to which they technically have a right. This is a beautiful gift that increases the safety, bonding, and trust in the relationship.

Clearly this would be beneficial for the relationship—and healthy relationships enrich the lives of the individuals in them. How can we tell if an agreement or compromise is healthy or unhealthy?

Healthy accommodations and healthy relationship agreements are the subject of the next chapter.

Part 3

Working Together

CHAPTER 8

Healthy Relationship Agreements

In this chapter, we will learn:

- what relationship agreements are and how they differ from individual rights
- how relationship agreements create safety and security in a relationship
- how to respond to relationship agreements ethically
- what you need to ensure that a relationship agreement is healthy.

What are relationship agreements?

In a way, relationships are defined by their agreements. Without relationship agreements, we are untethered individuals and nobody expects much of anything from us, other than a basic respect for their individual rights.

When we engage in a relationship, we make agreements with the other person or people that they can expect certain things from us: a certain amount of time, attention, a certain kind of affection, perhaps financial support, certain living arrangements, emotional processing, and more.

Some common expectations for attachment-bonded relationships include explicit or implicit relationship agreements to provide the ingredients for a safe haven, a secure base, and attunement. I'll discuss these expectations in chapter 10.

Each relationship agreement we make with another person is a commitment to not exercise some expression of one of our rights.

Monogamy can be whatever the people involved choose to make it, but for most people, sexual exclusivity is central to their understanding of the expectations of monogamy. The expectation of sexual exclusivity is an example of a relationship agreement. When two people agree to be sexually exclusive, they are both agreeing to not exercise a particular expression of their right to full bodily and sexual autonomy. They are agreeing to only have physical sexual contact with each other.

Similarly, if my nesting partner[58] and I want to have barrier-free sex, we might negotiate with each other about what we need in order to feel safe doing that. We may decide to always use barriers with other partners so that we can mitigate the risk of not using them with each other. This is also an agreement to not exercise our individual right to this aspect of full bodily and sexual autonomy.

This agreement doesn't mean either of us is giving up the entire right to full bodily and sexual autonomy. We have only agreed to not exercise this particular expression of that right. Most people, whether they are agreeing to sexual exclusivity or to the use of barriers with other partners, retain the right to decide for themselves when and how they will have sex with their partner or partners. They reserve the right to say yes or no to any individual sexual invitation from a partner. And they typically retain the right to determine for themselves other things related to bodily autonomy, such as if they want to get a tattoo, take up an exercise program, or have cosmetic surgery.

Another example might be a relationship agreement to share finances. Often, people choose to share finances with a nesting partner. When they do, they are agreeing to not exercise the right to autonomous control over how they spend their money. They make an agreement to discuss expenditures and make decisions together.

Some people may negotiate completely shared finances. Others will negotiate sharing a portion of their finances to pay shared expenses and retain individual allowances where they have autonomous control over deciding how to spend that portion of money.

For a relationship, an agreement means that each partner can now expect the other person or people to limit themselves and their behavior to fit the agreement they made together. Relationship agreements are both a

---

58 A nesting partner means a partner you live with. This term usually suggests a higher level of commitment, such as long-term planning, sharing a home life, and possibly raising children.

responsibility and an extension of trust. We have a responsibility to live up to the relationship agreements we make, and if we fail to do so, our partners may experience this as a violation of trust, depending on the circumstances and intent.

The many forms of dominant/submissive (D/s) relationships also include multiple freely negotiated relationship agreements. As in egalitarian relationships, in a D/s relationship, these are agreements to not exercise some iteration of our individual rights, and they create an expectation for both people that they can expect certain behaviors from the other person.

For example, if a submissive negotiates turning over decision-making authority regarding their wardrobe or food choices to their dominant, they have agreed to accept without resistance their dominant telling them what to wear or eat. Their agreement may be limited to certain circumstances, such as social occasions, or when going to the club, or it may apply all the time. And in order for the submissive to feel cared for and to trust the dominant with this authority, the dominant typically agrees to take the submissive's needs, wants, and goals into account. For example:

> Andrew had always been a picky eater. Early in the relationship, his dominant Kiara asked him in what parts of his life he would like to grow. Two areas he told her about were to better tolerate publicly embarrassing moments and to expand the variety of foods he likes or can tolerate.
>
> Kiara creatively combined these two goals and relished in finding public moments to instruct Andrew to eat something outside his limited palate. This was especially fun for Kiara at BDSM and Leather events because she could be open with the people around them and create an active audience for Andrew's act of submission. This increased the embarrassment for Andrew, giving him a better challenge to his limits.
>
> This arrangement was fulfilling for both of them. Kiara and Andrew both enjoyed Andrew's submission and over time, Andrew expanded his palate and became stronger in his ability to tolerate public embarrassment. Andrew felt cared for because he could easily see the effort Kiara put into taking his goals and needs into account. As well, if he ever experienced one of these moments as

harmful, rather than growth-inducing, they had a system in place for him to discuss this with Kiara.

Based on their freely negotiated agreement, Kiara could expect Andrew to submit to her instructions about what to eat without resistance, and Andrew could expect Kiara to tailor her instructions to things that would help him grow in certain areas of life.

With all relationship agreements, whether the relationship is egalitarian or some form of D/s, it's beneficial to have open communication where the people involved can continually check in with each other regarding how the agreements are working for each of them.

It's also important to be able to be flexible and remember the responsibility we have to adjust agreements. The rights we and our partners have chosen to not exercise due to an agreement are still always our respective rights. An agreement to not exercise a right must be voluntary and consensual at the outset and must continue to be voluntary and consensual throughout the relationship.

If an agreement is no longer working for our partner, they have the right to withdraw from that agreement. It benefits us and our partner to be flexible and willing to renegotiate when an agreement is no longer fulfilling for both people. If we really need that specific agreement in place, but our partner no longer wants it, then we may have to accept this as an incompatibility and thus it may signal the possible end of the relationship. Here's an example of an incompatibility in a D/s relationship:

When Condalese entered the Master/slave relationship with Dominic, she turned over control of her daily wardrobe. She assumed he would take her needs into account and didn't think to negotiate any details of what, when, or how this would apply.

When we met, she said to me, "Dominic gets really turned on dressing me up in very short skirts, heavy make-up, and low-cut tops. I don't mind wearing these things 90% of the time, but it feels really inappropriate to wear them to school-related functions for my kids.

"I worry that I'm embarrassing my children. It's very difficult to keep my undergarments covered when sitting on the bleachers during a sports event. And I worry what the teachers and other parents think of me and my parenting.

"I would want Dominic to care about these things too and not want me to make a poor impression in this area of life. I mean, surely he wouldn't dress me this way if I had to go to court for something, would he?"

I asked her how they negotiated this at the beginning of their relationship.

"In all honesty," she said, "I didn't want to negotiate details. I wanted to experience his control, and questioning him about how he would apply this before I agreed to it felt like I was still in control. It felt like a turn-off, so I didn't do it.

"But now," she continued, "I try to tell him about the problems this is causing for me and my children during our check-ins, but he's not changing anything. He says if I only wore these clothes when I wanted to, then he wouldn't really be in control. He still has me wearing super-short skirts and heavy make-up to my son's sporting events."

It turned out that Dominic and Condalese had very different and ultimately irreconcilable ideas about what they wanted from a power dynamic relationship. Condalese wanted to give up control to a benevolent dominant who took her needs and preferences into account. She imagined she would experience feelings of safety and love from this, and she wanted to succeed at living up to his expectations and be praised for her good and attentive service.

Dominic wanted to push past her limits and expected her to perform service with no expectation of praise. If she performed well under his expectations, this was a sign to him to push her further outside her perceived limits. He expressed that he only felt he had control when he was administering punishments. For him, the reward was in knowing she was submitting to something she genuinely didn't want, and when she hesitated, resisted, or failed, he had the power to punish.

Either model could be a workable power dynamic if both people involved truly experienced the model as rewarding. However, both Condalese and Dominic had expectations that weren't rewarding for the other person.

Condalese decided to take back control of what she wore when she felt Dominic's choices were damaging her or her children. Dominic experienced this as a violation of their relationship agreement. Because they had such different desires for a D/s dynamic, they were not able to renegotiate.

Eventually Condalese chose to end the relationship altogether. This experience helped her to learn about herself and what she needed in order for a power dynamic to be rewarding. Later, she used this information to query prospective masters before deciding whether to get involved.

Though it may be easier to imagine a dominant giving an instruction and a submissive either achieving or failing to achieve the expectation, dominants can also fail to live up to expectations. Being a dominant involves taking on responsibilities, and those responsibilities can sometimes be beyond the abilities or desires of a given individual. Here's an example.

Tanya didn't know what to do. She was in a D/s relationship with Kendal.

"I literally passed out on the MARTA train. [MARTA is Atlanta's public transit system.] Kendal is in charge of arranging for my basic needs like food. He tells me when and what I can eat," she began. "He's also been depressed a lot this whole year and has trouble getting up and moving in the mornings.

"We were meeting friends that day and we were running late, so we left the house without eating. Because I'm hypoglycemic, and because he's forgotten to ensure I eat in the past, he's told me to let him know when I need to eat soon. So, I told him when we were leaving the house that I needed to eat soon. He said he would take care of it.

"By the time we got to the train station, I was feeling light-headed. I told him again that I needed to eat soon. He said he would take care of it, that he intended to feed me after we met up with Bob and Karen.

"We got downtown and found Bob and Karen, but by then we were still running late and needed to get to the event, and find two more friends meeting us at the venue. So, we got back on the train to go to the event without feeding me and a few minutes later, I passed out. Completely passed out. I was lucky I didn't hit my head."

She felt angry about this and also sad and disappointed. She feared that taking back control of her food and eating would further depress Kendal and damage their relationship. But she also felt he wasn't capable, in his current depressed state, of living up to these expectations. "In fact," she said, "When he's depressed like this, he's not good at keeping up with his self-care. Expecting him to manage the self-care of two people just seems to overwhelm his mental resources."

Based on their agreement, Kendal expected Tanya to wait until he arranged for her to eat, and Tanya expected Kendal to prioritize the timing and substance of her food to fit her medical needs. Truthfully, Kendal also expected this of himself. But due to his inability to manage time and make flexible and assertive decisions, he was not able to live up to those expectations.

How do relationship agreements differ from individual rights?

Your individual rights are human rights. They are innate, and you never lose them. You might live many years without knowing what your rights are. You may negotiate them away for long periods of time. But you never lose them. You *always* have the right to take them back.

This is reflected in Right #12 from the list in chapter 5: You have the right to withdraw your consent to any previously made relationship agreement at any time.

Also, you don't need anyone's consent to exercise your rights. If you want to leave a relationship, you can leave it. Your partner does not need to agree. If you don't want to have sex, you don't have to. Your potential sex partner does not have to agree or be happy about it. Why? Because it's your body and you have the right to decide what you do with it. If you are the sole owner of a car, and you want to sell it, you can.

Relationship agreements are different from individual rights. First, a relationship agreement always involves more than one person. It can involve two people or any number of people.

Since the agreement doesn't belong solely to one person, one person cannot unilaterally change the agreement (except to withdraw from it). If my partner and I have an agreement to use barriers when having sex with other people, I can't just change the agreement without her consent. I can withdraw from the agreement without my partner's consent, because of Right #12. But that's a kind of nuclear option and can easily damage the trust and security in my relationship. Though I *can* withdraw from an agreement at any time, if I want a healthy, secure relationship, I must also show care and consideration for my partner's feelings, wants, and needs. Therefore, it's a better idea to renegotiate the agreement rather than unilaterally withdraw from it.

Remembering that I have the right to withdraw from an agreement without the other person's consent or approval is helpful when the other person refuses to be open to discussion or renegotiation, or when someone is being manipulative, coercive, or abusive.

Relationship agreements, like the relationship itself, belong to all of the people involved in the agreement. I do not have the right to change relationship agreements without the consent of the other people involved.

Here's an example. I have the right to control my career, livelihood and income. In my relationships, I haven't negotiated that away. But I know that many decisions I might make regarding my career could affect my relationships and the agreements I've made within those relationships.

If I make a career choice that would cause me to travel frequently or for long periods of time, this could impact the agreements my partner, my metamour, and I have about sharing a home, caring for pets, and spending a certain amount of time together. Such a choice would also impact my relationship with my girlfriend and agreements we have about the frequency of time we spend together. Therefore, I know that decisions about my career that would impact my relationship agreements should be discussed with my partner, metamour, and my girlfriend because they would be affected and they should have input into how these agreements are renegotiated.

I also know that their feelings of safety and security in our relationships are dependent on them knowing that their feelings matter to me. Therefore, I want to know how they each feel about potential changes. And I want them to know I will take their feelings into account before making decisions that will impact them. If I want to make a change, I have a right to make that change, but if any of them have feelings about it, we will either negotiate an agreement that resolves their feelings or they will work on resolving their own feelings. I will do my best to wait on implementing changes until that work is done and their feelings are resolved.

In short, any relationship agreement that my partner and I have is owned by both of us and requires us both to agree. Because my partner, myself, and my metamour live together, many agreements (such as where we will live, shared time together, vacation travel, monthly bills, and home repairs) belong to all three of us, and we must all agree.

We do not use a majority vote method because it could easily lead to one person feeling ganged up on by the other two. All decisions that affect all three of us are decided by a unanimous vote. If we don't all agree, we must continue discussing and exploring new options until we find one that we can all agree to.

Likewise, the agreements I have with my girlfriend belong to both of us. Because our relationship is of a lesser degree of commitment, we both assume our agreements are more flexible and more subject to change. But I would still seek her input and demonstrate that her feelings, needs, and expectations are important to me by trying to renegotiate how to meet her needs and mine given the new career and travel circumstances.

The second way relationship agreements differ from individual rights is that all relationship agreements are temporary. They can always be changed, ended, or renegotiated, and new agreements can be adopted to replace old ones.

We have an ethical responsibility to be open to renegotiation when someone in the relationship needs it. Because an agreement belongs to all the people in the relationship, if someone needs change, their only options are to renegotiate or withdraw from the agreement. Withdrawal is a nuclear option that will likely damage the relationship. If their partner shuts them down when they try to renegotiate, they can feel trapped and frustrated, and may begin to believe their feelings don't matter to their partner.

Remember the story of Bill and Carol in chapter 3? Bill wanted to introduce their children to his girlfriend Janet. Bill and Carol had an agreement to conceal their other relationships from the children until they were older. Bill wanted to renegotiate that agreement. At first Carol used "shut-down language" and this left Bill feeling hurt and unheard. The second time through, Carol was open to hearing Bill's feelings, what he wanted and why. By staying open to communication, they were able to collaboratively address Bill's feelings, yet they didn't change the substance of their agreement.

Being open to renegotiation doesn't mean always giving in and giving the other person everything they want. Their feelings matter, and your feelings matter just as much. Being open to renegotiation means being open to discussion and listening to their feelings and their requests. It means asking yourself if you can give an authentic yes. If not, ask yourself what you would need in order to get to an authentic yes. Also, explore with your partner what they want to feel and if there are other possible solutions that would create the emotional experience they want and to which you could more easily, and more authentically, say yes.

We, as individuals, change. Our lives change. Our relationships change. As long as we are able to engage in open, collaborative discussion, we are showing our partners that their feelings matter to us. This allows our relationship agreements to be flexible enough to change and keep our relationships together, healthy and secure for all the people involved, and moving forward.

Action item: Reflect on your current and past relationships. Did you or do you feel comfortable exercising your rights? Did you or do you take partners' feelings into account? Are you able to continue holding the space for negotiation until you reach a voluntary and unanimous agreement? Have your partners been able to hold the space for continued negotiation while you each also acknowledge and respect each other's rights?

Relationship agreements need to change as the relationship and the individuals in it change

For many people, the thought of relationship agreements changing can bring up some intense emotions such as anxiety, fear, anger, and sadness. Why? Because relationship agreements give us safety and security in relationships! When we engage in relationships that involve intimacy (emotional, physical, or sexual) we are vulnerable to being hurt. The more vulnerable we are, the more we will seek some sort of safety and security.

In a casual sexual encounter, we may not engage the vulnerability of deep emotions, but we do engage at least a physical vulnerability. We will usually negotiate some physical safety regarding protection from sexually transmitted infections. We may also negotiate physical safety in other ways—for instance, we may say there will be no use of restraints, or agree to check in with a friend by phone at a predetermined time.

The more intense the situation (whether that be intense BDSM play, intense emotions of love, or both), the more vulnerable we are and thus the more agreements we will likely want to negotiate in order to create enough safety to contain that vulnerability. Here's an example of a vulnerable situation two of my clients encountered.

Tom and Susan had been together 20 years and both knew they were bisexual from the beginning, but they had also always been monogamous with one another.

Tom found his desire to explore his attractions to other men growing and he wanted to act on it. He feared it would end his marriage, but when he told Susan, she suggested they open their marriage.

As they sat in my office, it was clear they were renegotiating the terms of their marriage. Their old relationship agreement of monogamy was out. A new openness was on the table and being negotiated.

At first, Susan was more comfortable with the extramarital relationships being casual hookups. But Tom didn't want to limit his explorations to casual sex. He wanted the possibility of meaningful relationships.

Susan was able to agree. "As long as we continue to have a real marriage. I don't want to live like housemates. I want us to put the effort in to have romance and desire with at least a moderate sex life."

Susan needed to know her marriage was a real relationship (based on her definition of what is real) in order to risk the vulnerability of an open marriage and not feel like she was being neglected or taken advantage of. This is what she needed to feel emotionally safe and to get to an authentic yes.

By suggesting this agreement, she was spelling out what behaviors she and Tom could expect from one another. Tom could expect that Susan would not object to him developing meaningful sexual and romantic relationships with other men. And Susan could expect that Tom would continue to put in effort toward keeping romance and sexuality alive in his relationship with her.

If Tom was not willing to agree to this and live up to that agreement, Susan had every right to withdraw her consent to opening up the relationship, or to being in it. If Tom knew he was unwilling to live up to this agreement, he could say so, and if they were unable to form a new agreement, this would likely end their marriage or end the possibility of opening their marriage.

The price of admission: Know yourself and tell others what you need up front

Each person is different. Each person wants or needs different things when they engage in relationships. Many of these are not actually rights, but things they need to negotiate in the form of agreements. A client of mine put it in a way I found insightful:

> James was relaying a story to me about how his primary girlfriend had anxiety anytime he was with one of his other girlfriends. She wanted to know, well in advance, where he was planning to be and what he was planning to do so that she could prepare herself emotionally.
>
> If his plans changed at the last minute, she would have a great deal of anxiety and her mind would plague her with thoughts that James was lying to her about many things, including how committed he was to her.
>
> James struggled under the weight of these requirements and found himself making mistakes that would trigger his girlfriend's anxiety.
>
> I asked him if he wanted to renegotiate this agreement with her… if maybe he didn't want to have to tell her his agenda in advance. I asked if he wanted to have more flexibility to be spontaneous when with his other girlfriends.
>
> "Sure I would," he said, "but I knew when I got involved with her that this was the price of admission. She's not able, or maybe not willing, to work on her anxiety. So, if I'm going to be involved with her, agreeing to do this to help her with her anxiety is the price of admission. And I'm willing to pay it."

We should all know ourselves well, and know what we need from others as our "price of admission." I've also heard these called "deal-breakers." Knowing ourselves and knowing what we need from a partner in a relationship is part of having a strong, clear personal identity. We all need our individual rights to be respected by our partners in relationships. And if we know our deal-breakers, we can present them early in a new relationship and get agreement from a partner that these will also be respected. Here's an example:

> Taniesha was a person with a history of childhood sexual abuse. Though she had done a great deal of healing, certain things were still triggering for her. After some thought and reflection, she decided that she needed the people she was involved with to be sensitive to the fact that she might get triggered. She wanted them to avoid talking about sexual assault around her. She wanted to avoid being exposed to news programs where she might see or hear stories of sexual assault.
>
> She reflected on her past relationships and breakups and decided she needed her current and future partners to respond by not taking it personally if she became triggered. She wanted them to respond by backing off and asking her what she needed. She needed them to be gentle, concerned, and attentive when she was triggered.
>
> As well, a few specific things or words were triggering to her. Even a casual sexual partner would need to agree, up front, to not do or say those things if they are going to be sexual with Taniesha. That was her price of admission. If anyone wanted to get involved but couldn't or wouldn't agree to those ground rules, Taniesha would end her involvement with them and walk away.

Remember, we have a right to make boundaries around things directly related to our human rights. Some of these are so universal that they're codified into our laws, allowing us to use the power of the courts to enforce our rights. However, most of the time, we're dependent on people voluntarily choosing to respect our rights, and this book is full of suggestions for how to talk with people in such a way as to encourage them to do so.

Price-of-admission or deal-breaker issues, and the boundaries we require around them, occupy a special category. Sometimes they are very clearly linked to our rights. Sometimes they are accommodations that would normally not be considered rights because they also infringe upon other people's freedoms. The more tenuous the connection between the accommodation and a right, the more a person should consider it a gift and express gratitude for it.

For example, due to Taniesha's history of sexual trauma, she may have a boundary prohibiting certain sexual experiences or touch. She absolutely has the right to demand a person only touch her in ways she agrees to. However, she may also feel triggered when walking into a room and someone else is watching a crime show with a sexual assault victim. Asking other people to not watch certain shows has only a tenuous connection to a right and is actually an accommodation she needs to ask for.

The difference is that with other accommodations, I have said that we can ask, but we must be prepared to gracefully accept no for an answer. With price-of-admission or deal-breaker issues, we need to ask, but also know that we can't really accept no for an answer without doing damage to ourselves.

It helps to own our issues when explaining deal-breakers to other people and to be careful to not lash out at them if they are unwilling to accommodate us. And we must also stand our ground, be true to ourselves, and gracefully explain that the closeness of our relationship with a given person is contingent on their willingness to provide this accommodation.

In practice, it might sound like this:

Taniesha: Because of my trauma history, I get really triggered when I walk into a room and hear a TV show or podcast talking about a sexual assault experience. If we are going to live together, I need to know I can move freely around the house without fear of overhearing that.

Her partner: But I really like crime shows. I want to watch them. I have a right to watch them if I want.

Taniesha: Yes, that's true. You do have a right to watch them. However, I also have the right to feel safe in my home, and my trauma history isn't something I can change. I need this if we are going to live together. Can we talk about ways you can watch these shows without me being exposed to them? I'd like us to have an agreement that allows you to watch them in a way that also protects me from overhearing them.

Mental health issues as disability

The concept of disability is one that some people fear, some resist strongly, and others embrace. I stated clearly that we have a right to disability accommodations. When it comes to mental health issues or diagnoses, when is something a disability?

I don't feel it's very helpful to look for some kind of outside metric such as governmental criteria where a person has to prove their symptoms are "bad enough" to qualify as a disability. Instead, I want to foster an ethic of compassion, mutual respect for the vast differences among people, and self-determination.

I am a psychotherapist and my job often involves educating clients about mental health symptoms, diagnoses, and treatments. I also help people accept where they are at the moment and to cope with their symptoms in ways that result in less pain and improved relationships. And I encourage interventions and treatments that can reduce people's symptoms, reduce their suffering, and even resolve their symptoms.

Each person has the right to decide for themselves what symptoms they wish to challenge, what interventions they are willing to do, and what symptoms they would rather accept and integrate into their identity.

Based on my knowledge and experience, some mental health symptoms are more immutable, and for these I believe it's important to aim for positive acceptance and integrate these into our identities. Some examples include symptoms of autism spectrum disorder (ASD), attention deficit disorder (ADD and ADHD), bipolar disorder, and brain changes due to post-traumatic stress disorder (PTSD). There's even a peer-based movement to include the many forms of hallucinations and psychosis as something we'd do better to live with and integrate than to fight against or highly medicate.[59]

Some mental health symptoms respond well to medication, such as anxiety, depression, the mood swings of bipolar disorder, and some ADD/ADHD symptoms. Other diagnoses have considerable potential for resolution through behavioral changes and talk therapy, such as anxiety, obsessive-compulsive disorder (OCD), depression, PTSD symptoms, eating disorders, and addiction. But "potential" means that although sometimes

---

59 Daniel Bergner, 2022. "Doctors gave her antipsychotics. She decided to live with her voices." *New York Times*, May 17. https://www.nytimes.com/2022/05/17/magazine/antipsychotic-medications-mental-health.html

the symptoms improve, sometimes they don't, even after considerable time and effort.

Whether a person is simply accepting where they are right now or has accepted some or all of their symptoms as immutable and chosen to integrate them into their understanding of who they are as a person, if they need accommodations from others for their mental and emotional health, I would consider those accommodations to fall under what I call disability accommodations.

For example, post-traumatic stress disorder (PTSD) is a mental health diagnosis that results in real, physical changes in brain structure, and is thus a disability for which accommodations are often needed. The brain changes that occur in PTSD are sometimes referred to as brain damage. I find that verbiage offensive. These brain changes are a form of neurodivergence, and like ASD or ADHD, they only become disadvantageous when the person is required to participate in a world designed for neurotypical or non-traumatized people.

These brain changes are in some ways beneficial and adaptive when a person is living in a dangerous environment. The resulting symptoms—hypervigilance, hyperarousal, avoidance, and multiple forms of dissociation—help a person survive, function, and avoid additional trauma when living in an ongoing trauma-inducing environment.

I encourage healing PTSD because some of its other symptoms—such as night terrors and flashbacks—are painful. As well, when we leave traumatizing environments and move to safer environments, symptoms that were once adaptive (hypervigilance, hyperarousal, avoidance and dissociation) can be maladaptive and become additional sources of pain.

The idea of healing is not meant to suggest a person returns to how they would have been if the trauma had never happened. We are forever changed by traumatic experiences and healing involves developing peace, happiness, and functionality that doesn't attempt to deny the powerful changes of our life experiences.

The same is true for a person with diagnoses of ADD/ADHD, ASD, or bipolar disorder. With ADD/ADHD a person might need accommodations such as compassion for their tendency to be late, lose things, or get distracted and leave a task half done, or they might need support for their need to take medication.

A person with ASD might need compassion for when they become overstimulated and need to escape to a soothing environment, support and appreciation for their special interests, acceptance of stimming behaviors, and forgiveness for their tendency to interrupt or monologue.

A person with bipolar disorder might need support for their need to take medication, support and assistance avoiding disruptions to their schedule that might increase the likelihood of manic or depressive episodes such as working overtime, losing sleep, or traveling, and compassion for the episodes that will most likely happen even with medication and stable daily routines.

When are symptoms of mental illness and neurodivergence a disability? They're a disability when a person decides they're a disability. Whether they accept the symptoms as immutable, they decide they no longer wish to challenge their symptoms, or they are simply honoring where they are at this time as they toggle back and forth between self-acceptance and working toward healing, they have the right to create boundaries and ask for accommodations around those symptoms.

In my experience, deal-breakers and price-of-admission accommodations are often built around mental health issues, diagnoses, and emotional vulnerabilities. Whether the accommodation you're asking for is practical or emotional, own it as yours. Accept that other people are free to say no. But with regard to deal-breaker issues, instead of encouraging you to question yourself, this time I'm encouraging you to stand your ground. It's wonderful to be willing to negotiate on *how* the price-of-admission need is met, but not on *whether* the need is met. If the other person won't agree to respect what you need, be prepared to limit the relationship, end the relationship, or provide some other solution that still works for you.

Action item: Reflect on your past and current relationships and what you know about yourself. Identify as best you can what you need in a relationship. Review the list. How many of these are your rights? Do you feel comfortable demanding these? How many of these are your deal-breakers or your price of admission? Do you feel comfortable requiring these accommodations? Could you walk away from, or reduce the depth of vulnerability in or commitment to a relationship with someone who declines to respect either your rights or your deal breakers? If not, why not?

Disability accommodations and abuse

I have also seen the concept of disability accommodations wielded in an abusive manner in relationships. Mental health accommodations, in particular, are easily abused by manipulative people. Here are some examples:

Panuk and Reginald lived together and came to me to work through some issues in their relationship. Panuk struck me as nervous and admitted that he felt like he walked on eggshells in every interaction with Reginald.

After a few sessions, I began to see a pattern. Anytime Panuk expressed that he felt unsafe, or felt fear or discomfort in the relationship, Reginald insisted this was a trauma trigger for him. He said that he experienced extensive teasing in school because he was big and strong and this trauma was triggered if anyone expressed fear of him. I also noticed that when Panuk tried to express that Reginald had engaged in behavior that harmed others and asked him to take responsibility, Reginald said this was a trauma trigger, too. He said his father humiliated him as a child by making him accept blame.

I expressed compassion for Reginald's trauma and expressed that for a relationship to be healthy, we need to be compassionate toward trauma triggers, but we also need to allow space for our partners to be honest about how they feel, and we need to apologize and make amends when we harm others. I then asked him how Panuk might say these things in a non-triggering way.

Reginald didn't answer my question, and an expression crossed his eyes that, in my opinion, was cold and frightening. They did not return for another session.

It's been my experience that when a person is consciously, intentionally manipulative or abusive, they rarely agree to therapy. When they do show up in therapy, they have been dragged there by their partner. When I begin to challenge their controlling or abusive behaviors, they find a reason to not return. Here's another example.

It had been nine months since the dramatic and traumatic end of Viraj's marriage. We spent the first month battling his suicidal thoughts. We spent the next couple of months decreasing his depression symptoms. Then, we worked on building his self-esteem and processing the damaging aspects of his relationship with his former spouse.

"I think I'm beginning to feel grateful that my marriage ended," he said. "I was always so tense around Brinda. She accused me of being abusive for the smallest things. The other day, I stubbed my toe and I yelled in pain. Then I felt panic because I yelled in the house. In the past, Brinda would have accused me of being abusive because I triggered her trauma, even if I wasn't yelling at her. Even if it was just a natural expression of pain or surprise.

"There are other things, too," he continued. "She accused me of being physically abusive when I came home wearing a cologne someone gave me at the office holiday party. She said I knew her allergies were so severe that it could be life-threatening to her. She accused me of trying to kill her!

"I don't dismiss allergies. They can be severe. But to accuse me of intending to kill her? That really hurt me. I thought I'd just forgotten. But she had me questioning if I am a bad person at my core. I think this had a lot to do with how depressed I became."

I'll discuss intentionally manipulative and abusive behavior in greater depth in my next book, but for now I want to acknowledge that abusive people can easily misuse the concept of mental health accommodations as a way of not accepting responsibility for their intentionally harmful behaviors.

I believe the key is in what attitude we have toward other people when we're seeking disability accommodations. If we use the concept as an entitlement to compassion and accommodations from others without also extending compassion toward them, and if we use this as an opportunity to tell others they are bad or abusive people if they don't give us the accommodations we want or need, then we are most likely being abusive in how we are employing this concept.

When we negotiate the accommodations we need for our mental and emotional issues, I encourage balance. Those of us with mental health diagnoses must remember that even though we have a right to the accommodations we need, our symptoms impact others, often in painful ways. We must always strive to remember to validate the other person's experience, and express compassion for any pain or harm our symptoms cause them.

This is where it helps to try and be flexible about how our accommodation needs are met, even as we stand firm that we need accommodation. Being flexible about how the need is met offers others the opportunity to meet our needs while we are also being compassionate toward theirs.

Respect for boundaries and agreements creates trust and safety

I believe that one of the reasons we think of personal boundaries as being in conflict with happy relationships is because we imagine individual boundaries as being about saying no to people, and happy relationships about saying yes.

All this talk of individual rights and boundaries might leave you imagining that I'm encouraging people to say no to each other a lot or to set a lot of limits and to be on the defensive. Nothing could be further from the truth! I encourage saying yes to our partners. As long as the yes is an authentic yes, said for the right reasons, and coming from a healthy place.

Knowing our rights and boundaries and the other person's rights and boundaries, and respecting those boundaries, creates safety and security in a relationship. Knowing that my partners, friends, and colleagues are on the lookout for my boundaries and intend to protect and respect them, whether I am aware and do anything to defend those boundaries or not, makes me feel respected, safe, valued, and loved.

The safety and security that come from healthy boundaries and relationship agreements, along with acceptance and affection, are what make true intimacy possible. When people violate each other's rights, stomp across each other's rightful boundaries, or violate relationship agreements, damage is done to the relationship. Trust is violated. Safety is compromised.

When a person doesn't feel safe in a relationship, when they don't trust a partner will abide by a boundary or live up to an agreement, they will likely seek safety in other ways. One way is to increase their control. They may do this with surveillance, monitoring, demands, or guilt trips. All of these behaviors tend to damage the relationship. A different way to seek safety is to withdraw. They may create physical or emotional distance. They may share less information or withdraw from physical affection. This also tends to damage a relationship.

Action item: Review your relationships. Can you identify patterns of control or withdrawal by you or any of your partners? Can you identify the safety issue that led to that behavior? Can you address this issue with yourself or your partner and discuss what rights need to be respected or what agreements need to be honored or negotiated to create the safety needed to either let go of the controlling behavior or re-engage instead of withdrawing?

How do you know if a relationship agreement is healthy?

Most often, when I see people violate relationship agreements, it's because they never actually wanted the agreement in the first place. Maybe they thought the agreement was silly or unnecessary, or they felt unfairly con-trolled by it. So, when they thought they might not get caught, they did what they always felt they had a right to do. Here's a scenario along these lines:

Ronald and Xander had been together for several years. Xander struggled to feel safe in an open relationship. Because of Xander's pain and emotional distress, Ronald had put his relationship with Jasmine on hold for months, though he also felt resentful and controlled.

Last week Ronald went to see Jasmine. He and Xander had agreed this was to be a get-together without sex. When he got home, Ronald said all had gone as planned. Three days later, Ronald admitted that he and Jasmine had sex during their meeting.

Upon questioning, Ronald said he was now telling the truth because Jasmine was telling her husband and Xander was friends with the husband. Ronald wanted to come clean before he was caught in the lie.

Each time Ronald failed to live up to a relationship agreement, Xander's ability to trust him was damaged. Why did Ronald agree to things he didn't actually want to agree to? Because he wanted peace. Xander would ask for limits that Ronald didn't want. When Ronald said no, Xander would become upset. He would become more animated. He would raise his voice. He would become distressed. The only way Ronald knew how to calm Xander down was to give in and agree to limits he didn't actually want.

When Ronald agreed to not have sex with Jasmine during his visit, this was not a healthy relationship agreement. Not because there was any objective measurement of whether this was a good or bad choice, but because he agreed under feelings of duress.

For a relationship agreement to be healthy, both people (or all the people) need to agree freely. The yes they give needs to be consensual and authentic.

Another reason I see people violate relationship agreements is when an old agreement is no longer working for them, but they don't feel comfortable initiating a re-negotiation of that agreement. Here's an example:

> Jorge and Sandra had been dating for some time and Jorge always used condoms due to an agreement with his wife Victoria. Sandra had no problem with the use of condoms other than they were sometimes a minor annoyance.
>
> However, Jorge had begun to resent the requirement. He believed Victoria would never agree to change this agreement and he predicted she would be really angry at him just for bringing it up. He knew he *should* bring it up, but he kept putting it off.
>
> While he was avoiding bringing this up with Victoria, he also found himself "forgetting" to put on a condom before having intercourse with Sandra.

By choosing to avoid facing an uncomfortable conversation, Jorge not only violated his agreement with Victoria, but he also delayed telling her about it, which violated her right to have information related to her consent given in an honest, clear, and timely manner.

Whether Jorge's apprehension was caused only by his fear or he had predicted accurately that Victoria would get very angry, he still had a responsibility to initiate this uncomfortable conversation.

Victoria had a responsibility to help create an environment where Jorge felt safe enough to bring up difficult topics. And they both had a responsibility to be willing to consider renegotiating agreements that were no longer working.

Notice that Victoria also has a responsibility here. It's possible that Jorge delayed renegotiating with Victoria due to the painful ways Victoria had responded to similar moments in their past. I can't emphasize this enough! Most of the time when I see a partner withhold important information, or delay bringing up difficult topics, it's because they don't feel safe. Sometimes they feel frightened or intimidated because their partner gets angry and raises their voice. Sometimes they feel shamed because their partner judges them, ridicules them, or employs guilt trips. Sometimes they feel confused because their partner intellectualizes and thinks circles around them. Sometimes they feel panicked and tortured by the emotional distress their partner displays.

If we want our partners to tell us the truth, especially truth that's difficult to hear, we must create an environment where they feel safe enough to speak their truth. They need to know we will not judge them, reject them, guilt them, or try to punish or control them if their truth is something we would rather it wasn't. We must show them we are strong enough and stable enough to accept their truth, even when we don't like it.

Action item: Reflect on relationship agreements you have made. Were any made under duress? Do you recall ever pressuring a partner to agree to something they didn't really want to agree to? Do you recall either you or a partner being so emotionally distressed that one of you may have made an agreement they didn't want, just to soothe the distressed person? In your past or current relationships, do you feel safe enough to speak your truth? Have you contributed to an environment where your past and present partners could speak their truth? Have anger, guilt, judgements, intellectualizing, punishments, emotional distress, or emotional displays by you or a partner interfered with anyone speaking their truth?

When people negotiate well, there are few things more beautiful than the love, care, and giving that happens in healthy, secure relationships. But to be healthy, the giving needs to be fully consensual, authentic, recognized, and appreciated.

Consent and authenticity

Let's address **consent** first. *Informed* consent is central to any agreement being truly consensual. In chapter 5, I was clear that one of the things we have a right to expect from others is complete, honest, and timely communication about the information we need in order to engage in informed consent.

Here's an example of where the absence of information makes a relationship agreement unhealthy:

Karen and John had been together for six years and Karen introduced the idea of opening up their relationship to polyamory. John was intrigued and also apprehensive. They did research and discussed. John was more comfortable starting with swinging and wanted both of them to be physically present during any sexual activity with other people. They agreed to attend some swinger events to see how it went.

On the surface, this appeared to be a healthy, consensual agreement. However, Karen withheld some information. She had already developed an attraction to John's cousin, Kevin. They had flirted extensively and had "accidentally" crossed a line at a Christmas party a few months earlier. She and Kevin had been drinking and kissed.

Rather than tell John about the months of flirtation and the "accidental" kissing, she hid that information and approached John about opening the relationship as if it were a totally unrelated topic.

Karen told Kevin she was working on getting John to agree to opening the relationship before John had ever agreed to it, in the hopes that Kevin would hold on to his interest in her. And she hoped that she would eventually be able to have relationships with John and Kevin at the same time.

This information might have (and probably would have) affected John's decisions regarding his willingness to consent to opening up the relationship, and thus, failing to disclose this information was a violation of his right to the information he needed in order to give his informed consent.

Open relationships require considerable trust. If he had known that Karen flirted with his cousin for months before the party, then kissed him at the party, then introduced opening the relationship without telling John this information, it is likely that John might not feel his relationship with Karen had a strong enough foundation in trust and emotional safety to agree to opening the relationship.

Authentic means that when a person is saying yes, they are saying it because they truly want to. It's important that they not be responding to internal or external obstacles. It's also important that they not be responding to some other motive such as, "If I say yes, then they will love me," or "If I say yes, this argument will finally stop and I'll get some peace." Here's an example:

Tonya and Michael had been doing polyamory fairly well for several years by seeing people who lived a long distance away. But when Michael met Jacki, someone local, Tonya felt threatened. She tried to be okay with it, but found herself inventing reasons to be upset with Jacki.

Tonya would feel particularly insecure when Michael was having a date with Jacki. Tonya would call and text Michael during these dates, asking for reassurance.

Jacki felt her very limited time with Michael was being intruded upon and asked that date time be respected and that Tonya only contact Michael for actual emergencies.

Michael stated he would like this too and presented this request to Tonya. Tonya felt this was a sign that Jacki was trying to isolate him from her and steal him away. She not only did not agree to restrict her reaching out to Michael during dates, but demanded that Michael agree to respond any time she contacted him for reassurance.

When Michael resisted agreeing to this, Tonya became distraught, and stayed distraught for hours, keeping Michael up almost all night on a work night. She threatened to end their relationship unless he ended his relationship with Jacki.

Before they became polyamorous, Michael and Tonya had settled many disagreements using the principle that the person who cares more about an issue gets their way. And Michael was tempted to break up with Jacki because Tonya clearly cared a great deal about this. But he knew he would resent Tonya if he felt forced to break up with Jacki when he didn't want to, and he also felt he and Jacki had done nothing wrong.

Had Michael agreed to break up with Jacki just to get peace in his relationship with Tonya, this would not have been an authentic agreement. He didn't really want to agree. He only felt tempted to agree because he felt pressured by Tonya's intense emotional response.

If we examine this issue through the lens of individual rights, Tonya does not have the right to require Michael to break up with someone. But Tonya does need a solution to her uncomfortable emotions of insecurity. She tried to solve that problem by asking for reassurance from Michael in the moment she was feeling the insecurity, but this became problematic because it prevented Michael and Jacki from actually enjoying their dates.

As difficult as it may be for Tonya to hear, her emotions of insecurity are primarily her responsibility to solve. Also, since this is a bonded relationship between Michael and Tonya, Michael should be very invested in helping Tonya get back to a place of security in their relationship.

If Michael and Jacki had no issue with Tonya asking for reassurance during dates, they could have continued with that method, as long as they both authentically wanted to say yes. But since that's not the case, they both need to remember that there are many possible ways to resolve Tonya's insecurity. Getting reassurance from Michael in the moment is just one way. Doing her own internal work is another way. Or they could brainstorm additional possible solutions. For instance, Michael could make a voice recording reassuring Tonya of his love and commitment to her that she can play when she feels insecure; Tonya could plan social activities to keep busy and distracted during Michael's dates; or she can compile happy photos and videos of Michael and Tonya together to look at during his dates.

This aspect of relationship agreements—that agreements need to be fully consensual and agreed to authentically—is one of the most difficult parts of building and maintaining healthy relationships. Our emotions of fear, anxiety, jealousy, and anger can be difficult to work with, and these same feelings in our partners can be difficult as well.

Gifts and appreciation

The easiest relationship agreements to negotiate are the ones where, upon discussion, you find that both (or all) people involved want the same thing. For example, when discussing safer sex practices to use with other partners, if you're both comfortable with condoms, and neither of you feels the need for dental dams, gloves, or prophylactic medications such as PrEP, this is an easy agreement to negotiate.

However, if one person is comfortable with only using PrEP and the other feels this is inadequate in order to feel safe, and they also want their partner to use condoms, gloves, and dental dams, this is a more difficult negotiation.

Good negotiation can begin with NVC and the Imago exercise. For now, I simply want to discuss the importance of having an attitude of appreciation and avoiding situations in which anyone involved in the relationship feels taken for granted. Here's an example showing where expressing appreciation was appropriate in a relationship negotiation:

Mike and Jermaine met as casual sex partners. Jermaine required they use condoms. This wasn't Mike's preference, but he understood that Jermaine had a right to require anyone having sex with him to use condoms. So Mike agreed.

Mike was primarily concerned about protecting against HIV. He wasn't that concerned about other STIs since most were treatable, and he didn't like the decreased sexual pleasure he experienced when using condoms.

Jermaine was very concerned about herpes as he knew people who experienced painful outbreaks. He also felt it was more socially responsible to not spread the treatable STIs, because some of their sex partners might not be able to easily afford medical treatments.

Two years later, they were in love and decided to move in together. They also wanted to negotiate not using condoms with each other anymore. For Jermaine to feel safe, and to feel socially responsible, he wanted both of them to take PrEP and use condoms with all other partners.

Mike never liked condoms and at first didn't want to agree to this. Jermaine expressed that he understood how Mike felt and didn't want Mike to have less sexual pleasure. He acknowledged that Mike had the right to make this decision for himself. Jermaine also expressed that he very much wanted to have condomless sex with Mike going forward, but would only feel safe if he knew that Mike was not having condomless sex with others.

"Please tell me if you can think of other ways to accomplish this, but the only two ways I can think of are for you to either use condoms with all other partners, or for you to not have other partners," Jermaine said.

Mike agreed that he couldn't think of other possible solutions. He expressed that he also wanted to be able to have condomless sex with Jermaine. He acknowledged to Jermaine that he had every right to determine what restrictions he needed to keep his body and health safe. He said he would think about his options.

Though Mike knew he wanted to be able to have condomless sex with both Jermaine and other partners, and wished Jermaine felt safe enough only using PrEP, he knew he didn't have a right to pressure Jermaine or judge his choices.

He knew he would have to choose. He could have the increased intimacy and increased sexual pleasure with Jermaine, and use condoms with others. Or he could continue using condoms with Jermaine and not use condoms with others (except when other partners also required condoms).

Ultimately, Mike came back and told Jermaine that he would agree to use condoms with all other partners, so that he and Jermaine could have condomless sex with each other.

Jermaine knew that Mike didn't owe him this. And he knew this wasn't Mike's preference. Mike was choosing what Jermaine wanted and this was a gift. Jermaine felt grateful for this gift, for this accommodation, and expressed that gratitude to Mike.

Mike felt appreciated.

When we are able to say yes to something a partner wants, even though we know we would be within our rights to say no, this is a gift. It's important that this gift be freely given and not pulled from us out of guilt or in response to manipulative or coercive tactics.

When I say that a gift needs to be **recognized,** this means that each person involved is recognizing each person's rights, and if someone is offering to give up acting on one of their rights, that is a gift. It should be recognized as a gift, not claimed as an entitlement.

When we claim these kinds of gifts as entitlements, our partners are likely to feel unappreciated, taken for granted, and possibly even controlled.

Appreciation is the appropriate response to receiving a gift. Others don't know you appreciate them unless you communicate it. Saying "thank you," or "I appreciate you," will let them know you appreciate the gift they are giving to you.

> **Action item:** Reflect on past and current relationship agreements. Did you ever feel unappreciated or taken for granted? See if you can identify the gift you were giving and how the other person could have expressed appreciation. Reflect again on relationship agreements. Can you identify a time or times when you could have expressed appreciation for a gift or accommodation and did not? Can you express that now?

Next, let's look at a more complicated example. In this story, both members of the couple choose to make concessions—eventually. Let's take a look at the beginning of their process.

Lisa and Susan had been together almost six years. They considered themselves nesting partners and shared a home in a suburb north of Atlanta. Lisa was dating another person named Deb and though Susan had been happy for Lisa at first, she had grown increasingly resentful of the money Lisa spent on dates with Deb, as they went out to eat and bought tickets to events and concerts. Deb was a graduate student on a tight budget and Lisa tended to pick up the tab most of the time.

It came to a head when Lisa said she wanted to have a weekend getaway with Deb to Tybee Island. Susan knew this would include an AirBnB rental, gas money, and several meals at restaurants.

Susan felt hurt and neglected and began to object to the situation. She said to Lisa, "I feel like second best, like the old doll replaced by a new, bright, shiny doll. You spend all this money on Deb, and you and I never go out and do anything anymore. I haven't had a weekend getaway with you in two years."

She then insisted on what she thought the solution would be: "No weekend getaway with Deb until I get one. Cut your spending in half for dates with Deb, and start taking me out. In fact, I'm your nesting partner, so I should get more than half. I think I'm being pretty generous."

Lisa felt confused and hurt and fired back at Susan, "You and I had an agreement to share living expenses, and for the last year, you've only worked part-time. I think I've been pretty generous to financially supplement you for the last year, but you're talking as though my money is your money. I'm not feeling very appreciated right now."

Susan began to cry and said, "We're nesting partners. That's like a marriage. I know we had that agreement, but when my current job dropped me to part-time, I thought we settled into a new agreement. I started doing more of the housework. You never complained. I thought you were okay with this."

Lisa said, "Well, I'm not. I don't want this to be a permanent financial arrangement. I've been waiting for you to get full-time employment and getting increasingly resentful that it doesn't look like you're trying."

Susan admitted that she felt considerable anxiety about the job-hunting process. She said to Lisa, "You've seen how my anxiety has gotten worse and worse. When my full-time job dropped me to part-time, I just couldn't face the interview process and the rejection of job-hunting. I thought that since you're my nesting partner, I should be able to count on you for financial support."

Susan insisted that her anxiety made the interview process impossible and she couldn't handle the stress of full-time work. She said she had tried to make up for it by doing more of the household chores, "and isn't that labor worth something?" And she reminded Lisa, "You were unemployed for four months, four years ago, and I paid when we went out together during that time." Susan still felt her demand for equity in the money spent on dates was fair.

Lisa felt torn and confused. She had compassion for Susan's anxiety, and it was true that they hadn't spent money on dates or travel, but she did spend more than 75% of her non-working time with Susan. They cooked at home and watched movies together.

Lisa also didn't like feeling pressured into becoming the primary breadwinner without getting a chance to consent or not consent. She was also feeling resentful that Susan seemed to be laying claim to having a say over how Lisa spent her money as though they had shared ownership of Lisa's money. She hadn't consented to that either.

But she felt guilty. Susan was making some relevant points. She believed that household labor was worth the same as paid labor, so maybe Susan was "working full-time." Was she being a bad partner by not recognizing and valuing this?

Deb had been working hard in her graduate program and Lisa really wanted to give her a treat. She wanted to plan this trip with Deb for the semester break coming up in eight weeks and time was running out.

Susan was clearly very hurt. And, since Lisa was not agreeing to make the changes she required, she began questioning Lisa's commitment to her and their relationship. She put her foot down and threatened to break up with Lisa if she moved forward with planning the trip to Tybee Island with Deb.

Lisa felt confused and backed into a corner. She knew if she agreed to what Susan was demanding, she would feel resentful. But she didn't know if her resentment was justified. She worried that she was being selfish, and a bad partner. Because she feared this might be true, she felt guilty and ashamed.

Guidelines

First, if Lisa or Susan agree to anything due to feeling pressured, these will not be healthy, consensual, authentic relationship agreements. In this scenario, Lisa is experiencing both internal and external pressure. Her internal pressure is the guilt and self-judgment she is experiencing. The external pressure is Susan's strong emotions, her rationalizations for why she believes her view is fair, and her threat to break up with Lisa if she doesn't accept the solution Susan presented.

For a relationship agreement to be healthy, it needs to be fully consensual and authentic, and gifts should be recognized and appreciated.

Fully consensual means:

- Based on full, complete, honest and timely information.

Authentic means:

- Not as a response to internal negative emotional pressures such as guilt or fear.
- Not in response to external negative pressures such as displays of anger, manipulation, emotional meltdowns, guilt tripping, or threats.

Recognized means:

- Each person involved recognizes the "rightness" of each person's rights and boundaries.
- Each person recognizes the responsibilities they have to act ethically and takes responsibility for their own emotions and actions.
- Each person recognizes the responsibilities they have to act ethically and adhere to relationship agreements.

Appreciated means:

- Each person recognizes when the other is voluntarily choosing to not act on one of their individual rights.
- Each person expresses appreciation for the other person's gift.

Analysis

There is a lot to unpack here. First, each person in the scenario has their individual rights. Susan has every right to communicate her feelings and ask for what she wants. Lisa has the right to decide how she wants to spend her time and money.

It's ethical to adhere to the relationship agreements that we make. They both agreed that they once had an explicit agreement to share living expenses 50/50 and they have not explicitly changed that agreement.

Susan's complaint about not feeling special and prioritized needs to be addressed. But the solution is not necessarily the one Susan came up with. Individuals have the right to construct boundaries around their individual rights without input from other people. But once we step outside our individual rights, solutions to relationship problems should be crafted by both people (not one person), in a way that respects both people's rights and takes both people's feelings into account (see the Imago Exercise in chapter 4).

When the issue of sharing finances was addressed directly, Susan admitted that in the past, before she and Lisa moved in together, applying for and interviewing for jobs was very anxiety-inducing. The pressure of having to financially survive pushed her through that process. She had quietly hoped that Lisa would rescue her from having to face that anxiety again. Lisa stated clearly that she did not wish to consent to a new relationship agreement to financially supplement Susan in the long term and did not wish to give Susan shared ownership of her money. Lisa stated, "I want you to be fully employed again and I don't see you trying to achieve that."

Notice that Lisa does not have the right to tell Susan that she must become employed full-time again. But she does have the right to say, "I will not agree to financially support you." If Susan had some other source of income, such as a trust fund, then she could pay her 50% of the household expenses without working full-time.

This issue of money was the first relationship agreement they addressed. Lisa allowed herself to be open to hearing Susan's feelings about job hunting and full-time employment and expressed compassion for her anxiety, and was also able to be honest and express that whatever solution they found together, she was unwilling to financially supplement Susan long-term.

They attempted to brainstorm solutions, but neither of them wanted to make the financial sacrifices that other solutions would require, such as reducing their standard of living so that Susan could pay her 50% with her part-time income.

This put them at an impasse. When at an impasse, we look at who is responsible for what. Susan agreed that she was responsible for her own financial support and for facing the feelings of anxiety that might involve. She decided she would need to either apply for government disability payments, supplement her income with self-employment, or seek full-time work.

Though she didn't rule out seeking disability payments in the future, she knew that would be a long process and that she might not qualify for them. She also didn't really want to give up hope that she could overcome her anxiety. She asked for my input on how she might begin making progress.

I didn't feel it was appropriate for me to try to treat Susan's anxiety; I was their relationship counselor and not Susan's individual therapist. But I did feel it was important to instill hope that she could achieve this goal.

I explained that the first question I would ask is whether the anxiety is based in a past trauma. If so, I would seek out a trauma specialist for individual therapeutic work, preferably someone trained in somatic work (based in polyvagal theory), EMDR (eye movement desensitization and reprocessing), clinical hypnosis, or ERP (exposure and response prevention).

If the anxiety isn't based in an identifiable trauma, then it's likely based in false beliefs or obsessive thoughts. In this case she might benefit specifically from working with an anxiety specialist who might use clinical hypnosis or ERP.

She might also want to consider talking with a psychiatrist or medical doctor for medications that could reduce the physical symptoms of anxiety, or study dialectical behavioral therapy (DBT) for coping skills to increase her ability to tolerate the discomfort of her anxiety. These options could help her to take action and do the things she wanted to do, such as job hunting and interviews.

I told her that I have seen many people overcome severe anxiety and that with the right treatment it was very likely she could achieve her goals and live a fuller life. I gave her a referral list of therapists and encouraged her to begin her individual work.

In our relationships, we are each responsible for our own feelings and emotions, and that includes anxiety, depression, trauma symptoms, and more. We aren't responsible for the experiences that caused those symptoms, but we are responsible for the impact our current behaviors (including those behaviors based in mental health symptoms) have on others and on our relationships with others. Sometimes our feelings and emotions feel like they are beyond our control. But that doesn't mean that they are beyond our ability to improve. Even when our emotions rise to the level of symptoms of mental health diagnoses, with proper treatment, there is a lot we can do to reduce the intensity of these emotional responses and even eliminate them.

What if Susan's anxiety regarding job-hunting was a disability? Based on right #3, we have a right to disability accommodations. Does this mean she has a right to require financial support from Lisa? Not necessarily. If Susan's anxiety disability was present before they moved in together, she might have presented it as a price-of-admission issue such as, "My ability to earn an income is limited by my disability. This is not negotiable. If we live together, we either live at a standard I can afford, or if we are going to live at a higher standard, you will have to be willing to pay for that."

If the anxiety disability developed later, after the shared home was established, they might renegotiate, and Lisa might get to an authentic yes regarding her willingness to financially support or supplement Susan. But it's during this renegotiation that Lisa has to ask herself if this yes is an authentic yes. Lisa still has to choose whether to agree and continue the relationship under this new expectation of financial support.

In this case, Susan was able to acknowledge she had been unfair about the money issue. Lisa had never agreed to financially support or supplement Susan, nor had she agreed to allow her money to be treated as "family" money such that Susan would have some say over how it was spent. Susan also admitted that by assuming an agreement that had never actually been agreed to, she had failed to recognize the gift Lisa had been providing for the last year by supplementing her income without ever having agreed to do so long-term.

Susan was now able to recognize this and thank Lisa for that gift. But she still felt hurt and "not special" in comparison to Deb. This was the second issue they needed to address. She acknowledged that she and Lisa spent enough time together, but they put little or no effort into making that time special. Lisa was able to gently explain to Susan that after spending considerable money supplementing Susan's bills, she didn't want to also spend money going out together, but did want to put effort into making their time together more special. After some brainstorming, they agreed to research free activities such as movies in the park and local festivals. They would pack their own food and drinks and make a point of doing an activity outside the home at least once per week. Lisa agreed to put time and effort into the planning to help Susan feel special to Lisa. Lisa even agreed to a weekend getaway to celebrate once Susan lands a full-time job.

Finally, Susan expressed that if she were not going to be financially supplemented by Lisa, then she didn't want to do more than 50% of the housework. Lisa agreed this was fair and they negotiated to return to equal sharing of housework as long as Susan put equivalent time into a combination of her part-time job and job-hunting.

What about the Tybee Island trip? Susan acknowledged that Lisa had the right to schedule the trip and she didn't have the right to demand that Lisa not go. But she was still feeling neglected due to them not making an effort to make special plans during the last year, and asked Lisa if she would consider postponing the trip.

Lisa was feeling more appreciated by Susan and that her rights were being acknowledged and respected. She wanted to say yes to Susan, and said, "I would need to talk to Deb first, but I think I would be willing to postpone the Tybee trip until spring break, which is five months away, instead of the semester break that is two months away. Would that help?"

"Yes," Susan said, "I know you have to check with Deb first, but thank you for offering that."

These new agreements met the criteria of fully consensual, authentic, recognized, and appreciated.

A note on precedents

Many, many expectations in relationships are not built on explicitly negotiated agreements, but rather on just the way the people have been doing things. This is natural. When both people or all the people involved seem to want the same thing, they fall happily into doing that without the need for cumbersome debate and negotiation.

When we engage in a pattern of behavior, or allow a pattern of behavior, it sets a precedent in our relationships that this behavior is okay or desired. If two people who really like each other fall into seeing each other every Friday and Saturday night, it's natural after a few weeks or months to expect this pattern will continue. If one person is unavailable or wants to do something else the next weekend, the other person is likely to be surprised, disappointed, or even hurt.

In a positive example such as this, it's important to remember that setting a precedent doesn't mean this pattern is now written in stone, but rather you should be aware your partner has a reasonable expectation the pattern will continue. If you need or want to change the pattern, be sensitive to your partner's feelings as you bring up your desire for change. Ask them how they feel about the change. If they have any painful or uncomfortable emotions, ask what the two of you can do to help them to feel better.

In the example with Susan and Lisa, when Lisa began supplementing Susan without objection, and this was allowed to go on unchallenged, Susan began to assume this was okay with Lisa.

It's important to remember that we must speak up when something is happening that we don't want in a relationship. Even if Lisa had said, "I can supplement you temporarily, but I don't want this to be long-term," then she has at least let her boundary be known, even if it has no clear timeline. But when Lisa said nothing, she helped set the stage for a slow, simmering resentment and feeling taken for granted.

Likewise, if in a new relationship the other person does something inconsiderate (takes your car without asking, or leaves you waiting for hours without communication) or does something abusive (calls you names, throws something at you, pulls your hair), if you allow this to pass unchallenged, it sets a precedent that they expect they can get away with this behavior in the future.

It's very important in abusive situations to ensure your safety first. Abusive people frequently respond to limits by attempting to increase their control and sometimes increasing the abusive behavior directed toward you. As well, although it can be empowering to understand that you can help shape your relationship experience by objecting to unacceptable behavior and enforcing your boundaries, even if you have not done this, another person's abusive behavior is never your fault. It's also important to acknowledge the reality if a power imbalance leaves you unable to enforce your boundaries successfully. This is also not your fault. Engage self-compassion, and consider seeking assistance in advocating for yourself and improving your situation.

When to include other people in relationship agreement negotiations

"Nothing about us without us" —South African disability activists Michael Masutha and William Rowland

Relationship agreements sometimes affect people who are not in the relationship. Which raises the question, "When is it ethical to make a relationship agreement without including other people, and when must we include other people in order to be ethical?"

There is no easy answer to this question. But the first question I would ask is: Does this relationship agreement require the consent or cooperation of someone who is not present? If so, it's likely they should have a say, or at least an opportunity to have input.

In the example, Lisa said she needed to check with Deb before she could agree to postpone the Tybee Island trip. Since Deb would certainly be impacted by a postponement, it is considerate and ethical to allow her some input.

Since no concrete plans were made, and since Lisa was planning to pay for the trip, it's not likely that Deb will argue that they must continue with the trip during the semester break.

Deb would still need to be fully included in any new plan to do the Tybee Island trip during spring break as she may have other plans for that bit of time. But if the circumstances were different regarding the end-of-semester break—for instance, if concrete plans had been made and Deb scheduled time off from work, or rearranged child visitation schedules with her ex—then Deb might have reason to object to a change in plans.

For another example, let's turn back to the safer sex question.

If Jermaine and Mike have just negotiated that they will use barriers as part of their safer sex practices with all other partners so that they can have barrier-free sex with each other, does that negotiation need to include other people?

If neither Jermaine nor Mike currently have any other sexual partners, and this agreement will only impact people they haven't yet met, then no, this negotiation doesn't need to include other people. However, I do think that it's important that both Jermaine and Mike present this boundary as their own personal boundary when they meet a new prospective partner. When negotiating sex with a new partner, they simply need to say, "Barriers are a requirement for me."

If they present it as a relationship agreement, it may feel to the new person like relationship privilege is being voiced and established early and can feel like a power play. Also, it's a short step from here to throwing your partner under the bus by saying, "I'd love to have unprotected sex with you, but my partner insists we use barriers." This would be unethical toward the established partner and also sets up the new partner to resent the existing partner.

What if Jermaine and Mike are discussing the use of barriers and Mike has another partner, Ted, with whom he has had barrier-free sex for some time? If Mike shows up to the next date with Ted suddenly requiring barriers, this is likely to be upsetting for Ted. If Mike tries to claim it's just his (new) personal boundary, Ted is likely to wonder why Mike suddenly feels unsafe with him.

If a new relationship agreement is going to affect or impact another person, and essentially will require their consent or cooperation, then they should have some input. Bringing a third person into what may feel like an intimate, inner-circle relationship conversation may feel awkward. You could choose to do it face-to-face and in real time. You might choose to do it in a relay fashion (Jermaine and Mike talk, then Mike and Ted, then Jermaine and Mike again). Or you may choose to use email, text, Evernote, or some other format where all three of you can talk to each other.

Ideally, this will result in outside-the-box thinking and solutions that would not have happened otherwise. What if Ted has no other sexual partners, is very trustworthy, and agrees to use barriers with any other partner he may have in the future? What if Ted is very willing to use barriers with Mike and simply appreciates being included in the conversation? What if Ted is unwilling to use barriers under any circumstances?

This is where it becomes difficult. If Ted refuses to use barriers, and Jermaine is unwilling to have barrier-free sex with Mike unless Mike uses barriers with everyone else, then Mike may have to choose. And no one likes having to choose.

If Mike chooses to make the agreement with Jermaine, he may lose his relationship with Ted. Ted will feel hurt and it will communicate that Jermaine is more important to Mike than Ted is (which might very well be true). If Mike chooses to not make the agreement with Jermaine, hopefully Jermaine can accept that gracefully, but he may be hurt and may come to wonder if Ted is more important to Mike than he is.

But, like any other relationship agreement, it must be unanimous, or changing it is not ethical. Jermaine and Mike have been having sex with barriers before now. The only way for Mike to be able to agree to use barriers with his other partners would be to stop seeing Ted (if Ted refuses to use barriers). If he is unwilling to break things off with Ted, then he and Jermaine can't have this new agreement.

But if Ted is not an emotionally significant relationship, and if advancing his relationship with Jermaine is very important to him, Mike may choose to end his involvement with Ted because he wants to make a new agreement with Jermaine.

In situations like this, the more deeply involved anyone is with the third person, or the more important the issue is to the third person, the more they should be included or have input in the discussion. It's also difficult to say when "input" crosses over to decision-making power. But if it would be unacceptable to you that the third person might choose to walk away rather than abide by the new agreement, then they should probably be included in the decision-making process and have a say, rather than simply input.

> **Action item:** Reflect on your past and current relationship agreements. Do any of them impact another person besides the partner you have the agreement with? Really stretch yourself to consider how other people might be impacted. Imagine how it might have been different if you had included the third person in the discussion. If this feels threatening, imagine the third person is friendly and respectful during the discussion. Try imagining you switched roles with the third person. How would you feel about being either included or excluded from the discussion of the agreement that impacted you?

Ethical behavior

Most people want to be ethical. There is a reason we call what we do "ethical non-monogamy." And ethics can be complicated. It may help to think of relationship ethics in a triage-like order. In the next chapter I present a personal responsibility flowchart to help guide you through solving relationship disagreements. But for now, I'll say that the first priority is respecting each person's individual rights. And a very close second is living up to our relationship agreements.

Mastering the relationship skills outlined in this book is like playing a complicated game, while having access to the rule book and adhering to the rules of the game. You know that violating the rules will cause the other players to not want to play with you.

When players see other players voluntarily hold themselves to the rules of the game—even when it costs them something they want, even when they might be able to get away with bending the rules—they develop trust in those other players to play fair.

Referring to the rules and properly applying them makes the game more enjoyable for everyone. When people have fun together, they bond and want to come together again and again to play. Also, just like with playing a game, we need to develop the ability to accept that sometimes the rules don't allow us to fairly take an action we want to take. And that might mean not advancing in the game.

We all need to learn how to accept disappointment in this context and lose things we want without lashing out at other players. In games, we all need to learn how to lose gracefully so that others get to enjoy when they do well. Following the rules helps everyone enjoy the game and makes it more likely that all the players will want to continue to play.

If we apply this analogy to our relationships, there will be times that we want something, but have to tell ourselves no because it would violate a relationship agreement or someone's rights. There are times we will have to tell our partners no because we can't get to a yes authentically. And there are times when we will need to do real work to get to the authentic yes that we want to get to, for our own sake, our partner's sake, and the sake of the relationship.

The next chapter clarifies when to stand up for our rights, when to negotiate or renegotiate relationship agreements, and when to take a long hard look at ourselves and accept the responsibility to address our own emotional issues.

CHAPTER 9

Personal Responsibility: Who Has Work to Do?

How can you use the information about rights, boundaries, and relationship agreements to determine which person in a disagreement may have an issue they need to work on? The personal responsibility flow chart will help you determine when you need to take responsibility for yourself, and when you may need to require that someone else take responsibility for themselves. It can also help you see when you may need to renegotiate a relationship agreement.

In this chapter I teach a method for how to begin the process of taking responsibility for ourselves, our thoughts, and our emotions as they relate to conflicts in our relationships. It's best if we initiate these internal investigations for ourselves. But since we often become aware that we have work to do when in the context of an argument or conflict with a partner, sometimes our partners will make us aware of it. We may become aware that we have work to do when a partner pushes back on the things we want, when they are unwilling to give us an accommodation we think we need, when we fail to live up to an agreement, or when they point out we're violating one of their rights.

The first step in resolving a relationship conflict is to approach the conflict as a team, using the Imago exercise with NVC (see chapters 3 and 4). It's ideal if people can resolve a conflict by accessing compassion, validating each other's feelings, and taking each person's needs into account. Ideally, we want any relationship agreements to come from an authentic yes.

But sometimes after the Imago exercise, the people are stuck and can't seem to brainstorm solutions that work for everyone. And sometimes one person's feelings seem completely out of line to the other person, and that other person doesn't want to take those feelings into account in the solution.

In these situations, it helps to be able to identify who is responsible for what. I don't think of this as a case of one person being wrong and one person being right. Everyone's feelings are valid, and no one is wrong for feeling what they feel or wanting what they want. Rather, I think of it as, "It's ethical for me to take responsibility for myself. I need to examine this situation and make sure I'm not trying to make my partner responsible for my stuff."

Often, if someone's feelings seem totally out of line, it's helpful to separate their feelings from the solution they're asking for. Once you identify what they feel and what emotional need they are trying to fulfill or meet, brainstorm other ways that need could be fulfilled.

For example, if you're feeling insecure when your partner is on a date with someone else, but they are unwilling to reassure you during their date, feeling secure is your goal. What other things could help you feel secure during those dates? Can you have a physical token to hold, or a recording of your partner's voice reassuring you of their commitment to you? Could you look through photos of you and your partner together, or would you benefit from distracting yourself with movies, social activities, or exercise?

The intensity of someone's feelings has no bearing on whether the solution they are asking for is ethical in terms of respecting your rights. If the solution they're offering (or demanding) is a violation of your rights, and you don't authentically want to give it as an accommodation, don't give it.

We can look at each person's rights, the ethics of respecting other people's rights, and the need to take responsibility for ourselves, and we can use that information to identify whether someone has internal mental and emotional work to do. This work could include examining their thoughts, beliefs, and values or implementing coping skills to see if they can shift how they feel about a given issue. These are alternatives to expecting their partner to give in to the solution they think they need, or expecting their partner to compromise and meet them partway when that would be damaging to the relationship. As one of my clients put it, "Compromise is not always a viable option. If two people are trying to decide what to have for lunch and you want to eat pasta, and the other person wants to eat you… you can't compromise with that!"

We can only call a compromise a healthy agreement if all the people involved are agreeing authentically and willingly. If we cannot agree authentically and willingly (such as agreeing to allow a person to cannibalize a part of us rather than all of us) then the so-called "compromise" is still a violation of our rights.

Remember, if someone is violating our rights, it's damaging to our self-esteem and self-respect to not defend our rights (or not be able to due to a power imbalance). It's also damaging to the relationship because our sense of safety is damaged when a partner violates our rights. Therefore, if we're feeling angry, hurt, or afraid under these circumstances, I don't recommend trying to change our feelings to make those actions okay, or trying to compromise with someone by making it acceptable for them to violate our rights.

When two people are having an argument, sometimes the painful or unpleasant emotions that result are a sign that we need to do some internal work on ourselves. Sometimes they are a sign that the other person needs to do some work. Often both people need to do some work.

In other words, sometimes we need to take responsibility for ourselves, and sometimes we need other people to take responsibility for themselves and change their behavior toward us. Knowing when to do the former and when to do the latter is fundamental to applying ethical principles in polyamorous relationships.

This chapter is about that process. In this chapter you will learn:

- What questions to ask yourself to analyze a disagreement and determine if you have a responsibility to own up to.
- How to forgive others and yourself.
- Why taking responsibility for your feelings, thoughts, and actions is ethical.
- That hurt feelings alone are not a good indicator of whether you are the victim in a disagreement.
- And why sometimes other people are responsible for our feelings.

Who has work to do?

Try really hard not to think of this as being an effort to discern who is wrong and who is right. I've explained why making one person right and one person wrong damages relationships, but I will say it again:

First, when we make one person wrong without hearing and validating their feelings, all they tend to hear is, "Your feelings don't matter to me."

Second, it's a power move. Exerting power in an egalitarian relationship is an abuse of power (unless you are using that power to defend your rights).

Third, power can be abused in a power dynamic relationship, too. In a power dynamic, the use of power should stay within the limits of the areas of life and the ways of asserting power that have been consensually negotiated. Any use of power outside those limits would be an abuse of power.

Fourth, if we insist on being completely the victim and making the other person completely the perpetrator, without compassion for the other person's experience and without taking their intentions into account, then we are insisting on shaming the other person. We're setting up a situation where we insist the other person take complete responsibility and grovel to get back in our good graces. This is also unethical.

Instead, think of this next section as a way to determine when one of you has work to do for the sake of your own personal growth. Most of the time it will be both of you, in different areas of the disagreement. I strongly encourage us all to take the initiative and engage assertively in self-exploration. It's hard enough to take responsibility for ourselves. It's harder when someone else is pointing out our flaws. Sometimes, when we aren't proactive enough, it's necessary for someone else to encourage us to examine ourselves. But it's much more palatable when our self-examination is self-initiated.

Personal responsibility flow chart

Here, I present the whole flow chart for you. Following that, I will break it down into two charts and explain how to use them.

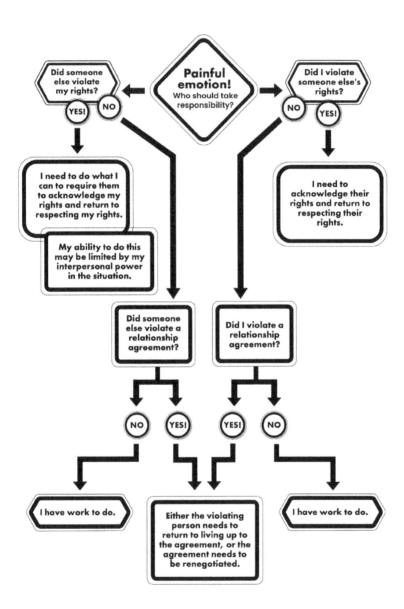

When rights are violated

Let's go directly to the pain point. When someone's feelings are hurt, they're upset, sad, angry, disappointed, anxious, guilty, ashamed, or afraid. Let's say I am the person feeling these painful emotions and I've just had an argument with someone. We have both walked away feeling upset. It appears we both feel like the victim in the situation.

As I begin to reflect on the situation, the first question I want to ask myself is, "Not including a relationship agreement, did someone violate someone else's rights?" I need to ask this question in both directions: "Did someone violate my rights?" and "Did I violate someone else's rights?" To figure this out, I might want to review and reflect on all 13 rights.

The first question in the personal responsibility flow chart presented next explains the course of action if the answer to either question is yes.

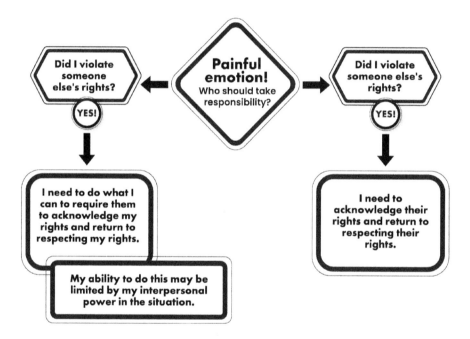

The diagram begins with a painful emotion and asks, "Who should take responsibility?" Following the left side of the diagram, I ask myself, "Did someone violate my rights?" If the answer is yes, I need to do what I can to require the other person to acknowledge my rights and return to respecting those rights. My ability to do this may be limited by my interpersonal power in the situation.

Returning to the beginning of the diagram and the painful emotion, I also ask myself, "Did I violate someone's rights?" Following the right side of the diagram, if the answer is yes, I need to take responsibility for my behavior. I need to acknowledge the other person's rights and return to respecting their rights.

Let's look at an example. If my partner and I are arguing and I'm trying to express myself and she mocks me, this is disrespectful. She has violated one of my rights: to be spoken to respectfully and treated with dignity. (Follow the left branch of the diagram.) I may have other things to answer for in the argument, but I need her to take responsibility for her behavior and to acknowledge that it's not okay to talk to me disrespectfully, and I need her to agree to not do that again.

On the other hand, if I am the one who spoke disrespectfully to her during the argument, I need to acknowledge that I did that. (Follow the right branch of the diagram.) I need to take responsibility for my actions. I need to apologize. And I need to agree to not do it again.

When rights are not violated

But what if the answer to both of the questions is no? What if no one's rights were violated? Then we move on to the second question on the personal responsibility flow chart, which is, "Did someone violate a relationship agreement?"

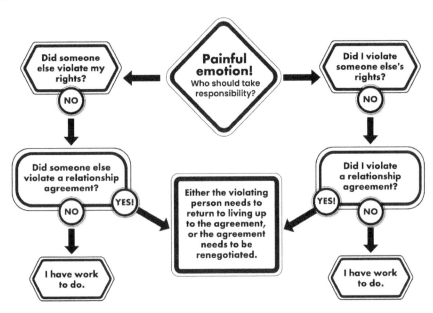

In this second section of the flow chart, we continue with our investigation of the same painful emotion. We follow the left side of the diagram and ask the question, "Did someone violate my rights?" This time, the answer is no. We then ask the second question, "Did the other person violate a relationship agreement?" If the answer to this question is no, then I have work to do. I need to examine why am I upset. If the answer is yes, and the other person did violate a relationship agreement, then either they need to return to living up to the relationship agreement, or we need to renegotiate that agreement.

Starting at the beginning and following the right side of the diagram, we ask, "Did I violate someone else's rights?" If the answer is no, we ask the second question: "Did I violate a relationship agreement?" If the answer is no, then I have work to do. I need to examine why I am feeling this painful emotion when I haven't violated anyone's rights, nor have I violated a relationship agreement.

If the answer is yes, and I did violate a relationship agreement, then either I need to return to living up to the relationship agreement, or we need to renegotiate that agreement.

If no one violated anyone's rights, and no one violated a relationship agreement, and I've identified that I have some internal work to do, I might begin by asking some of these questions: Why am I upset? What does this situation mean to me? How am I interpreting this experience? Do I know if my interpretation is factually correct? How can I find out?

I may also decide that creating a relationship agreement could help, and I can ask the other person if they are willing to negotiate an agreement.

A good example of this situation is the story of Khyree and Simone in chapter 6, where Simone was upset because Khyree had a night to himself and he decided to have a bachelor night rather than spend the extra time with Simone. He had not violated one of her rights. Nor did he violate a relationship agreement. She could have asked for a new agreement, such as, "Anytime you have a free night, I can expect you will spend it with me." But I doubt Khyree would have been willing to agree to that. Therefore, Simone had some internal work to do. She examined her thoughts, beliefs, and interpretation of the events. She asked Khyree for his perspective to "reality check" her interpretations. In the end, she found emotional peace by deciding to change what she believed.

She also did something of great benefit to her relationship. By taking responsibility for solving her own painful emotions, she spared Khyree from the stress and drama of a relationship crisis over something he had a right to expect: that he could decide what to do with his extra night. This absence of drama and conflict increased Khyree's feelings of safety in knowing that Simone has the emotional strength to recognize and respect his rights and had the relationship ethics to do that internal work.

On the other hand, sometimes the upset feelings we have are guilt or shame. Sometimes we are taking responsibility for our partner's feelings when we shouldn't. Caring about our partner's feelings is not the same thing as taking responsibility for them. We should always care about our partner's feelings, especially if they're in pain. But taking responsibility for their painful feelings means we have taken on the responsibility of fixing them, or finding and implementing a solution to their pain. I'll explain toward the end of this chapter when we are responsible for others' feelings and when we are not.

If my life partner asks me to cancel my date with someone, and I really don't want to, she might say, "Why can't you do this for me?!" If she is clearly still in pain and struggling, I might feel guilty. I might feel torn. I might not know what to do. I examine the list of rights. I ask, "Did I violate one of her rights?" … No. "Did I violate a relationship agreement?" … No. Then I have some internal work to do to solve my misplaced guilt. I still need to help my partner with her pain, but that's not the same thing as me being responsible for resolving her pain.

If I agree to cancel my date when I don't want to, I wouldn't be agreeing authentically. If my partner continues to pressure me or begins demanding that I cancel my date, that could be considered a violation of my rights to determine what I do with my time. It would be helpful for my partner to acknowledge her responsibility in this situation. In turn, I can help by showing compassion for her pain and my willingness to help her if I can. That help could come in the form of giving her reassurance, helping her understand my intentions and motives, or negotiating a new relationship agreement.

What kinds of agreements might we negotiate? That would depend on what we learned when we did the Imago exercise on this issue. What if my partner has no objection with me having this date, but she just needs more forewarning to emotionally prepare herself? Or she's having anxiety about me driving a long distance and is afraid for my safety? Or does she fear the person is impressive in some way she's not, and she is feeling insecure?

To help her with her painful emotions, we could make any number of agreements that I could get to with an authentic yes, without canceling my date. I could agree to provide more forewarning in the future. I could agree to turn on my phone GPS so she can see that my car is still moving. I could agree to give her heartfelt reassurances of my love and commitment to her.

What if she wants me to cancel my date because there is a true emergency? What if someone close to my partner died that day and she is feeling fragile and needs my emotional support? What if our dog got loose, she's frantically worried for the dog's wellbeing, and she wants me to cancel my date and help her search for the dog? Chances are we have an explicit or implicit agreement that as life partners she can expect me to prioritize providing emotional, material, and physical support to her in moments of high distress or emergencies. In this case, I may not want to cancel my date, but I need to live up to my relationship agreements. If I don't, I will damage my relationship.

When relationship agreements are violated

If someone violated a relationship agreement, then that person needs to acknowledge what they have done. They need to take responsibility for their actions and apologize or make amends if possible. They may decide to keep the relationship agreement, in which case they would need to recommit themselves to living up to the agreement. Or they may decide that this is a sign that they need to renegotiate.

An example of this situation would be the story of James and his anxious girlfriend from chapter 8, who wanted to know all his dating plans well in advance. James repeatedly failed to live up to these agreements. His girlfriend was justified in being upset with him. He readily acknowledged that he had made the agreement and failed to live up to it. He apologized for hurting her each time. He truly wanted to live up to this agreement but was unable to. His options were to either renegotiate the agreement to make it something he could live up to, or continue to reapply himself to the original agreement while exploring what inner or outer obstacles were interfering with his success living up to that agreement.

In another example, from chapter 7, Keshav found himself repeatedly failing to live up to the agreements he made with his husband Colin to be home at an agreed upon time after his dates with Jared. During the Imago exercise, we learned that Keshav didn't really want to agree to those limits, but would feel frustrated in the face of his husband's jealousy and agree to limits he didn't want in order to pacify Colin.

While it might appear that both of these examples are examples where the agreements that were violated appear to be unfairly restrictive, either one of them might be a deal breaker or price-of-admission requirement for the other person.

Here's another example. Margo felt she had adjusted pretty well to polyamory. She'd had very few struggles with her husband's last relationship, and she had some fun dating experiences for herself. But there was an issue with his new girlfriend. Margo thought she was high-drama and her husband seemed totally sucked in by that drama. He would make agreements with Margo to be home by noon the day after a date with the new girlfriend so they could have lunch or go to the park with their son, and the girlfriend would start a crisis at 11 a.m. Margo's husband would be delayed, sometimes for hours. Margo was ready to put her foot down: "He needs to teach this girlfriend to accept limits, break up with her, or be prepared for me to separate from him."

In this example, the restrictions don't seem unreasonable. I provide it here as a reminder to avoid getting distracted by whether someone else's relationship agreement appears reasonable to us from the outside. Only the people involved can decide that. This is about determining who has work to do when a relationship agreement has been violated.

When a relationship agreement has been violated, painful emotions are to be expected. Relationship agreements provide the safety we need in order to contain our vulnerabilities. Violating a relationship agreement can leave us or our partners feeling vulnerable, unsafe, hurt, betrayed, or angry. We all need solutions to painful emotions. The solution outlined in the personal responsibility flow chart is that the people need to either recommit themselves to the original agreement or renegotiate that agreement.

Each person will need to do some self-examination regarding whether they agreed to the original agreement authentically or under internal or external pressure. Agreements decided under pressure should be renegotiated until they are fully consensual and authentic.

The people involved should also examine whether they are capable of living up to the agreement. Asking a partner to attend frequent parties and family gatherings sounds reasonable and the partner may want to live up to that agreement. But when we add the information that the partner has severe social anxiety, we may need to face that the partner isn't capable of living up to that agreement no matter how much they authentically want to.

If a partner no longer wants to be held to an agreement, then either we need to accept that this painful emotion falls back into the category of being our responsibility, or we need to accept that it is a deal-breaker or price-of-admission issue for us. If having this agreement is an absolute must, and our partner is no longer willing to abide by it, then we must face that this is an incompatibility that may lead to the end of the relationship or a fundamental change in it.

Relationship repair, forgiveness, and self-forgiveness

When trust has been violated in a relationship, it can be a real challenge to repair the damage. Typically, we have taken an action or spoken in a way that was a violation of an agreement or a violation of our partner's rights. The behavior shows a disregard for our partner's feelings or wellbeing. Therefore, the trust that needs to be rebuilt is twofold. Our partner needs to be able to renew their belief that we genuinely care about their feelings and wellbeing, and they need to rebuild trust in our ability to demonstrate that care through our behaviors.

When clients come to me to discuss trust violations, first I take them through the Imago exercise, sometimes several times, to give each of them ample opportunity to hear how the other felt, and to give each other the opportunity to validate their feelings.

One of the challenges here is that the "wronged party" may be very resistant to validating the feelings of the person who "wronged" them. They sometimes fear that this will let the other person off the hook.

Let's use the example of Jorge and Victoria in the last chapter. When Jorge eventually told Victoria that he had "accidentally" had barrier-free sex with Sandra several times, Victoria was very upset. Victoria had requested this restriction because she was very concerned about sexually transmitted infections, and Jorge had waited so long to tell her that she had also had sex with Jorge since then and now felt exposed and at risk.

Jorge had already admitted that he was wrong and that he should have told her immediately. He validated her feelings, expressed regret, and agreed that her trust was violated. It's *very* important that this be done first and thoroughly! The person whose trust was violated must be validated first.

When it was Jorge's turn to speak in the Imago exercise, however, Victoria resisted allowing him his turn. She felt he was 100% responsible and she didn't want to empathize with or validate how he felt or hear what led up to him violating this agreement.

How do we reach a place of forgiveness when our partner has violated our trust? And what does that even mean? When a partner violates our trust, not only does it damage our sense of safety with them in the relationship, but how we see them has changed. Before, we held them in high esteem. Now, our opinion of them is lowered. They are not who we thought they were.

To forgive, repair, and rebuild means that in the end, we will hold the person in high regard again. We will believe our feelings matter to them again. And we will have new reasons to trust them again.

If we allow ourselves to hear what led up to or contributed to them violating our trust, we open the door to compassion and understanding. We need that in order to separate out their overall character—as someone who cares for our feelings—from this one act of violation. In other words, if we are ever going to be able to hold them in high esteem again, we need to be able to see that their overall character is good (by your own, unique definition of good), they are someone we can trust to care for our feelings, and this violation of trust is an anomaly. It's not representative of who they are overall or who they are in the relationship.

If we truly believe that the violation is representative of their character, then that is who they are, and we would be ill-advised to trust them again. They are destined to commit the same violation in the future. If this is a deal-breaker issue for us, we should probably reduce the depth of our involvement with them or seek to end that relationship rather than rebuild it.

An exception to this might be if a violation is within their character, but it can be mitigated through preventative measures, such as when an alcoholic or addict is in recovery. They may feel that addiction is part of their character, but they don't want to drink or use and they can typically prevent it by going to self-help meetings or participating in other treatment options.

The desire to shame a partner who violated our trust can be strong. The desire to avoid feeling any compassion for their experience or hearing what contributed to their violation of our trust can also be strong. Sometimes we simply need time for our pain or anger to soften. But in order to access constructive forgiveness, we need to be able to access compassion for the partner who hurt us.

When Victoria's hurt and anger softened and she was ready to hear Jorge's experience, she had to face some uncomfortable truths. Jorge had grown up with a mentally ill mother, and strong displays of emotion caused him to go into freeze mode (recall our discussion of the three Fs—fight, flight, or freeze—in chapter 2). In the past, when he made smaller mistakes, Victoria, who had grown up in a very expressive family, engaged in emotional displays that Jorge could barely tolerate.

He knew he should have sought to renegotiate the boundary around condom use before he violated it. But every time he thought about how upset he predicted Victoria would be, he would shut down. After he violated the agreement, he imagined her response would be even more exaggerated and he just couldn't bring himself to tell her.

When Victoria validated Jorge's experience and his feelings, she had to also face the fact that she hadn't known the impact of her expressiveness on him. Given his history, she could understand his avoidance. And she realized that she bore some responsibility, not for the violation of the agreement, but rather for not creating an environment where her partner felt safe enough with her to speak his truth.

The five-step apology

Repairing damage done in a relationship sometimes requires more than the standard apology. Typically, we think of an apology as an expression of regret for hurting another person. Even so, we tend to apologize in a way that expresses regret or wrongness for our actions rather than for the emotional harm done. "I shouldn't have done that," or "I'm sorry for what I said."

An effective apology is about taking full responsibility for our behavior, whether we think of it as wrong or not, and expressing regret for hurting the other person. The best apologies also include an expression of compassion for the other person's feelings and some assurance that we will take action to correct our hurtful behavior in the future.

I believe that the common way we apologize is sometimes insufficient for a true mending of the harm done in a relationship. Here, I outline five steps to a thorough and effective apology.

Step 1. Admit to what you did. This is simply pointing out the facts and taking responsibility for your behavior. If your behavior was wrong, be secure enough in yourself to say so.

Examples: "I interrupted you when you were still speaking," or "I went out Saturday night and didn't call you when I said I would. And that was wrong."

Step 2. Identify how the other person felt. If you're sure you know how the other person felt, just say it. If you're not sure, you can either ask or you can take a guess and then ask if you got it right.

Example: "I can imagine that if I were you, I might feel hurt by that. Is that right? Is that how you felt?"

Be open to hearing corrections or additional details such as, "No, not really. I felt angry. I felt dismissed."

Step 3. Apologize for how your actions made the other person feel and express that their feelings matter to you! If appropriate, *also* apologize for your behavior. This is the most important step.

Example: "I'm sorry I interrupted you and I am very sorry that you felt dismissed and unimportant. Your feelings matter a lot to me and I actually do value what you have to say, even though my behavior at the time didn't show that. It was wrong of me to interrupt you."

Or, "I went out on Saturday night and didn't call you when I said I would, and that was wrong of me. I'm very sorry that my actions caused you to feel dismissed and angry. I care very much for your feelings and would not want you to feel this way."

Either way, take responsibility for your behavior. Don't offer excuses or justifications. Chances are, you already spoke those in the discussion that happened before you decided to apologize.

Step 4. Explain what you will do to ensure you don't hurt the person in the same way in the future. This can include any new relationship agreements you have come to as a solution to the problem. This is the step people almost never take, and yet it's vitally important to rebuilding safety and trust.

Example: "I'm going to work really hard to not interrupt you in the future and I would like you to please point it out to me if I do interrupt you. That will help me to break this habit."

Or, "From now on I will always put my plans on our shared calendar so you can see if I have plans to go out."

Step 5. Ask for forgiveness or ask for the opportunity to make amends (if possible) and repair the rift in the relationship. "I will replace the broken item." "Can you forgive me?" or "What can I do or say that will help repair this damage?"

After talking through the issue, if you and your partner or partners decide to renegotiate a relationship agreement, step 4 can be modified. Instead of saying, "Here's how I will prevent myself from doing this again," you can say, "And here's why I think I can live up to this new agreement."

In the case of Jorge and Victoria, if Victoria commits to working with Jorge to create an environment where he feels safer talking with her about tough topics, he can say that he believes he can speak up about difficult topics knowing that she now understands and that she will put effort into curbing her emotional expressions when she's upset with him.

What about the case where no one is actually upset with us, but we feel guilty, afraid, ashamed, or anxious anyway? We can still apply the same questions. For example, Jorge felt terribly guilty for weeks before he told Victoria about the agreement he had violated.

First, we ask, "Did I violate someone's rights?" If the answer is yes and if we want to foster a real intimacy in our relationship, we should consider telling our partner the truth.

If we feel guilty because we violated the other person's privacy, withheld information they had a right to, or some other violation that they are unaware of, we need to take responsibility, consider telling them the truth, apologize, and make amends if possible.

Keep in mind that when they learn the truth, they may feel violated, the relationship may be damaged, or they may end the relationship. If the relationship is damaged by the truth, but we are able to repair it, it will likely be stronger and more honest than it was before.

What if we violated one of their rights, and they already know? What if they are not upset with us, but we are upset with ourselves? First, try to determine if they are not upset because of low self-esteem. Are they not upset with us because they don't believe they deserve to be treated better? If so, validate their rights! Encourage them to own their rights, improve their self-esteem, and embrace that they should be able to expect that their rights will be respected. Yes, I'm saying that under these circumstances, we should encourage our partners to expect more from us and require us to respect their rights. This may lead to them feeling upset with us, but this would also be growth for them, and ultimately good for our relationship with them. When we violate a partner's rights, we should take responsibility for our behavior, apologize, and make amends if we can.

But what if our partner knows what we did and they are not upset with us because they have already forgiven us? They agree that what we did was a violation and that they deserve to have their rights respected, but they have graced us with the gift of forgiveness? Then the issue appears to be that we have not forgiven ourselves.

Self-forgiveness

The process of forgiving ourselves is very similar to the process of forgiving someone else. Many people don't realize it, but we have a relationship with ourselves just as we have relationships with other people. At minimum, we can think of ourselves as having two parts: the "I" and the "me." The "I" is the actor and the "me" is the observer.[60] Sometimes our "me" is a benevolent friend. Sometimes, it's a vicious critic.

Freud divided our inner world into three parts: the id, the ego, and the superego. Internal Family Systems theory allows for a multitude of inner characters of all ages and qualities. However you choose to imagine your inner world, we want to focus on that internal judgment when it comes to achieving self-forgiveness. Just like our partners, we can feel hurt and betrayed by our own failure to live up to our agreements or values. And also, just like our partners, we can lose respect and esteem for ourselves when we fall short of who we thought we were.

In order to forgive ourselves, we need to be able to access compassion for ourselves while also holding ourselves accountable for our behavior

---

60 George Herbert Mead, 1967. *Mind, Self, and Society from the Standpoint of a Social Behaviorist.* University of Chicago Press.

and providing an avenue by which we can either redeem our character or improve upon it.

Consider taking an issue and going through the Imago exercise from the two perspectives of your "I" and your "me." Then do the five-step apology.

Here's an example:

Maria was still angry and ashamed. Her involvement with Taylor had only lasted for about two years, but there was so much damage to repair. Her bank account was empty and her credit ruined; she had barely saved her home from foreclosure. Her teenage children were estranged, and worst of all, the dog she loved, Sadie, was gone.

Several years had passed, but Maria still found herself having imaginary arguments with Taylor. And she felt deeply ashamed that she had allowed a romantic partner to control and manipulate her into behaviors that violated her values and hurt herself, her children, and a dearly loved pet.

She knew she had let herself down and she wanted to be able to forgive herself, learn what she could from her experiences, and let them recede into the past.

She started by writing in her journal, using the Imago exercise, and let her inner critic express herself first.

> I'm so angry at you. How could you be so weak and stupid as to let him pressure you into leaving the dog outside? You knew there was a hole in the fence. But you couldn't stand up to him. You let him do so much damage. Your kids lost respect for you. I just don't know if I can trust you to ever select another partner. And if I could walk away from you I would. I'd be done. I've lost respect for you, too.

She thought about what she'd written and the NVC requirements of the exercise and tried again.

> When I think of how you allowed Taylor to pressure you into doing things you knew were wrong or damaging, I feel angry. When I see the lost respect in my children's eyes, and in my own mind, I feel ashamed. I feel deeply sad that I've lost my dog and I feel guilty and ashamed when I think of the suffering she may have experienced when she was lost, if she went hungry, or if she got hit by a car.

She responded with the validation step.

> I completely understand why you feel this way. You thought you could trust me to live up to our values. But when it came to being in a relationship, I seemed to lose that ability and I really let you down. I care about how you feel. (I care how I feel about myself.) And I want to work with you to find a way to redeem myself and forgive myself.

Next, she turned her perspective around to explain herself.

> Before I met Taylor, I was so lonely. I'd been single for years. My girls lived far away with their father. I'd never had a good relationship. I just couldn't seem to get it right and I had no idea what I was doing wrong. I made a decision to try as hard as I could to make the next relationship work with whoever showed an interest in me. I know now that was a poor decision.
>
> I did try to stand up for myself in the beginning. But Taylor would talk circles around me. He'd tell me that's why I never had a relationship work, because I didn't know how to compromise. When I tried to tell him I thought some choices were just wrong, he told me I was judgmental and thought I was better than him. Eventually he wore me down and I stopped trying to stand up to him. The last time I tried to stand up to him, he kept me awake all night on a work night until I finally gave in just to get some peace. Then his drinking got worse, and he stopped going to work. I felt so powerless and hopeless. When the arguments got bad, I found myself giving in just to avoid conflict. The arguments were such torture.
>
> Then there was the night he made me put Sadie outside. I knew it was wrong. I knew there was a hole in the fence. I knew being outside at night was just not something she had experienced before, and she might be frightened. I prayed she'd still be there in the morning. But I was so beaten down by then. And I was exhausted, and just needed peace so I could go to sleep and get up for work the next day… I took the chance that she'd stay in the yard.
>
> I know I'm at fault. I feel so guilty and ashamed when I think of these memories. I'm so sorry I let myself down. And I'm so sorry I let

Sadie down. I pray she didn't suffer. I hope she was found by kind people, right away. But I'll never know.

I also feel angry at Taylor. I was responsible for standing up to him, but I would never have done any of those things on my own. I didn't create any of those situations. He was responsible for putting me in those positions and for the pressure he applied to try and make me violate my principles.

Validating this perspective was difficult, but she kept at it until she did.

I understand the loneliness you felt. Companionship is a normal human need and you'd been alone for a long time. I also understand the decision you made to try and make it work. You assumed the problem was with you and you were really trying to create a positive relationship in your life. Your intention was good. I also understand the helplessness you felt. Once you were living with him, he worked hard to make you feel trapped. Remember when he said you'd have to evict him, and he'd drag it out and destroy your house before the courts made him leave? Anyone would have felt trapped.

I understand your grief and sadness. You loved Sadie. She was a great dog and a great companion. Of course you miss her. And I understand your guilt and shame at failing to live by your values and failing to defend the good things you had built up in your life.

I care about how you feel and I want to get to a place of forgiveness.

What do we need to rebuild trust and forgive? I need to know you've learned from this experience and you won't allow us to get trapped into a relationship with an abusive person again.

I've learned that it's better to be alone than in a bad relationship. I've learned that when someone tries to pressure me into things I'm not ready for (like moving in together, getting a joint bank account, or getting rid of a pet) that's a big red flag, and rather than feel pressured to give in, I should feel increased pressure to resist or get out of the relationship.

And I don't think I'd get involved with someone like Taylor again. But I'm sure there are lots of ways a person can be manipulative and controlling and I might not recognize those traits until after I feel trapped. What can we do to build safety around that problem?

We can agree to read about manipulative, abusive people and try to learn all we can, and agree to stay single for a while. We can also agree to rethink this concept of trapped. Is a person ever really trapped? Or are they just not willing to accept the consequences of leaving? If I had it to do over, would I rather have Sadie and my self-respect, but lose my house? Maybe so.

Let's decide to be very slow to let people in or get entangled. And if I feel pressured to violate my values, especially if it hurts an innocent like Sadie, I'll pay whatever price I must to resist that pressure.

That covered trust. Now let's address forgiveness.

Can you forgive me? Can I forgive myself? I can forgive myself for making that decision to try so hard to make it work. I was lonely and I assumed the problem with my past relationships had been me and that if I just tried really hard and stuck it out, I'd learn how to have a good relationship.

Can I forgive myself for what happened to Sadie? I remember how trapped and hopeless I felt. I was so much weaker after two years with him than I was in the beginning. Deep down I knew if I resisted, he would just keep me up all night and then he'd do something to her after I left for work. He'd chase her off and claim she must have escaped through the hole in the fence. I knew once he decided she was the problem, something was going to happen.

She couldn't excuse what she had done, and she couldn't absolve herself. But she could say she had learned and changed. Now that she had experienced the guilt and shame of failing Sadie, she could say she had learned to never allow anyone to pressure her into hurting or neglecting the needs of a pet. She could ask herself to forgive herself for not knowing how bad this would be, and to put her trust in the new Maria, who knows now to never let that happen again.

For the first time in years, she felt better. She still wasn't sure she could trust herself to keep herself safe, but at least she identified what was important to learn from her past experience. Now, she had a game plan for how to learn more about abusive and manipulative people and how she would respond if she found herself in a similar situation in the future.

Post-traumatic growth

After a painful experience, healing is a return to baseline. It's a return to a similar level of peace and functionality we had before the painful event happened. Sometimes we accomplish this through intentional work we do with our thoughts, feelings, or body. Sometimes it's simply the passage of time, expressions of love and acceptance from others, or an epiphany that results in healing.

Growth is surpassing baseline. Growth doesn't require a painful experience but is often prompted by one. Growth is when we achieve a level of happiness, peace, resiliency, or functionality beyond what we had before.

In the example in the previous section, for a long time Maria was damaged by her trauma. Eventually she healed, and then it became a source of growth.

Life inevitably includes painful, sometimes deeply traumatizing experiences. Sometimes people are deeply damaged by those experiences, sometimes they heal, and sometimes they grow and become stronger, better versions of themselves.

Post-traumatic growth (PTG)[61] is the phenomenon where after a life-altering traumatic event, subjects report and show evidence of great mental and emotional growth, and sometimes even express gratitude for their traumatic experience—not for the trauma itself, but for the growth that came as a result.

When it happens, the characteristics of post-traumatic growth are[62]:

- A greater appreciation for life
- A greater appreciation and strengthening of close relationships
- Increased compassion and altruism

---

61 Jim Rendon, 2015. *Upside: The New Science of Post-Traumatic Growth*. Simon & Schuster.
Victor E. Frankl, 1959. *Man's Search for Meaning*. Beacon Press.
62 Scott Kaufman, 2020. "Post traumatic growth: Finding meaning and creativity in adversity." *Scientific American*, April 20. https://www.blogs.scientificamerican.com/beautiful-minds/post-traumatic-growth-finding-meaning-and-creativity-in-adversity/

- Identifying new possibilities or purpose in life
- Increased inner strength
- Increased awareness of and ability to utilize personal strengths
- Enhanced spiritual development, life philosophy, and ability to find meaning in adversity
- Creative growth

Post-traumatic growth is not about overcoming trauma or disability. It's about integrating our painful experience in such a way that it fosters healing to baseline and growth beyond baseline.

I have experienced incredible healing and post-traumatic growth. Yet my brain and I are forever changed by my trauma. Because I live in a world designed for neurotypical people, I still need accommodations for my complex PTSD. (I explained some of my personal history in the introduction of this book.) Anyone who is going to have a close relationship with me must agree to those accommodations, or I don't let them get close enough for me to be hurt by the lack of those accommodations. Requiring these accommodations is an integral part of my self-care, and the people who truly care for me defend those accommodations as if they were their own. There are members of my family of origin whom I still keep at a distance because they don't acknowledge my trauma or respect the accommodations I need. This is also an integral part of my self-care.

If you choose to keep family (or anyone else, for that matter) at a distance for the sake of your mental health, please know that this is sometimes essential. I encourage you to resist any tendency toward feeling guilt.

Choosing to seek post-traumatic growth is completely voluntary, and should come after extensive healing and be done on the traumatized person's timeline. If a person pushes themselves or is pushed by others to "look at the bright side" and seek PTG too soon, this is greatly damaging, dismissive of their pain, and invalidating of their experiences.

It's also okay if a person doesn't seek PTG. It's not a requirement in order for healing to be complete or even effective. I have found, however, that when the traumatic event involves regret, such as in Maria's story earlier, that post-traumatic growth can help a lot toward the goal of resolving intrusive thoughts, shame, and guilt.

If a person can find or create meaning for the traumatic event in their life, figure out what they've learned from it, see how healing from it has changed them for the better, and possibly feel grateful for their growth that came from the trauma, this often helps solidify their self-forgiveness.

Taking responsibility for ourselves is ethical

I want to revisit the concept of rights, boundaries, and ethics. The way I stated it before was: It's damaging to our self-esteem and self-respect to allow other people to disregard our rights and disregard the boundaries that we make around our rights.

But if we reverse those roles, and I am the person who has violated or disregarded someone else's rights, my actions run the risk of damaging that person. I run the risk of damaging their self-esteem, their self-respect, their standing in the community, and their perception of safety, self-efficacy, or personal power.

If I do that and don't acknowledge it, apologize, express regret, or attempt to correct the damage I've done, I will damage their feelings of safety in their relationship with me, and I will damage the relationship between us.

Disregarding or violating someone else's rights or the boundaries they make around their rights would be unethical behavior on my part. Therefore, it's ethical for me to take responsibility for my actions. It's ethical for me to pay close attention to whether or not I am violating someone else's rights and to be proactive, if possible, in respecting their rights.

When people are having disagreements or arguments, they each tend to feel hurt, angry, or afraid. When we don't take responsibility for our own feelings, we use verbal justifications for why the other person is responsible for resolving our hurt feelings.

Remember the rock-climbing example from chapter 6?

"How can *you do this to me*?" (Meaning: You are doing this to me.)
"How can *you put me through this* again?" (Meaning: You are putting me through this again.)

Other justifications might be:

"Well, that's how I feel, and if my feelings don't matter in this relationship, maybe I shouldn't be in it." (Meaning: You have to give in to what I want, or it means you don't care about me and I will threaten to end the relationship.)

"Everybody knows that! It's just normal!" (Meaning: What you want is not normal, therefore wrong, and you should be willing to give it up.)

"I was just joking. You have to learn to take a joke." (Meaning: When you call me out on my hurtful behavior, I'll deny that I meant it to be hurtful and refuse to take responsibility for its hurtfulness.)

Remember, when we don't take responsibility for our own emotions and actions, we put emotional pressure on the other person. This pressure can be coercive, and no agreement can be truly consensual when made under pressure or due to coercion.

Power and power imbalances are created in our interactions with other people. If we value consent, whether that be in an egalitarian relationship or a power dynamic, it's ethical to pay close attention to those moments where power can be created and act accordingly. If we're in an egalitarian relationship, the ethical response would be to seek to re-equalize the power between the two people as quickly as possible. If we're in a power dynamic, we need to evaluate whether the power difference created in that moment falls within the parameters of the consent given. If not, seek to re-equalize the power until it can be discussed in a fair manner, free from coercion or pressure.

Coercion is an abuse of power. In a love relationship, both people have made themselves emotionally vulnerable. This gives both people power to hurt each other. We have been entrusted with the ethical care of each other's vulnerable emotions. Coercion involves applying pressure to gain cooperation without genuine consent.

Force is also an abuse of power. Coercion can be mental, emotional, financial, or legal. Force tends to be the use and abuse of physical power but can also be financial or legal.

When our rights or relationship agreements have not been violated, and we fail to accept responsibility for our own emotions, and we tell ourselves stories about why the other person is responsible and should resolve this for us, we justify why it's acceptable to apply pressure (coercion) to that person. That pressure can take many forms: judging our partner, threatening to break up, emotional meltdowns, yelling and using aggressive body language, keeping someone awake until they give in, giving them the silent treatment or the cold shoulder, stonewalling, and more. When we don't take responsibility for our own emotions, we let ourselves down, we hurt our partner, and we damage our relationship.

Hurt feelings indicate a problem, not an outcome

We tend to become aware there's an issue anytime a disagreement or hurt feelings arise between two or more people. Unfortunately, in almost every disagreement, all the people involved tend to have hurt feelings. All the people tend to be upset. All the people tend to be convinced that they have been wronged.

Let's take a simple example:

Many years ago, I had a housemate, and he was also a friend. He needed transportation to work and asked if he could borrow my electric bicycle. It was a very expensive bicycle and it meant a lot to me, but loaning it would not have inconvenienced me.

My housemate was a good and honest person, but also forgetful and easily distracted. He had lost many things, left many things unlocked, and had many things stolen. His need for transportation was real. And I knew his intention would be to take good care of my bike. But I also believed that no matter how hard he tried, he would probably get my bike stolen or damaged.

I wasn't willing to risk losing my bike, so I told him no.

He was really upset with me. He reminded me of the many things he had done for me in the past. He tried to create feelings of guilt and then use that guilt to apply pressure. He insisted he could keep the bike safe and he could pay attention well enough to not damage or lose the bike. He accused me of being an ungrateful person and a bad friend.

He felt hurt that I didn't trust him with my bike. He felt hurt that I didn't show the gratitude he felt was appropriate for the things he'd done for me in the past.

I felt hurt that he called me ungrateful and a bad friend. I felt angry that he seemed to feel entitled to use my bike. And I also felt guilty for telling him he couldn't borrow my bike.

In this scenario, both of us felt hurt. Each person had their own unique perspective on the argument. Each person created their own interpretation of what was happening. Each person had a story they told themselves about why they were the wronged party. The hurt feelings we each felt were a result of our interpretations.

If we follow the personal responsibility flow chart, we ask, "Did anyone violate someone else's rights?" The answer is no. We can acknowledge that I have the right to control my material property, and the bike is my property.

"Did anyone violate a relationship agreement?" The answer is also no. He might have argued that I was violating an implicit agreement—the friendship norm of reciprocity. However, I would have argued that I was willing to repay his previous kindness, but I still have the right to determine how I would do that. I also felt that his attempt at using guilt to pressure me was coercive.

Our hurt feelings were an indicator that there was a problem in our relationship. But since both people were feeling hurt and upset, those feelings don't give us any clue as to which one of us had violated the rights of the other, was being unethical or abusing power, or needed to look inward and reexamine their interpretation of the situation.

Sometimes, we may feel the appropriate response is to defend ourselves as individuals, to defend our boundaries, and protect our self-esteem and self-respect. At other times we may feel the right thing to do is acquiesce for the sake of repairing the relationship.

As I stated in chapter 1, I believe this is why people tend to think of defending boundaries as being in opposition to maintaining happy relationships. However, I believe we can do both if we understand the difference between when acquiescing means we are taking responsibility for our own emotions and actions and when it means we are taking too much responsibility for the emotions and actions of others.

As you can see, when someone is violating one of our rights and we choose to stand up for ourselves and defend that boundary, we are doing what is best for the individual, and we are also doing what is best for the relationship. It would be toxic for any relationship to allow a pattern of behavior where one person is acquiescing when they shouldn't, and one person is abusing, coercing, or disrespecting the other and getting away with it.

Conversely, when we realize that we have violated the other person's rights, what's best for both individuals and the relationship is to acknowledge that we are in the wrong, express respect for the other person's rights and boundaries, and correct our behavior.

Additionally, if we have found that we have violated a relationship agreement, this is unethical behavior. Unethical behavior is damaging to the individual who engages in it, damaging to the individual on the receiving end of it, and damaging to the relationship between the two people.

In summary: When there's a disagreement between people, or when someone is feeling hurt, we often make the mistake of interpreting those hurt feelings *as evidence* that we have been hurt or wronged. That is only the case sometimes! That is only the case when our rights or relationship agreements have been violated. Otherwise, the hurt feelings are evidence that we have internal work to do or we need to negotiate a new agreement if we can.

When others are responsible for our feelings

We've all heard it said, "You're not responsible for other people's feelings." But how can this always be true? If someone steals from us and we feel violated, aren't they responsible for how we feel? If someone knowingly withholds information applicable to our informed consent and we feel angry about that when we learn the truth, aren't they responsible for how we feel? Shouldn't they be held accountable for their unethical behavior?

I would say a qualified yes to these questions. Remember the distinction I made early on that feelings are always valid but not always justified by the facts? In these examples, we are justified in feeling upset when someone violates our rights, violates our trust, or fails to abide by a relationship agreement. They're responsible for their behavior, and they are responsible for the painful feelings we might experience as a result.

That's why, in the five-step apology, they take responsibility for their actions, they apologize for their actions, *and* they apologize for how we felt as a result of their actions. If that person wants to repair their relationship with us, they are responsible for resolving our painful emotions through the use of apologies, making amends, and asking for forgiveness.

It's important for our self-esteem and self-respect to require people to do this repair work before allowing the relationship to move forward. Many clients have expressed to me their frustration when others want to move forward without actually resolving a conflict. When someone's rights are violated in a disagreement, they're left with their unresolved feelings, their safety and trust is damaged, and their self-esteem and self-respect may also be damaged if they allow the issue to be swept under the rug without proper resolution.

I gave a qualified yes because the degree or intensity of our feelings will also be impacted by our personal histories. If I'm an even-tempered person and someone accidentally leaves a bag of garbage behind my car and I run over it, I may feel frustrated. But if I have anger management issues, I may feel livid. The other person is not responsible for my history or for the hurt others have done to me in the past that might magnify my emotional response.

That's why we need to inform partners about relevant parts of our personal histories, and ask for accommodations around trauma triggers and sensitive topics. Disability accommodations are a right, and in the case of trauma triggers and other mental health needs, they are very specific to the individual and often invisible to others. That's why we need to talk with people about what we need and get their intentional agreement to provide those accommodations.

When I say we have a right to these accommodations, I don't mean we have a right to control the other person's behavior against their will. They are also human beings with their own needs and limitations and may not be able to provide the accommodations we need without damaging themselves.

When I say that a disability accommodation is a right, what I mean is that we should not feel guilty because we need it, and (depending on what the accommodation is) we may also have a responsibility to our own self-esteem and self-respect to distance ourselves from a person who declines to provide that accommodation.

It might be helpful for me to use a concrete example. Imagine I have physical limitations and cannot climb stairs, and I start dating a new person who lives on the third floor of an apartment building that doesn't have an elevator. I have a right to disability accommodations, but what form of accommodation is it fair to expect from my new dating partner? This is what I mean when I say we need to be flexible about *how* the need is met, not *whether* the need is met.

It's highly unlikely that my new dating partner would have the means to add an elevator to their building, or to move to an accessible location right away. Instead, if we are going to date, we will need to negotiate spending our time together in places that are accessible for me. On the other hand, if we're still dating a year or two in the future and they choose to move to a new location, it would be reasonable for me to request they move to a place accessible for me, if possible. And, if for some reason it's not possible (say, if all of the accessible apartments available are more expensive than they can afford), they can still verbally validate my right to these accommodations and their desire to provide it, even though they lack the resources.

Unfortunately, there's no clear line between what disability accommodations a person needs and should require from others versus what accommodations are beyond the other person's ability to provide. They are unique to each combination of people and the unique histories and resources of each person.

The most important thing to remember is that all the people involved should be spoken to respectfully and treated with dignity. This is not about laying blame or telling someone they're a bad person if they are unable to provide what we need without harming themselves.

Conclusion

By using what we've learned about rights, boundaries, and relationship agreements, we can examine our role in any argument or disagreement and determine what internal work we might have to do, when it's healthy and ethical to take responsibility for ourselves, and when it's healthy and ethical to stand our ground.

When we need to stand our ground and defend our rights or our rightful boundaries, it can be difficult to communicate to our partner that they might have some internal work to do. It's best if this is initiated by the person who needs to do the internal work as part of their commitment to be ethical in their relationships. But if we find we need to point this out to a partner, it's best done gently, compassionately, and with an offer to help them with their emotional struggles as long as we can make that offer authentically.

Building a happy, healthy relationship is a beautiful, sometimes delicate dance of both people shifting back and forth between fostering connection and encouraging independence and personal responsibility. It's important to approach this exchange with the generous and loving attitude described when I discussed the spirit of healthy relationships in chapter 1. But it's equally important to have the tools for how to do it and a solid understanding of the reasons why these tools work.

In the final chapter, we're going to revisit attachment theory and explain how and why each tool and concept we've learned fits into the goal of creating a securely bonded attachment in our adult relationships. And we'll see how employing them with a generous and kind attitude can succeed at creating an earned secure attachment even for those of us with mental health struggles that would normally interfere with this goal.

CHAPTER 10

Creating Earned Secure Attachment

The beginning of a relationship is usually the easiest part. New relationship energy (NRE), being fascinated with each other, wanting to learn everything about each other, a lack of painful past interactions, and sometimes a strong sexual attraction adds up to people greatly enjoying each other and what feels like an easy development for the beginnings of a bond.

Growing that bond into a secure relationship and keeping that bond healthy and strong takes skill.

If we've never seen a healthy relationship in action, it's difficult to know what to do to keep a relationship in good condition and even more difficult to access the information on how to repair a relationship when it's damaged. And for those of us with attachment injuries or current mental health struggles, we can make a lot of mistakes—not out of malice, but out of our own fear, pain, or lack of skill.

Imagine if you've never had a pet, and if you've never been close to anyone who was caring for a pet. The closest you've ever been to a pet is seeing other people walking dogs in the park. Now imagine you suddenly have a new puppy. How would you know what to feed it, how much to feed it, and how often? When do you let it outside? How do you house train it? What toys are safe for the puppy? What houseplants are poisonous? When should you take it to the veterinarian? Without advice from other pet owners, books, or internet sources, a person would be completely lost.

Like a puppy, a relationship is a living thing that needs continual care and maintenance. Secure attachment (or earned secure attachment) isn't a destination. It's not something you achieve once and then it's done. It's a process that's lived, every day. It's a pattern of interactions, and an attitude toward the other people involved, that all the people in the relationship must do well enough to keep the relationship healthy and thriving.

What are the essential elements to maintaining secure attachment in a bonded relationship? What skills do we need to have in order to enact these elements? When we have attachment injuries, what struggles are we likely to face as we try to live these essential tasks? And how do the skills learned in this book apply to each of these tasks?

Let's revisit attachment theory now and see exactly how the tools we've learned work to create the best potential for loving, secure, bonded relationships in our adult lives.

Childhood attachment

The attachment experiences we have as children with our caregivers (in Western industrialized countries) create our first template for intimate and romantic relationships as an adult, for friendships, and for our general feelings of safety in the world. As I explained in chapter 1, the attachment style we learn as infants is not permanent or immutable. We continue to change with each new interaction and each new meaningful relationship. Understanding how to create and maintain secure adult attachments is easier if we first understand what children need from caregivers in order to develop secure attachment.

Once we understand childhood attachment needs, and we understand how our own childhood attachment pattern may have been damaged, we can better understand our current needs and communicate them to our partners. Furthermore, we can better understand the comfort or discomfort we may feel when we try to meet our partner's relationship needs. And finally, if both partners are engaged in this work, we'll be better able to hear our partners' needs, allow them to meet our needs, and come together as a team to repair ruptures as they happen.

To develop secure attachment as children, we need our caregivers to provide both a safe haven and a secure base for us. For the caregiver to be a safe haven, a child must feel loved and accepted for who they are. This is how we learn we're valued, and also how we learn to value ourselves. Some of the behaviors and attitudes the caregiver will need to show toward a child are physical touch and soothing, joy in spending time with and interacting with the child, attentiveness, attunement to the child's emotional state (this includes appropriately shifting their own emotional state as the child's emotional state changes), and being mentally, emotionally, and physically present.

Attunement does not mean acting as an exact mirror of a child's emotional state. Simple mirroring is fine when the child is happy, safe, or calm. But when the child is upset, in pain, or feeling fear or any other form of distress, the caregiver must shift their state to one of concern while also maintaining emotional equilibrium and validating the child's experience, pain, or distress as justified given the circumstances. By doing this, the caregiver creates a safe container for the child's distress. This communicates that it's safe for the child to be distressed, even to the degree of losing awareness of their environment or control of themselves, because they know their caregiver is in control and will keep them safe.

A secure base is a platform of security and consistency that allows a child the courage to disengage from the caregiver, or go out into the world and explore. For the caregiver to be a secure base for us, we need to know that when we return, the caregiver will be accepting and supportive and the positive relationship will not be changed by our explorations. These experiences provide us the opportunity to develop our sense of personal competence and healthy autonomy.

A securely attached child experiences the ebb and flow between their safe haven and their secure base in this way: The child comes to the caregiver to feel acceptance and attunement, to experience the safe haven, and fill their emotional gas tank, so to speak. When it's full enough to induce feelings of safety, they feel free to go out and experience things away from the caregiver. This fulfills their need to experience autonomy and develop self-mastery. If they continue to feel safe, their fuel lasts longer. If they experience something frightening or painful, their tank empties more quickly. As their emotional tank empties, they circle back to the caregiver to refuel with more acceptance and attunement.

Therefore, attunement to the child's emotional state and current need must include an awareness of the child's need for autonomy, exploration, and opportunities for self-mastery as well as their need for comfort, reassurance, acceptance, and safety. When the child is ready to explore, the attuned caregiver will also feel safe allowing this temporary disconnection. They will encourage the child and express confidence in the child's budding self-mastery. They will exhibit a "go have fun, you can do it" attitude.

Mistakes, misattunement, and ruptures in the relationship are inevitable. Therefore, the caregiver also needs to notice when ruptures happen, identify the child's underlying emotional need, respond to that need, and repair the relationship bond.

Non-secure attachment patterns

Though our childhood attachment pattern is not written in stone, unless it has been fundamentally altered (for better or for worse) by later experiences, it does tend to serve as a baseline for us, even in adulthood. This means that when triggered or under stress, we're more likely to revert to our original attachment patterns. And the more stress we're under, the more we might feel the pull of our early self-protective strategies.

This is also true for people who are simply in an adult relationship that lacks secure attachment. Non-secure attachment styles are adaptive strategies meant to protect people when their relationships hurt them. When we have a non-secure attachment pattern as our baseline, the healthy skills described in this book can feel risky, unsafe, or frightening.

One of my goals in writing this book was to explain what's healthy for individuals and for relationships, and to describe the benefits of healthy bonded relationships, so that readers with attachment injuries can find the courage and strength to face the emotional risk to employ these healthy behaviors in their relationships.

Here are some of the ways a person with attachment injuries might experience distress when trying to employ healthy relationship skills, based on their baseline attachment style.

Anxious preoccupied

Adults with this attachment pattern (if it's based in their childhood experiences) most likely experienced inconsistency from their caregivers. Their needs for attunement, safe haven, and secure base were sometimes met, and sometimes not.

Children need connection and attunement with their caregivers. When caregivers are sometimes able to provide that, children learn that it's possible to get those needs met. When their caregivers are inconsistent in providing that connection, children learn to try harder because they know that connection is possible.

When people get a benefit inconsistently, and the pattern of when they get that benefit is random, this is called intermittent reinforcement. Intermittent reinforcement is the most powerful type of reinforcement.[63] When a benefit stops altogether, people tend to give up trying pretty quickly. When a benefit is given at regular intervals, people tend to learn and only seek the benefit when it's available. But when the benefit is given randomly, like pulling a lever on a slot machine, people try longer and harder to get the benefit because they know it's there, and they might succeed at getting it at any time.

Because of this, people with an anxious preoccupied attachment style are often tenacious and will continue to try and try and try to make their relationships work. This is one of the situations where a person gives and gives, and does way more than 50% of the work in the relationship, and hopes that if they finally give enough, it will pay off with the other person finally seeing their value.

Some of the challenges for them and their growth toward earned secure attachment will be in learning to assess when they should set boundaries and require the other person to step up, and when they should stop trying altogether and walk away.

It may also be the case that the damage is not just related to the inconsistency they've experienced, but also the lack of genuine or skillful repair of relationship ruptures caused by the inconsistencies. Therefore, learning healthy rupture repair techniques will be important. But equally important is that their partners be willing to learn healthy rupture repair techniques and use them. When their partners won't try or use the techniques, not only will the anxiously attached person end up doing more than 50% of the work in the relationship, but their other issues, such as being intrusive, will be triggered.

---

63 Also known as the "variable ratio reinforcement schedule" in B. F. Skinner's experiments with rats. See Saul McLeod, 2018. "What is operant conditioning and how does it work? How reinforcement and punishment modify behavior." *Simply Psychology*, January 21. https://www.simplypsychology.org/operant-conditioning.html

These interaction patterns trigger a fear of abandonment in anxiously attached people. They never know when a partner will show up for them and when they won't. If a rupture happens, they have no reason to believe it will be effectively repaired. Therefore, any rupture could be the last.

People with an anxious preoccupied attachment pattern very much want a bonded relationship, and believe that it's possible, but also believe that the likelihood that their partner will abandon them, betray them, lose interest in them, or not be there for them consistently is high. Their life experience provides proof their fear is valid. This characterizes the anxious part of the "anxious preoccupied" label.

Their adaptive strategy has been to be vigilant and intrusive with their partners in order to not give their partner a chance or opportunity to let them down. What I mean by intrusive, is the person violates their partner's rights related to autonomy and privacy, and their partner will likely experience them as either controlling or clingy. This might include watching every little expression and every change in tone of voice; picking apart every word their partner says; reading their journal, emails, or text messages; wanting to know where their partner is at all times, who they're with, and what they're doing; or wanting to basically read their partner's mind and emotions at all times for signs that the partner may be souring on them. This is the preoccupied part of the anxious preoccupied label.

Dismissing-avoidant

Adults who grew up to have this attachment pattern most likely experienced their caregivers as consistently abusive or neglectful. Sometimes they also develop this attachment pattern when their caregivers were very rigid, authoritarian, or overly demanding. As children they basically decided to turn away from their caregivers and give up. They consistently did not find a secure base or safe haven with their caregivers and they learned to not expect their needs to be met.

A dismissing-avoidant attachment pattern can also happen in adulthood when a person experiences an abusive partner. When they leave the abusive relationship and try to establish new relationships, they discover they've become "gun-shy" in a way. They may now show a pattern of keeping their distance until they experience enough consistency in being treated well that they begin to feel safe trusting the new person.

When a person has a dismissing-avoidant attachment style as their baseline, they may avoid initiating contact, asking for help, or engaging in other proximity-seeking behaviors. They may become very self-reliant. The person may also prefer to be alone when feeling distressed instead of turning toward their partner for reassurance or comfort. They may become distressed or overwhelmed when their partner seeks proximity, soothing, or reassurance from them. And they may struggle to engage in collaborative problem-solving, which is often a requirement for healthy relationship agreements.

And while the anxious-preoccupied person tenaciously works hard to fix a damaged relationship, the dismissing-avoidant person is more likely to cut and run in order to avoid painful conflict or the abandonment they believe is inevitable.

Unresolved disorganized attachment

Unresolved disorganized attachment is another term for fearful-avoidant attachment. When this happens in children (called disorganized attachment), it's caused by severe abuse where the child is harmed, hurt, and terrified by the caregiver, but the caregiver is also their only source of comfort and intermittently offers that comfort. When this happens, two separately evolved protection systems clash within the child's nervous system and can cause incredible harm.

Because the caregiver is the source of fear and pain, the sympathetic nervous system (the fight or flight response which we share with fish, reptiles, and other mammals) is triggered and the child feels compelled to flee or hide. But due to isolation (physical, mental, or emotional), if that same caregiver is the only source of comfort, and sometimes provides soothing, approval, and expressions of love (often in exchange for some degree or cooperation or submission to the abuse), the child's bonding and attachment system (which we share with other social creatures, such as other primates as well as dogs and wolves) compels the child to seek comfort and closeness with that caregiver.

The result is a powerful disconnection between (or dissociation from) the child's own perceptions, sensations, emotions, and cognitions. This can lead to a fractured sense of self, or of the world around them. It can also lead to a fracturing of the caregiver into two or more identities in the child's mind.

This process is called splitting, where the abusive caregiver is split into a good version and a bad version. Only the good memories are linked to the good version, and the abusive memories are linked to the bad version.

All of this makes it much easier for an abuse perpetrator to groom a child to accept violations of healthy boundaries, to compel the child to accept the perpetrator's explanations and protect the perpetrator's secrets. And it makes it easier for the child to dismiss their own internal danger signals regarding the perpetrator.

Growing up under these conditions can result in the child developing PTSD with dissociative symptoms, dissociative identity disorder (DID), or borderline, histrionic, or narcissistic personality disorders.[64]

An adult with unresolved disorganized attachment will appear to have confusing, contradictory responses to relationship distress. Sometimes they will cling tenaciously and be intrusive, sometimes they will cut and run. Sometimes they will lash out, and sometimes they will withdraw.

The label "unresolved disorganized attachment" can be misleading because it sounds as though the disorganized attachment style must have been initiated in childhood and simply remained unresolved in adulthood. That's one possibility, but unresolved disorganized attachment can be acquired in adulthood. This can happen when a teen or adult finds themselves in an abusive and isolating relationship where the partner who is the source of their pain is also their primary or only source of comfort. It's also what happens when people are drawn into cults or other totalistic social systems.[65]

Unresolved disorganized attachment to a specific person is also sometimes referred to as a trauma bond, and the techniques that create it in adults are called brainwashing, undue influence, mind control, conditioning, and neurolinguistic programming. If we've had these experiences in childhood or adulthood, developing a secure self-attachment will be most important for being able to create an earned secure attachment in our current relationships.

A person with this attachment pattern will struggle with second-guessing themselves. They will struggle with naming their emotions. They'll struggle greatly with self-validation and identifying when to stand their ground versus

---

64 A diagnosis of a personality disorder is not given until adulthood.
65 Stein, 2016.

when to require their partner take responsibility for themselves. These skills are also very important for being able to know when they are giving an authentic yes to a relationship agreement. Without these skills they may struggle with saying yes to agreements only to find later that agreement to be very painful and beyond their abilities.

A secure self-attachment is what gives us the ability to assess our perceptions of our internal and external realities and validate our own feelings and experiences. We need this ability to identify what we feel, what we want, and what we value. These skills are central to being able to identify the boundaries we need and the coherent independent identity that grows directly from that.

Keep all of this in mind as we translate these needs and responsibilities into understanding how to ethically navigate the ebb and flow of interactions in our adult bonded relationships.

Adult attachment

The biggest difference between our childhood/caregiver attachment expectations and our adult relationships is that relationships between adult peers are two-way relationships. Both people have some power, knowledge, and skills relative to the other, and both people have needs they want fulfilled as well as responsibilities toward the other person.

The expectations we put on our adult relationships vary greatly. We place fewer expectations on our acquaintances, and more on those we consider friends, close friends, family, and some kinds of casual sexual partners. The greatest and most intense expectations are typically placed on bonded relationships such as romantic partners, life partners, nesting partners, and spouses.

Let's look at the closest, most bonded relationships. Jessica Fern, author of the book *Polysecure*, calls these our attachment-based partnerships.[66] She rightly suggests that even though we may not feel attaching to another person is a choice, we should discuss our relationship expectations with the other person and seek mutual consent regarding whether to be bonded attachment figures for each other and the expectations we have for each other as a result.

---

66 Jessica Fern, 2020.

In our attachment-based partnerships, we tend to want the functions of attachment relationships. This means both members of the relationship seek to experience having a safe haven and secure base in the other person, and both people provide the nurturing and security that results in a safe haven as well as the mutual respect for autonomy that results in a secure base for their partner. We need to be able to sometimes do all of these simultaneously and sometimes toggle back and forth between skills, and we need to be able to determine when it's appropriate to seek support versus when it's appropriate to give it.

We create secure attachment in our adult relationships through these essential elements:

1. We provide a safe haven for our partners.
2. We provide a secure base for our partners.
3. We allow our partners to provide a safe haven for us.
4. We allow our partners to provide a secure base for us.
5. Each person has an internalized secure attachment with themselves.
6. Each person strives to be attuned to their partners as much as possible, and notice or communicate misattunements promptly.
7. Each person responds to misattunements and ruptures with the skills to come together as a team and repair the relationship bond.

Creating secure attachment in a relationship is not a pass-or-fail experience. Think of it as a scale or spectrum. If you or your partner in one of your relationships is not feeling secure in the relationship, try to identify where you can strengthen the relationship on any of these seven points so it can be more secure than it was. The more secure a bonded relationship is, the more peace and joy both people get to experience.

Secure self-attachment (item #5) plays a prominent role in our ability to provide a safe haven and secure base for our partners. Secure self-attachment is when we're able to take the secure attachment we learned from our upbringing (or earned later in life) and internalize it so that we can carry it with us and integrate it into our internal dialogue and self-soothing skills. I've said many times to clients that when we have trauma or attachment injuries from childhood, one of our tasks is to learn how to be a good, kind, loving parent to ourselves. When we are able to do that, and internalize it, we can validate ourselves, and we can also provide a safe haven (kind, accepting, forgiving) and a secure base (flexible, encouraging, consistent) within ourselves through our inner dialogue.

Additionally, each person needs to stay attuned to their partners as much as possible (item #6), notice when misattunement or ruptures happen, and take action to repair the ruptures and misattunements that will inevitably happen in any relationship (item #7).

It can be difficult to understand the difference between a misattunement and allowing for the freedom and independence to temporarily stop focusing on a partner in order to be present with whatever we're doing when we're away from that partner. It's okay to lose focus on each other at times. If anyone experiences a rupture to the relationship bond during this time of independence, it's important to communicate promptly with their partner, and the partner then re-attunes and joins in repairing the rupture.

Not only does all of this sound like a lot, but like most things, it's easier said than done. I've listed the essential elements for creating secure attachment in our adult relationships, and now I will spell out the mental, emotional, and behavioral skills needed in order to be able to do these things, and refer readers back to the chapters where I taught those skills.

What is our part in providing a safe haven for our partners?

When we seek to provide a safe haven for our partners, the tasks involved are similar to those of the caregiver in the caregiver/child relationship. However, we must remember that our partners are not children, and they retain their autonomy and need for mutual respect, even in their moments of need.

As described previously, to provide a safe haven for our partners we must express to them that they are accepted and loved for who they are. We express this to them by showing an interest, showing joy when we're spending time with them or interacting with them, sharing physical touch and affection, engaging with them in interactions and conversations, and voluntarily taking actions meant to meet their needs. We also actively avoid criticizing them or rejecting core elements of who they are, what they value, or what they enjoy.

This attitude of openness and affection is reflected in what I called the spirit of healthy relationships in chapter 1. When our partners are in distress, and they seek us out as a safe haven, it's our role to validate their experience, validate their feelings, and agree that their feelings are justified given the circumstances, if we can say that authentically.

I taught you nonviolent communication (NVC) and the Imago exercise in chapters 3 and 4. These tools are great for helping us validate our partners' experience and show nonjudgmental acceptance for who they are, even when they're upset and not at their best. As I've said many times in this book, if we want our partners to share their truth with us, we need to provide an environment where they feel safe doing so.

What is our part in providing a secure base for our partners?

Providing a secure base in our relationships allows our partners to have the freedom to develop self-mastery and explore the outside world without fear that their bonded relationship with us will be damaged in the process.

We can mess this up by expressing doubt or lack of confidence in our partner's ability to do things or navigate the outside world. We might express this through our fears and anxieties and block our partner from exploring. We might also express it by being critical or insulting of the results when our partner attempts to show self-mastery.

When we are not secure enough to provide a secure base for our partners, we may become angry or even distraught and punish them for wanting to explore away from us. This teaches our partner that the relationship with us is too fragile to remain undamaged if they choose to go out and explore.

Additionally, we might fail to provide a secure base by not showing encouragement and by being uninterested in our partner's activities or explorations, or on the opposite extreme, we might be overly intrusive and overly invested in our partner's activities or accomplishments (such as when we insist on all outside relationships or activities being shared with us when our partner doesn't want this).

It's vitally important for those of us practicing ethical non-monogamy to learn how to be that secure base for our partners. We've embraced a lifestyle that allows our partners to go out and explore the world, often without our presence, sometimes including loving or being sexual with other people, and it's our job as a secure base to manage our emotions so that we can say, "Go have fun; I believe in you," as they go out the door. We also need to show them that we and our bonded relationship with them are undamaged and unchanged by their explorations.

This may seem similar to compersion, but it's not exactly the same. Attributed to the Kerista Community in the 1970s, compersion is the state of feeling joy and happiness when our partners experience joy and happiness (including sexual fulfillment) when they're with someone else. When we're trying to provide our partners with a secure base, compersion can be helpful, and providing a secure base is much easier to do if you're feeling it. Compersion would make it easy to be encouraging about our partners going out and exploring the world and enjoying other people.

But it's not necessary to feel compersion in order to provide a secure base for our partners. We could feel completely neutral about whether or not they're experiencing joy with someone else. We might even feel some resentment, anxiety, or fear. Although it becomes more difficult to provide a secure base for our partners if we feel painful emotions while they're trying to experience joy with someone else, it's still not impossible to provide a secure base under these conditions.

To provide a secure base for our partners, it's essential to have the ability to assess whether our painful emotions are our responsibility to resolve, or if our partner has violated our rights or a relationship agreement. Chapter 9 explains how to do this using the personal responsibility flow chart, and how to respond to each combination of circumstances. If we find we should take responsibility for resolving our own painful emotions, we can still encourage our partners to go out and enjoy their experiences while away from us. When we're successful at this, our partners can enjoy the secure base of knowing we will not intrusively put the responsibility of our painful emotions on them. And, if we're able to either resolve or cope effectively with our own painful emotions, our partners can go out and enjoy themselves and know that their relationship with us is not damaged or changed as a result.

At the same time, we benefit from being able to be honest with ourselves about our actual limits, and if we can't resolve our painful emotions on our own, we can ask for accommodations from our partner as described in chapter 8. By approaching this as a request and expressing appreciation if it is granted, we are again taking verbal responsibility for our painful emotions. Even as we ask our partners to do something for us, we still let them know we are not being intrusive in our demands and they are safe with us.

This also applies to many other situations besides when our partners have dates with other people. Any time our partner does something independently of us, does something that involves exploring the outside world, or they seek to experience self-mastery, it's our job as a bonded partner to have a supportive and encouraging attitude if possible.

A good example is when Sarah wanted to climb the rocks in chapter 1. Jenny was afraid and at first insisted that Sarah not climb the rocks. Sarah was offended. She believed Jenny was expressing a lack of confidence in her abilities (self-mastery), and this was hurtful to Sarah. However, when Jenny was able to communicate this as her own fear, and her own lack of confidence in her own self-mastery, this helped repair the rift between them. Though Jenny didn't ask for an accommodation, Sarah offered one that preserved her independence and also created safety for Jenny's fears which, in the moment, Jenny was not able to overcome on her own.

Providing a secure base for our partners doesn't mean always blindly supporting everything our partner wants to do no matter how much fear, anxiety, or apprehension we might feel. It also doesn't mean lying and pretending to not feel those things when we feel them. It means learning to communicate about those fears in such a way that we take ownership for our feelings and our limits, rather than expressing a lack of confidence in our partners' abilities or blaming them for causing our pain.

What is our part in allowing our partners to provide a safe haven for us?

Many of us have difficulty allowing another person to be a safe haven for us. Our ability to gracefully accept our partners expressing that they value us, want to be attuned to us, and want to meet our needs is directly related to our ability to value ourselves, be attuned to ourselves, and prioritize our own needs. Therefore, this ability is directly related to having or developing a secure attachment within ourselves.

When someone expresses that they think we are wonderful, we need to be able to believe them in order to internalize that and translate it into feeling safe with them. If we are unable to believe that someone could find us wonderful, their pronouncement will trigger suspicion rather than security. We might be concerned that they're lying in order to get something from us or manipulate us. We might think we temporarily have them fooled and soon they'll see through the ruse and be angry or disappointed. Or we might begin to devalue their opinion. If their judgment is so poor that they would think we are wonderful, then their opinion isn't worth much. A humorous example is this quote by Groucho Marx, who wrote in his autobiography, "I don't want to belong to any club that will accept people like me as a member."[67]

The same is true for when a partner tries to prioritize our needs. If we feel unworthy of that effort and attention, we'll struggle to accept this gift. We may feel confused, or even deeply uncomfortable. We may even reject or attempt to reject this offering. Or we may feel we have an internal accountant who keeps track of each nice gesture and requires us to repay these gestures tenfold in order to not feel we're a burden to others.

For us to allow our partners to be a safe haven for us, we need to not only be willing to accept these wonderful gifts of affection, acceptance, attunement, and prioritization, but we also need to have the courage to be willing to be vulnerable with our partners. We need to be willing to share who we are, what interests us, what we value, and risk being rejected. We need to be willing to turn to them for support and validation when we're upset, frightened, or hurting. We need to be willing to turn to them for validation and encouragement. And we also need to be willing to ask for their help.

When we've been hurt by caregivers during our upbringing, or by people in our past relationships, what skills or abilities do we need to develop in order to learn how to be vulnerable again? In addition to developing a secure attachment within ourselves, we need to have confidence in our ability to assess the meaning of the other person's response and a belief in our own strength and resilience that we can risk being hurt because we know we can recover from new hurts.

If we risk being vulnerable with a partner and we get a positive or nurturing response, we need to be able to internalize it and allow ourselves to add this to a growing foundation of trust and safety in the relationship. And if we get a negative or damaging response then we need to have confidence in our ability to effectively protect ourselves and defend our rightful boundaries. We need to employ the skills to repair the rupture and allow our partner to do the tasks related to repairing the rupture with us.

---

67 Groucho Marx, 1959. *Groucho and Me*. Bernard Geis Associates.

I taught DBT skills in chapter 2 that will be very helpful in developing the emotion regulation skills to take the risks I listed. Learning about your rights in chapter 5 and using the cognitive behavioral skills in chapters 6 and 7 will help a person develop a stronger sense of themselves, what they think, feel, value, and who they are. Practicing the skills in chapter 8 and asking for what you need in relationship agreements is great practice for prioritizing your needs. Using the personal responsibility flow chart in chapter 9 is good practice for self-validation.

What is our part in allowing our partners to provide a secure base for us?

Allowing our partners to be a secure base for us means having the courage to go out and explore the world, or go out and develop self-mastery, while also being able to believe that our relationship with them will be unchanged when we return.

This can be frightening for those of us with attachment injuries. If we feel anxious when our partners encourage us to go out and explore, we may take this as a sign that they aren't adequately invested in their relationship with us. Or, we may fear that they're not telling us the truth and they secretly resent our explorations and will punish us when we return.

What skills do we need in order to accept that our partners are a secure base for us? First, I believe we need to be able to use the skill of tracking evidence from Cognitive Behavioral Therapy that I describe in chapter 6. This will help us to assess whether our partners are telling us the truth when they say it's safe for us to go out and explore. If they are being truthful then we need to take personal responsibility for the anxiety we feel, as I describe in chapter 9. Again, this will allow us to begin building a foundation of trust in the relationship.

It also helps to be able to trust that our partners are being honest with themselves and us about their actual limits and have asked us for the accommodations and relationship agreements (from chapter 8) that they need in order to feel safe as we go out and explore the world. Like the rules and limits placed on us by caregivers when we were children, our relationship agreements serve as clear boundaries that help us to feel more confident that as long as we stay within those limits, we can go out and explore without doing damage to our attachment-based relationships.

Secure self-attachment and its impact on our relationships

Consider a healthy, loving relationship between a caregiver and a child. A caregiver will typically have boundaries around how they'll allow a child to treat them. Most caregivers don't allow children to treat them disrespectfully without employing consequences for the child. When we're children, seeing that our caregivers have the self-esteem and self-respect to require that we respect their rights (and their authority), and seeing that they have the interpersonal power to enforce those boundaries, is often our first template for understanding that others have the right to be treated with respect, care and consideration.

If being loved, accepted, and enjoyed by our caregivers communicates to us that we're valued and provides the first building blocks to our self-esteem and secure self-attachment, then we must also look up to and value our caregivers so we can value their assessment of us. I think we all know that children usually look up to and admire their caregivers (at least before the teenage years). It takes some pretty severe failures on the part of caregivers for young children to turn away in disgust, and no longer value whether their caregivers accept or approve of them.

In our adult relationships, a similar exchange is at play. Our partners tend to want us to hold them in high esteem. To be valued by us adds to their self-esteem, and feeling loved and accepted by us is central to them experiencing the relationship as a safe haven. But our valuing of them only adds to their self-esteem if they value us and our opinion of them. And it helps them to value us if they can see that we value ourselves. One way for us to show that we value ourselves is by knowing our rights, having boundaries around what behaviors we will accept from others (including our partners), and using our interpersonal power effectively and ethically to enforce those boundaries.

What skills do we need in order to value ourselves? Self-esteem and self-respect derive directly from recognizing our individual human rights and erecting boundaries around those rights. All the skills described from chapters 5 through 9 help us to know our rights, determine if we are within our rights in a given disagreement, and assess how to respond and ethically use our interpersonal power if necessary.

Other ways we can show that we value ourselves is by prioritizing our own needs, speaking up for ourselves, and engaging in self-care. These are also the signs of secure self-attachment.

This process of seeing a person's value works both ways: It works as I just described and it works in reverse, in that we want our partners to hold us in high esteem. If this is going to enhance how we feel about ourselves, we need to be able to value our partners' opinions. And to do that, we need to be able to see that they value themselves.

Along similar lines, we can't very easily appreciate a partner being attuned to us if we're not attuned to ourselves. When someone is paying enough attention to notice and reflect back to us our internal state, the typical result is that we feel seen; we feel understood. This only happens if we have the ability to be attuned to our own internal state. If I am unaware, and unable to be aware, of my internal state, then I can't match what my partner is saying with how I feel inside. My internal experience is a blank to me. I can't feel seen if I can't see myself.

Attunement

Attunement in a relationship is the ability to "be in tune with" another person's inner emotional experience. To do this well, we need to know them well enough to know their typical signs of being in "safe and social" mode, and their signs of distress, worry, fear, anger, as well as excitement, elation, and pride. In addition to noticing their emotional state, we need to be invested enough in them to want to keep our focus on them and their inner world, and we need to be willing to shift our emotional state to be in tune with theirs and respond appropriately when their mood shifts.

When a partner comes into the room and is clearly happily excited about something, we're attuned with them when we notice and our mood shifts to a state of positive expectation. We engage with them and ask them to share whatever it is they're excited about. Then we celebrate with them whatever that good news is.

Imagine how alone you might feel if you told a partner that you got a promotion at work and they were uninterested in hearing about it, or said something that diminished this accomplishment.

When a partner is distressed, if we are attuned with them, we know them well enough to recognize the signs and we shift our attention away from whatever we had been doing to ask our partner about their inner experiences. We take the time to listen to their story of what happened to them and how they interpreted the meaning of the event. We validate their feelings. We express compassion. We tell them their feelings are justified by the facts (if we can). And we offer our help with the problem if that offer would be welcome.

When we are spending time with a partner, we might demonstrate this through being mentally and emotionally present rather than distracted, and when we are not present, we can demonstrate attunement by checking in with them or initiating contact as frequently as both partners feel is beneficial.

Attunement also means being able to gauge when a partner needs us to provide that safe container, which involves adjusting to their emotional state and showing concern while also maintaining our emotional equilibrium as much as possible so that they can feel safe and comforted.

Using emotion regulation skills, such as those I described from dialectical behavioral therapy in chapter 2, helps us to maintain our emotional equilibrium so that we can hear their truth. Emotion regulation skills also help us to keep our emotional equilibrium when our partners are in distress, and help us to provide that safe container for our partners' painful emotions so they can feel safe leaning on us and allowing themselves to be in distress in our presence.

Additionally, if we're able to stay attuned to our partners, we can often stop ruptures to the relationship bond before they happen. I describe this in the latter part of chapter 4. By staying emotionally connected with our partners, noticing the first signs of their distress, and responding with attentiveness, curiosity, and compassion, we can often stay true to ourselves AND avoid creating a rift in our relationships.

Misattunement and repairing ruptures

Ruptures are inevitable in any relationship. No one can stay perfectly attuned to another person indefinitely. A misattunement can expand into a rupture or argument when one or both people respond in a hurtful way to the misattunement. Diana Divecha wrote, in her review of *Raising a Secure Child*, that "ruptures, small and large, happen all the time in the fabric of human relationships, and so it becomes important that repairs, small and large, become second nature to parents."[68]

---

68 Dr. Diana Divecha is a developmental psychologist, an assistant clinical professor at the Yale Child Study Center and Yale Center for Emotional Intelligence. Diana Divecha, 2017. "How to cultivate a secure attachment with your child." *Greater Good Magazine*, February 3. https://greatergood.berkeley.edu/article/item/how_to_cultivate_a_secure_attachment_with_your_child

This is also true in our adult relationships. What skills and abilities do we need in order to repair the ruptures and misattunements that will inevitably happen in our relationships? Nonviolent communication (NVC) from chapter 3, the Imago exercise from chapter 4, and the personal responsibility flow chart and the five-step apology from chapter 9 are excellent tools and skills for repairing relationship ruptures when they happen.

Conclusion

Relationships don't have to be a confusing enigma. The art and science of creating and maintaining healthy, securely attached relationships are a matter of understanding what's needed for secure attachment to exist, and learning and practicing the techniques that create the opportunity for it to happen.

I say they "create the opportunity for it to happen" because there are no guarantees; we can't control whether the other person is willing or able to do their half of a healthy relationship. That's where we need techniques that nudge them in that direction, and also a way of deciding when and how to stop trying with a particular person.

Conclusion

I've noticed a curious pattern when doing therapy sessions with clients. The session usually begins with brief updates about what's going on in their lives and they may say a few random things that don't seem connected in any way to the work we are doing. Then we get into the session based on either a current struggle or their long-term treatment plan.

By the end of the session, something profound often happens. Some of the random stuff from the very beginning of the session turns out to be a key lynchpin or important clue to helping them resolve the overall issue for that session.

What I've determined after years of doing this work is that the subconscious speaks to us in a number of ways, and this is one of those ways. The client's subconscious knows what the client needs for healing and resolution and is dropping hints, like breadcrumbs in the forest, hoping we'll find them and use them to make the journey home.

Writing this book has been a similar journey for me. It began as several articles meant to clarify healthy boundaries and relationship agreements. Then I realized I needed to explain more fully the psychological and therapeutic basis for why some boundaries and agreements where healthy and some were not, and how autonomy and connection are both needed, and work together, symbiotically, in a healthy relationship.

I worked for three and a half years on expanding these concepts into the book you now hold in your hands. During this multi-year journey, this book has become far more than I intended it to be in the beginning. It's no longer just about boundaries and agreements in relationships. It's become a complete guide for creating and maintaining secure attachment in bonded relationships.

Additionally, for those of us with attachment injuries, this book teaches us how to create, maintain, and repair earned secure attachment with a partner or partners while also having compassion for our mental health issues and those of our partners. When we have attachment injuries or mental health issues, creating secure attachments in our relationships can be challenging. I hope this book has given readers an understanding of how secure attachment is created and maintained, and the quality of interactions needed for the care and feeding of the living bonds that exist between people.

If you've gone on this entire journey with me, you may have learned a lot and tried a lot of new things!

In the realm of theory, you've learned about the physiology of our emotions through polyvagal theory. You've learned about how we bond with others through attachment theory. And you learned some of my ideas regarding human rights in relation to other people, and the importance of balancing individual rights and responsibilities with attending to our relationship bonds and respecting the feelings and rights of others.

You've also learned a lot of skills. You've learned how to take breaks when distressed and how to soothe that distress using dialectical behavioral therapy techniques. You've learned how to communicate using nonviolent communication and the Imago exercise. You've learned how to validate yourself and hold others accountable by reflecting on rights and agreements. You've learned how to identify when you might have work to do by using the personal responsibility flow chart. You've learned skills to help ensure that relationship agreements are truly consensual, and you've learned when it's appropriate (and even essential) to express appreciation for relationship gifts.

If you've done some or all of the action items, you've done a lot of self-reflection. You've done a lot of thinking, and examined your feelings and your beliefs in a way you might not have done before. And you've probably communicated with a partner or partners about your relationship patterns and how to interrupt damaging patterns and begin implementing new behaviors.

You deserve a lot of credit for being willing to do this work.

Even as I close this book, I'm aware there are unanswered questions. I've mentioned that improving our relationships works best when all the people involved are willing to learn and use the tools I've taught in this book. But what if the other person or people are unwilling to learn these techniques, or they haven't had the opportunity to learn them? How can we respond constructively in those situations?

I've also mentioned interpersonal power, and abuses of power such as manipulation, coercion and abuse. When someone is intentionally abusing a position of power, they won't want to use mutually respectful, egalitarian relationship techniques. How can we identify the difference between someone who doesn't know these skills, someone who wants to use these skills but is struggling, and someone who is intentionally not using these skills? How can we strengthen our abilities to identify and protect ourselves from manipulation, coercion, and abuse?

I've also mentioned the need we all have to be able to assess our relationships and decide when there's hope for improvement versus when it would be better to end a relationship and move on. What are some of the ethical factors we need to consider when ending a relationship?

I'm well underway on another book that will address these questions. Every book has to have parameters. I've built this book around teaching practical tools for improving relationships you deem worth keeping and improving. I decided to save the discussion of relationships that may not be worth keeping for a different book.

Here, I wanted to present not only a practical, applicable self-help book for people doing ethical nonmonogamy, but also a foundation upon which to continue building upon concepts of ethics, power, and harm. I hope the theories provided have given you a mental framework for understanding emotions, and relationships so that the tools you'll be using actually make sense, and you know why you're using them. Understanding the theories behind the tools gives you the flexibility to successfully improvise in unique or unexpected situations.

It's my hope that readers will use these tools, not just in their bonded relationships, but in all kinds of relationships. Lots of people suddenly respecting each other's human rights, treating each other with respect, taking responsibility for themselves, and inviting compassionate teamwork to resolve disagreements would literally change the world.

About the Author

Thank you for reading **Cultivating Connection: A practical guide for personal and relationship growth in ethical non-monogamy**.

If you enjoyed this book, please consider writing a review of your honest impressions on Amazon, Goodreads, or the platform of your choice. Reviews greatly help other readers decide if this book will benefit them.

If you would like to connect with others who are implementing the principles in this book to their lives and relationships, consider joining the **discussion group** at: http://www.facebook.com/groups/cultivatingconnectiondiscussion/

About the author: Sander T. Jones, LCSW, LISW-CP, CCH is a clinical social worker, certified hypnotherapist, and author in Atlanta, Georgia. Sander has over 10 years' experience working with people in ethically non-monogamous relationships, people in the kink/BDSM/Leather communities, LGBTQ+ communities, and people doing voluntary sex work. You can follow Sander, their blog, email list, and news about events and future books at SanderTJones.com